The Wharton School
University of Pennsylvania

venture design

Entity Press

Printed in the United States of America

Knott, Anne Marie

   Venture Design / Anne Marie Knott

cm.

   Includes bibliographic references and index.

      1. Entrepreneurship 2. New ventures

Library of Congress Catalog Card Number: 2001093833

ISBN: 0-9713076-0-1

Book design, cover art and production by:

The Floating Gallery, 331 W. 57th Street, #465

New York, NY 10019

www.thefloatinggallery.com

acknowledgments

I would like to thank the following faculty for very helpful comments on the manuscript for this book. They have made many suggestions for additional material that could not be incorporated in this edition, thus all errors and omissions are mine: Richard Arend, New York University; David Audretsch, University of Indiana; Henry Beam, Western Michigan University; Michael Card, University of South Dakota; Ed Chung, St. Norbert College; Robert D'Intino, Penn State University, Capital College School of Business; Harry Domicone, California Lutheran University; James Fiet, University of Louisville; Brenda Flannery, Minnesota State University; Daniel Forbes, University of Minnesota, Carlson School; Lisa Gundry, DePaul University; David Hoopes, Southern Methodist University; Michael Leiblein, Ohio State University, Fisher College of Business; Ugbo Mallam, Jarvis Christian College; Thaddeus McEwen, North Carolina A&T State University; David Olson, California State University, Bakersfield; John O'Neil, Johnson and Wales University; Michael Rubach, University of Central Arkansas; Peter Russo, Boston University; Elton Scifres, Stephen F. Austin State University.

Two other people require special thanks. I'd like to thank Colin Kelley for the original inspiration to do the book, and for his guidance and encouragement throughout the process. Finally, I would like to thank to Kyle Kuvalanka. His research assistance and enthusiasm while an MBA at Wharton made this project possible as well as fun.

contents

chapter 1

introduction

Let me start by saying something about the heroics of entrepreneurship. Entrepreneurs ARE heroes. The Olim brothers started CDNow because they were sitting in Providence, Rhode Island without access to music stores, and felt they could solve the problem through the Internet. While most of us recognize that the structure of the industry was such that this was a short-term play, it was a wonderful short-term play. CDNow and subsequent entrants into the field have forced the adoption of Internet distribution by the established firms. Almost immediately after the birth of the firm, the entire distribution of who purchased music changed, because people now had an easy means to locate and purchase more obscure works. Not all ventures are as heroic, but I think most of you are creating something of value beyond profits.

INSPIRATION VS. PERSPIRATION[1]

What makes entrepreneurship heroic is NOT the idea. Students have been trained to think that their ideas are the source of value in new ventures. They take great pains to protect their idea—asking for non-disclosure agreements from faculty, students and investors. The fact of the matter is that few ideas are unique. Venture capitalists claim they see thirty versions of most ideas. In some cases they actually view this multiplicity as a good thing—a sign that there is critical mass for industry emergence. Moreover, even if the initial idea is unique, it rarely is preserved in its original state. You will see this evolution of an idea in the case that is carried throughout the text. You are also likely to witness it in your own ventures.

While you need an idea, it is the *entrepreneur* rather than the idea that is the source of value. This was nicely demonstrated in two recent books that examine the origins of successful firms: Collins and Porras', *Built to Last*,[2] and Amir Bhide's, *The Origin and Evolution of New Businesses*.[3] None of the eighteen visionary companies in *Built to Last* started with a unique idea, and only 6% of the 100 firms in *The Origin and Evolution of New Businesses* started with a unique idea. Yet all of these firms were tremendously successful.

This relative insignificance of the idea is not merely a recent phenomenon.

As early as 1942, Joseph Schumpeter in his book, *Capitalism, Socialism and Democracy*[4] characterized entrepreneurship in much the same way:

> *We have seen that the function of entrepreneurs is to reform or revolutionize the pattern of production by exploiting an invention or, more generally, an untried technological possibility for producing a new commodity or producing an old one in a new way, by opening up a new source of supply or materials or a new outlet for products, by reorganizing an industry and so on.*

> *...To undertake such new things is difficult and constitutes a distinct economic function, first, because they lie outside of the routine tasks which everybody understands and secondly, because the environment resists in many ways that vary according to social conditions from simple refusal either to finance or to buy a new thing, to physical attack on the man who tries to produce it. To act with confidence beyond the range of familiar beacons and to overcome that resistance requires aptitudes that are present in only a small fraction of the population and that define the entrepreneurial type as well as the entrepreneurial function. This function does not essentially consist in either inventing anything or otherwise creating the conditions which the enterprise exploits.* **It consists in getting things done.**

Venture capitalists embody this thinking in the decision criteria they use for selecting which ventures to fund. A proprietary idea ranks tenth out of twenty-four criteria.[5] Ranking above the idea are three criteria dealing with the entrepreneur's personality (capable of sustained effort, able to evaluate and respond to risk, articulate in discussing venture), and three more dealing with the entrepreneur's experience. Thus venture capitalists are looking for evidence that the entrepreneur can indeed *get things done.*

THEN WHY DO I NEED A COURSE IN ENTREPRENEURSHIP?

In many cases you don't. When I've asked students who have taken other introductory courses whether they liked the class, they've emphatically said, "Yes". They say they love the stories, and they enjoy hearing about other students' ventures, and hearing the students' and professors' comments on their own ventures. But usually within a few minutes, they all add that they didn't really learn anything. This was made most salient when I brought a former student from a different class to guest lecture for my course. She too answered that she loved the entrepreneurship class, but said it hadn't helped her in her new venture.

She said that for the first month of the venture the three-person team was completely immobilized—there was so much to do, they didn't know where to start. Having taken the traditional introductory course had not prepared her for entrepreneurship. While one month of immobilization may not seem critical, the team and its investors felt that the venture started only two months ahead of its rivals in a setting with first mover advantages. The immobilization cut that lead in half.

I had to agree with the students. When I taught the course in a traditional way I found that students had great ideas, but by the end of the semester they weren't any more developed than they were at the beginning. In short, it appeared that students were unable to make the link between their ideas and all the coursework that ought to translate those ideas into outstanding ventures.

Since what I would love most is to see all students start their ventures, I redesigned the course to increase the likelihood that that actually happens. The revised course captured in this text is a mechanism for breaking down the vast challenge of designing a venture into a sequence of critical decisions. Each decision takes advantage of tools developed in other parts of the BBA and MBA curriculum. The text reviews those tools, shows you how these are applied to new ventures, then links the decisions and tools to show you how a decision made in one part of the venture design flows through to other parts of the design.

The theme of the text is that thoughtful experimentation with your venture design is healthy, but that it is most healthy when that experimentation takes place on paper rather than in the real world. When the experimentation takes place on paper it is costless (more or less)—thus you will do more of it, and will ultimately arrive at a better design. If you were to introduce an arbitrary venture design into the real world, that initial design would be in essence an experiment. You would need to expend substantial funds to conduct that experiment, and if it was a poor design, you might not have enough funds to support the second experiment. Not only is real world experimentation costly to conduct, but it may lead to irreparable confusion on the part of the customer. This may render all subsequent experimentation infeasible.

Thus this course takes a "learning *before* doing" approach. Studies of firms who learn before doing, indicate that they not only start with better competitive postures, but they actually learn faster than their rivals, and respond better to change.[6] Thus firms who learn-before-doing are also better at learning *while* doing.

While the most *visible* output of the text will be a business plan, the most *valuable* output will be the venture simulation you will have created to support your decision making. By the end of the text you will have a set of spreadsheets that stretch from the demand curve for your product or service to the valuation for the entire venture. If you want to modify your strategy at any point in the future you can test that change in the simulation in minutes before you test it in the real world. If a new competitor enters your market with a different product configuration, you can go back to your raw data to see which product each customer will choose. You can do that not only for your current product configuration/price, but for alternative configurations/prices. This kind of costless experimentation makes adaptation far more likely and effective. This is one tangible component of why learning-before-doing might produce learning-while-doing.

Finally, one subtle role of the book is that by forcing you to actually do much of the venture design work, it will give you momentum. You will find that you have a substantial sunk investment in your venture by the end of the text. Accordingly, you may decide that the marginal effort to start the venture is relatively minor. If so, the book will have exceeded its goals!

Note that this text ends with a paper design. While this will be of tremendous value, and will have required considerable work, this is only the beginning of the entrepreneurial process. Once you move from design to implementation, you will need additional skills to actually acquire and manage the resources you identify in the plan. These are the subject of entrepreneurial implementation texts.

WHY THE DECISION-MAKING APPROACH?

This book offers a decision-making approach to venture design. The basic premise of the approach is that the quality of a venture is in essence the sum of its decisions. Decisions in turn are a function of the depth of information applied to each decision and the adequacy of the tools used to interpret that information. The basis for this perspective comes from "success curves".

A success curve is a means of depicting the survival odds of venture ideas as they pass through stages of development. The conventional wisdom from evaluating success curves across several industries is that it takes 3,000 raw ideas to produce one new commercial success.[7] This general ratio seems to hold not only for new product development inside large firms, but also for venture ideas posed by entrepreneurs. Exhibit 1-1 compares the success curves for the venture capital (VC) process against those for large firm new product development (NPD). The interesting distinction between the VC and NPD processes is that the VC "failures" take place on paper rather than the lab. Thus, they are costless. While the VC process thus seems harsher (funding fewer projects), large firms maintain the intellectual capital (both knowledge and people who have developed that knowledge) that is created as a byproduct of the NPD process. This knowledge has spillover benefits to other projects inside the firm, effectively increasing the returns to any project. This is not the case for Venture Capital—once a venture fails, the associated intellectual capital is dispersed.

Good decision-making allows you to distinguish good ideas from lesser ideas, and also to enhance the execution of the ideas that are carried forward to

Exhibit 1-1. Venture success curves

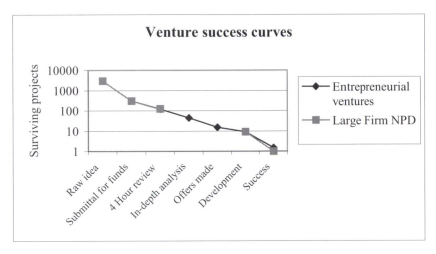

Source: Stevens & Burley, Research - Technology Management. May - June
1997. Reprinted with permission of the Industrial Research Institute.

launched ventures. The success curves in Exhibit 1-1 are close to ideal. These
are the curves for organizations whose main charter is discriminating between
good and bad ideas—firms with well-honed decision-making skills. Such decision-making skills shift the timing of "failure". NPD functions recognize early
that a venture will inevitable fail, and thus never launch it—the venture fails on
paper or in the lab, rather than in the market. Thus, 60% of their launches
become economically profitable,[8] whereas only 20% of independent firms survive past year eight.[9] The contrast is understandable. Entrepreneurs may only
attempt one new venture. Accordingly they have not developed the discrimination capability of VCs and large firm NPD.

Our goal in this book is to translate the collective wisdom of venture capitalists and large firm NPD, into decision-making skills that help you enjoy their
success curves rather than that of independent firms.

COMPETITIVE ADVANTAGE FROM DECISION-MAKING

Exploiting Decision Biases

One of the things I find when I ask students about their willingness to invest
in various ventures, is, they tend to reject ventures. While the 1:2999 odds of success suggest students aren't out of line, often the ventures they evaluate are ones
that have already succeeded. Since the students who take the course are by self-
selection those most likely to become entrepreneurs or venture capitalists, the

tendency to reject ventures is a little unsettling.

The problem in some sense is that we get students too late in the curriculum. While completing the core curriculum ensures students have the requisite skills, it also means they have adopted a large firm bias in favor of rejecting ideas. This bias is best described in terms of Type I and Type II errors of decision-making. The Type I/Type II error framework compares decisions against outcomes (Exhibit 1-2). Type I error is rejecting a venture that ultimately would have succeeded. Type II error is pursuing a venture that ultimately will fail. A perfect decision-maker makes no errors—it accepts all ventures that ultimately succeed and rejects all ventures that ultimately fail (or would have failed). Unfortunately, as seen earlier in the success curves, not even seasoned venture capitalists, whose job it is to discriminate between good and bad ventures, are perfect decision makers. Venture capitalists need to extract 50 to 70% annual expected returns across all ventures to compensate for those ventures on which they lose their initial investment.

Thus, decision-makers are characterized by their bias toward Type I versus Type II error. Type II error is an acceptance bias—in an effort to be a perfect

Exhibit 1-2. Decision Errors

True outcome

		Failure	Success
	Reject	Correct Decision	Type I Error
Funding Decision			
	Accept	Type II Error	Correct Decision

α = P(Funding a venture that ultimately fails), Type I Error
β = P(Rejecting a venture that ultimately succeeds), Type I Error

A perfect decision-maker is one where α and β are BOTH 0
(Can always make one 0 by either accepting all ideas (α = 0) or rejecting all ideas (β = 0)

decision-maker, you are happier accepting ideas that ultimately fail, than reject-ing ideas that ultimately succeed. Venture capitalists tend to favor Type II error.

Type I error, in contrast, is rejection of ideas that ultimately succeed, over accepting ideas that ultimately fail. This rejection bias is characteristic of large firms. A number of hypotheses have been set forth to explain the bias: reward systems with short time horizons, greater stock market penalties for poor per-formance than gains for comparable improvement in performance, and catas-trophic impact (termination for managers with visible failures). We are less interested in what causes the bias than in its regularity.

What is most alarming is that the bias seems to be inculcated in the MBA pro-gram itself. The most notable source is industry analysis. In general, the con-clusion students reach from industry analysis is that either the market is unat-tractive because it is too easy to enter, or it is attractive because it has formida-ble entry barriers. In the first instance, you can enter, but don't want to; in the latter, you want to enter, but can't. This tends to mean there is no opportunity for entrepreneurs. In the early days of examining CDNow, for example, students felt that the firm was doomed because established music retailers would ulti-mately displace the firm. What they ignored was the fact that in the meantime, CDNow could be quite profitable. Perhaps less foreseeable was the ultimate out-come—the firm had developed Internet resources that were easier for competi-tors to obtain via wholesale acquisition of firms, than by internal development. Thus, CDNow was acquired by Bertelsmann in September, 2000 for $117 million.

While we will address this "entry barrier paradox" in the next chapter, the point here is that part of the mission of this book is to reverse the large firm bias—to make students more sanguine about the fate of new ventures.

Fortunately, the large firm rejection bias is one of the major sources of entre-preneurial opportunity. Large firms reject new ventures for two reasons: risk aversion and unattractive scale. Risk aversion offers temporary advantage: large firms will wait to invest until the payoff uncertainty in reduced. Entrepreneurs who perceive venture payoffs with greater certainty have an opportunity to estab-lish footholds in new markets before large firms enter. Often when such firms do enter, they do so through acquisition, rather than through greenfield start-up. Thus not only do the new ventures enjoy an uncontested market for a short peri-od of time (and the associated monopoly profits), but they may also find that acquirers pay them the net present value of uneroded future profits.

While large firm risk aversion creates temporary opportunity, their small-scale aversion creates durable opportunity. Large firms leave several otherwise attractive opportunities on the table because the market is too small. Manufacturers of ethical drug equipment sell high-priced, large-capacity equip-ment to pharmaceutical firms. They were unwilling to develop a lower-priced, lower-capacity machine for pharmacy schools and small labs because the total market was only $10 million. This $10 million market, while trivial for large firms, created a very attractive opportunity for a student entrepreneur. Moreover, this initial opportunity may provide a steppingstone to follow-on products for the same market. In an interesting irony, Xerox sold off several of its own internal ventures due to the scale bias. In a recent study, it was shown that the market capitalization of these abandoned ventures actually exceeds that of Xerox.[10]

These large firm (and consequently MBA curriculum) biases against small and finite (no replacement) markets manifest themselves in a student evaluation of the potential for phyto-remediation technology developed at the University of Pennsylvania. The student team was asked to assess whether the University Center for Technology Transfer should create a venture around this technology, or whether they should license it to a large firm. Ultimately, the students concluded that while the technology was superior to other technologies currently available for remediating or cleaning hazardous waste sites—i.e., that it would do so at less cost and lower risk—the venture was unattractive. The primary reason for rejecting the venture was that the market was finite and shrinking. Before you jump on the bandwagon, let me point out that the size of the finite market was $300 billion.

Exploiting Raw Data

One of the conclusions I have reached as a result of several years' industry experience and teaching experience is that few people look at data, and therefore there is tremendous advantage for anyone willing to do so. I don't mean a career of data management, but rather of data examination as means to superior decision-making. This conclusion hit home first when I worked at Hughes Aircraft (now part of Raytheon). Once General Motors purchased Hughes, the company began to cut R&D spending, particularly for early stage projects. Such projects are ones for which the commercial potential is at least ten years in the future, for which their prospects are highly uncertain, and for which the government requires co-investment by the contractor. My concern with the cutbacks was that failure to participate in early stages was mortgaging the future—without early stage experience we would be unqualified to participate in later stage developments. To determine if this was the case, I wanted to understand the "demand" for early stage projects. This, in essence, is the inverse of what has come to be called the success curve—I wanted to know how many early stage projects Hughes needed now to ensure a single commercial success ten years in the future. I initially assumed that someone in marketing would have computed success probabilities from one stage to the next. Not only was that untrue, but worse, the raw data was almost irretrievable.

Hughes is not the exception. People are far too willing to trust their level of knowledge. In a really nice experiment,[11] students took on the role of hotel managers and were asked to choose a firm strategy. Students were given an initial strategy of being independent or part of a chain, and in the experiment were asked whether they wished to change their strategy. There were two stages to the experiment. In each stage students were given performance data on chain and independent hotels. In the first stage, the data were raw—tables where each row represented one hotel. Each hotel was identified as being either independent or chain, and a number of metrics were given for its performance. In the second stage, the same data were presented as summary bar charts of chain versus independent performance. In both stages, students received cash awards for making the correct decision.

The experimental results indicated that in the second stage almost all students made the correct choice, because the figure made the advantage of chains obvious. In the first stage, however, almost all students ignored the raw data and retained their initial strategy. Students were unwilling to make the effort to look at the data, despite the fact that it was well organized, that the experiment had no time constraint, and that they obtained a higher cash award if they chose the correct strategy in the first stage.

The implication is that because information flow is NOT efficient, there is entrepreneurial opportunity in exploiting even readily available information. Most people are unwilling to look at data, much less gather it. Persuaded by information efficiency arguments, they tend to believe they already know everything they need to know—that if anything REALLY important were in the data, it would make its way to them.

This, then, is the theme of the book: that you as an independent entrepreneur can approach the new venture success of NPD organizations and venture capitalists. This is possible through an information intensive and analytically rigorous approach to decision-making, using tools you likely already possess. The remainder of the book steps through each of these decisions. Each chapter is devoted to a particular decision, and is organized as follows: *Goal* of the chapter, theoretical *Principles* that enlighten the decision-making approach, the actual steps in the decision *Process*, and, finally, application of the decision process to the *Epigraphs* example.

FLOW OF THE BOOK

As mentioned previously, the book is organized around the decisions an entrepreneur faces in designing a venture. Each chapter in the book corresponds to a particular decision and the tools facilitating that decision. These decisions are nested, such that the outputs from each chapter feed into the decisions of subsequent chapters. These decisions and their interactions are captured in some detail in Exhibit 1-3.

The earliest decisions, Chapters 2-4, are considered feasibility assessments. They involve early, and reasonably inexpensive, methods for determining whether there is an opportunity worth pursuing: will the industry support entry, is there an unmet need in the market, and is there profitable demand for that unmet need.

Chapters 5-9 involve strategic decisions for the firm: what is the optimal price and configuration for your offering, what distribution channel and advertising program best exploit the potential demand, and what activities should the firm outsource versus retain.

Having made the strategic decisions (venture design), Chapters 10 and 11 define the resources necessary to implement that design (human and physical, as well as financial). Finally, Chapter 12 ties all the analyses, decisions and designs into a single document, the business plan. A sample plan is presented in Appendix 1. We now discuss each of these chapters in a little greater detail.

Chapter 2 (Industry Analysis) is the first stage in assessing the feasibility of your venture. The goals of industry analysis are two-fold. The first goal is to assess whether the industry will be hospitable to your particular venture. If so, and this is likely for most ventures, the subsequent role of industry analysis is to immerse yourself in the operational and competitive details of the industry. These details inform later decisions.

Chapter 3 (Perceptual mapping) is the second stage in the feasibility analysis. Perceptual mapping is a tool to characterize the way customers view your offering relative to competing or substitute offerings. The goal of perceptual maps is to determine if the proposed offering satisfies a clear, but currently unmet, need. The chapter introduces two tools: the perceptual map itself, and focus groups—the technique used to gather the primary data from which the perceptual map is derived.

Conjoint analysis, the technique introduced in *Chapter 4,* is the centerpiece of the venture design process. Its use marks the transition from feasibility analysis to venture design. Conjoint analysis is an extremely powerful tool consisting of primary survey data and corresponding statistical analysis. Conjoint analysis closes feasibility analysis by defining whether the unmet need identified in the perceptual map has sufficient demand at a profitable price. Conjoint analysis opens venture design by characterizing the demand curve for the product as a whole as well as each of its attributes.

Chapter 5 (Competitive Strategy) utilizes the demand curves derived from conjoint analysis to choose the optimal price and product configuration for the venture. The basic premise underlying the analysis is that, as a new venture, you will have some market power. The chapter applies principles of decision theory and game theory to a variety of industry conditions. With these tools you can

Exhibit 1-3. Book flow chart

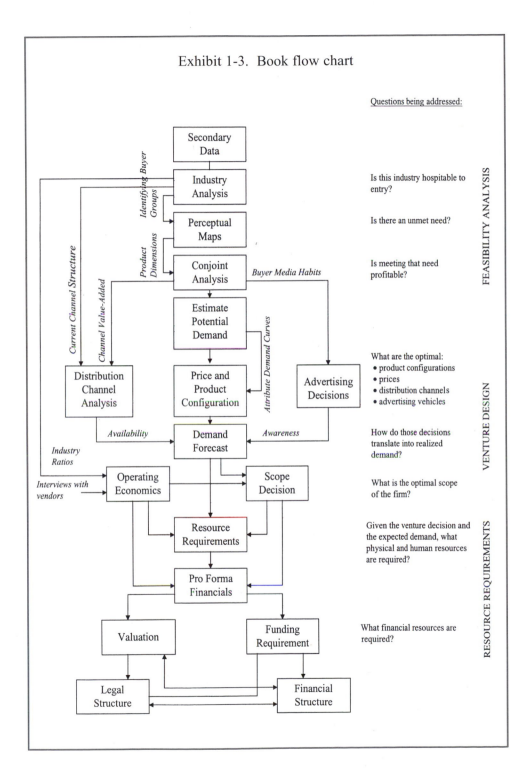

Questions being addressed:

Is this industry hospitable to entry?

Is there an unmet need?

Is meeting that need profitable?

What are the optimal:
- product configurations
- prices
- distribution channels
- advertising vehicles

How do those decisions translate into realized demand?

What is the optimal scope of the firm?

Given the venture decision and the expected demand, what physical and human resources are required?

What financial resources are required?

FEASIBILITY ANALYSIS

VENTURE DESIGN

RESOURCE REQUIREMENTS

Secondary Data

Industry Analysis

Perceptual Maps

Conjoint Analysis

Estimate Potential Demand

Distribution Channel Analysis

Price and Product Configuration

Advertising Decisions

Demand Forecast

Operating Economics

Scope Decision

Resource Requirements

Pro Forma Financials

Valuation

Funding Requirement

Legal Structure

Financial Structure

Identifying Buyer Groups

Current Channel Structure

Channel Value-Added

Product Dimensions

Buyer Media Habits

Attribute Demand Curves

Availability

Awareness

Industry Ratios

Interviews with vendors

determine whether to use market power to maximize current profits, or to condition entry, and thereby maximize lifetime profits.

Chapter 6 (Marketing Channel Decisions) deals with the choice of marketing channel (one of two choices involving the level of vertical integration). The chapter reviews principles from the vertical contracting literature in economics and the distribution channel literature from marketing. These qualitative insights are combined with quantitative techniques such as optimization and break-even analysis using the demand curves from Chapter 4 to derive a distribution strategy that maximizes lifetime profits.

The ultimate goal of the advertising program *(Chapter 7)* is to stimulate purchase through a paid program of communication to the target market. In the context of our venture, conjoint analysis reveals potential demand to a group of customers who are fully aware and informed about the product. The advertising program ensures the target market is aware and fully informed about the product. A single chapter is insufficient to provide enough guidance to develop a complete advertising campaign. However, we review the micro-principles of individual decision-making and the macro-principles of diffusion to help the entrepreneur become a sophisticated buyer of advertising, define the campaign goals, characterize their impact on demand, specify a budget likely to accomplish those goals, and understand message design and characteristics of advertising vehicles.

Demand forecasting *(Chapter 8)* is the linchpin of the entire business plan. The goal of demand forecasting is to generate reliable estimates of future revenues, and to support well-informed decisions about the levels of physical, human, and financial resources. Because the demand forecast is so critical, we tackle it from two different analytical approaches—the first bottoms-up approach that applies the reach of the distribution channel and the awareness from the advertising program to the "potential demand" from conjoint analysis to unfold demand over time. The second, top-down, approach is historical analogy to the diffusion of prior comparable products. Comparison of the two approaches not only leads to forecasts with higher reliability, but also provides insights into how demand can best be manipulated to the benefit of the venture.

One of the most important strategic decisions that a firm makes is that of its operational scope *(Chapter 9)*—which activities should the firm execute internally versus those which it should outsource to other firms. What makes the scope decision strategically important are the facts that it is largely irreversible, and that it affects the long-term viability of the firm. The chapter draws on vertical contracting theory, transaction cost economics, and resource-based theories, to develop a framework for determining which activities to outsource and which to execute internally. The objective in making the decision is to provide reliable provision of high quality goods and services at the lowest cost today, while building/preserving the capabilities that lead to sustained competitive advantage in the future.

While chapters 4-9 deal with strategic decisions (whom to target, with what product, at what price, through what distribution channel and advertising medium, and with what internal operations), chapters 10 and 11 treat their implementation—given the decisions we have made, what resources are required to execute them.

Chapter 10 (Establishing Resource Requirements) considers physical and human resource requirements. The goal of careful resource planning is avoiding both *under-investment* (which renders the firm unable to satisfy demand, and thereby leads to permanent losses in market share) and *over-investment* (with attendant high carrying costs that could strangle an otherwise healthy venture). The chapter reviews tools such as operating cycles, bills of capacity, and master output schedule, and applies them to the demand forecast (Chapter 8) to specify calendarized resource requirements. These tools ensure that internal resources are commensurate with demand.

Chapter 11 (Valuation and Financial Requirements) translates the decisions in all of the preceding chapters into a cash flow statement for the firm. This cash flow statement defines the finances required for implementing the venture design, and provides the foundation for a valuation. Since the valuation is the basis for equity financing, the cash flow statement (in conjunction with standard discount rates for various funding sources) also defines the amount of equity the venture must exchange for the needed funds.

Chapter 12 (The Business Plan) ties together all the prior feasibility analysis, strategic decisions, and resource requirements into a single document. The Business Plan basically serves two purposes for the venture—as a planning tool for the founders, and as a sales document for potential investors and other resources. This leads many people to conclude that there should be two separate documents—one that provides substance (the planning tool), and another that provides flash (the sales document). We argue, however, that given the criteria of venture capitalists, the well-conceived planning tool is also the best sales document. To make this argument, we first review the decision criteria of venture capitalists in an effort to characterize what would make a good sales tool. We then review the elements of an effective planning tool. Finally, we show how all the tools in this book form a business plan that satisfies both objectives.

EPIGRAPHS

Epigraphs is a new venture that was developed in conjunction with the book. Its purpose is to provide a fairly straightforward venture with which to demonstrate the tools in the book. Thus, you will see not only how to execute each of the tools, but also how the tools are linked—how, for example, the survey results translate into product designs; how those designs translate into demand forecasts; and how the demand forecasts translate into resource requirements and, ultimately, valuation. While this is depicted graphically in Figure 1-3, the case will provide nuts and bolts detail of how the spreadsheets are linked.

Because you will be living with the case over the next several weeks, we thought it would be worthwhile and possibly fun to know something about the venture's inception and the actual timeline of development. In fact, we even thought about subtitling the book, "The 100 Hour Venture". Ultimately we concluded that the 100 hours in the title might convey the wrong message—our real message is that the quality of the venture is a function of the qualities of the information and the decision-making. The subtext is that each of these can be accomplished within a reasonable length of time, i.e. good design does not take significantly more time than weak design.

What is Epigraphs? Epigraphs is a wall-covering product that is a substitute for wallpaper. The idea for Epigraphs was motivated by the limitations of wallpaper for a particular room I was trying to decorate. I had found a wallpaper that was nice for a library: Waverly's Alphabet from their Renaissance collection. However, when I began to estimate the amount of wallpaper needed, I noticed that the room was actually too "cut up" for wallpaper. In particular, there was ductwork that protruded along two of the walls, moulding on some but not others, five windows, two large entryways, and a fireplace. This meant that there would be lots of mismatching in the pattern, and tedious labor—almost no length of wallpaper could be applied without special cutouts. This problem defined the "need" for a new alternative.

Paint was an obvious solution, but I had grown attached to the look of the wallpaper. The next thought was that I could stencil letters of the alphabet on the painted wall. This took me in two directions. First, if I were daunted by the labor of wallpapering, I certainly would be more daunted by stenciling—what stencils, how many stencils, creating the stencils, and actually applying the stencils. The second direction was the expansive direction,—Why be constrained by the repetition of wall covering? Why not use whole quotes—favorite quotes from various sources? This implied hand painting, which was far more effort than I was willing to expend.

The incubation process of idea generation is often described as a garbage can approach.[12] At any given time you, carry around a set of "needs," such as how to decorate a wall, and a set of "solutions." The set of solutions any individual carries is a function of prior education and experience. An "idea" is thus the matching of a need and a solution. In this case, "the top-of-the-head" solutions were stenciling and hand painting, both of which were too labor intensive. The "Aha" solution was to take advantage of recent sign technology.

Because I had a friend who founded a sign company several years ago, I had fairly detailed knowledge of the technology. In particular I knew that almost any graphic could be computer-generated and cut from strips of self-adhesive vinyl. I could create a text file, choose a font and size, and the company could produce a set of quotes that could be applied to the wall. Thus I could solve my own decorating problem, but since I was also working on the manuscript for this book, it occurred to me that perhaps this was an opportunity to solve similar problems of other consumers. This in short was the link between an individual problem and a venture idea.

What follows in the succeeding chapters is the process of converting the venture idea into a comprehensive venture design. Exhibit 1-4 chronicles the process. In all, the process took approximately 100 hours extended over several months. This process can be compressed (and will be for a semester long course). Part of what extended the process is the fact that I was refining the process and documenting it for this manuscript, concurrently with designing the venture.

I should note that this is the length of the process for someone engaged in something else full-time, e.g., where venture design is done in stolen hours. This is likely the case for full-time students and is certainly the case for someone who is currently employed, but contemplating their own venture.

While it is possible that the process could be compressed even further, I believe the venture design improves if it has a chance to let information, analysis results, and design alternatives incubate. Two of the critical decisions for Epigraphs were changed: the distribution channel and the product technology. Not only did they change from my initial intuition, but they also changed from the decision reached from the corresponding analysis.

The implication is that 1) good designs evolve, and 2) it is better to have the venture evolve on paper than in practice. If I had committed to the technology or the distribution channel at the initial decision point, I might have wasted critical resources. Even worse, I might have committed myself to an inferior design.

Exhibit 1-4. Diary of the Epigraphs Venture

Date	Event
Aug 22	Need recognition (Original search for wallpaper/attempt to measure wall)
Aug 22-25	Consider alternative solutions: hand-painting, stenciling Begin collecting quotes in palm pilot
Aug 26	Venture idea: Combine need with Gerber technology Map out venture schedule
Sept 7	Initial e-mail to Kyle
Sept 7	Online research of wallcovering industry using Library
Oct 1	Initial meeting with Kyle—layout schedule
Oct 4	Industry analysis using secondary data
Oct 7	Obtain estimate for focus group cost
Oct 11	Obtain materials samples, place order for prototype quotes
Oct 11	Complete moderator guide and screener for focus group
Oct 12-19	Recruit participants for focus group
Oct 13-15	Obtain mail list for consumers
Oct 22	Create prototypes by mounting quotes on mat board
Oct 25	Focus group with interior designers
Nov 1	Analyze focus group data; create perceptual map
Nov 4	Create draft of conjoint survey
Nov 8	Distribute survey: Create/print cover letter mail merge, copy survey, mail
Nov 10-30	Surveys returned
Nov 22	Marketing channel analysis
Nov 29-Dec 2	Regression analysis of survey data
Dec 2	Optimal price and product configuration analysis
Dec 4	Meet with manufacturer to obtain production cost estimates Develop resource requirements Create demand forecasts/financial forecasts
Dec 8	Media kits from advertising media

notes

1   Edison, Thomas A., "Genius is one percent inspiration and ninety-nine percent perspiration," Life, 1932

2   Collins, James C. and Jerry I. Porras, 1994. "Built to Last: Successful Habits of Visionary Companies" New York: Harper Business.

3   Bhide, Amar V., 2000. "The Origin and Evolution of New Businesses," New York: Oxford University Press.

4   Schumpeter, Joseph A., 1942. "Capitalism, Socialism and Democracy," New York: Harper & Brothers.

5   Macmillan, Ian, Robin Siegel, and P.N. Subba Narashima, 1985. "Criteria Used by Venture Capitalists to Evaluate New Venture Proposals" Journal of Business Venturing 1, pp. 119-128.

6   Pisano, Gary, 1997. "The development factory: Unlocking the potential of process innovation" Boston: Harvard Busness School Press.

7   Stevens, Greg A. and James Burley, 1997. "3,000 Raw Ideas=1 Commercial Success," Research Technology Management, May-June 1997, pp 16-27.

8   Stevens & Burley (cited above)

9   U.S. SBA (cited above)

10 Chesbrough, Hank, 2000. "Creating and Capturing Value from Research Spillovers: The Case of Xerox's Technology Spin-off Companies," Harvard Business School Working Paper.

11 Ingram, Paul and Gaurab Bhardwaj, 1998. "Strategic Persistence in the Face of Contrary Industry Experience: Two Experiments on the Failure to Learn from Others." Columbia University Working Paper.

12 March, James and Johan Olsen, 1976. "Ambiguity and Choice in Organizations, Bergen: Universitetsforlaget.

assessing feasibility

chapter 2

industry analysis

INTRODUCTION AND GOALS

Industry analysis is the first stage in assessing the feasibility of your venture. The goals of industry analysis are two-fold. The first goal is to assess whether the industry will be hospitable to your particular venture. If so, and this is likely for most ventures, the subsequent role of industry analysis is to immerse yourself in the operational and competitive details of the industry. These details inform later decisions.

Up to 98% of firms involved in the creation of concentrated industries ultimately fail.[1] Industry analysis helps us to determine whether a particular industry is likely to become concentrated, and if so, which firms are most likely to survive. This kind of dramatic shakeout is currently taking place in the Internet. While the Internet is more a distribution channel than an industry, the pattern of growth and shakeout resembles that of concentrated industries. In the midst of the growth frenzy, students felt that the Internet was so new and different, normal analytical techniques did not apply. A recent study indicates that in fact they do still apply.[2] The survivors in the Internet arena are firms who moved early in sectors where there were classical "first mover advantages." Two things should be noted here: one, first mover advantage doesn't require moving first, and two, there is still opportunity for firms that ultimately will fail (as the founder of ValueAmerica can attest).[3] This chapter will help you understand whether an industry is likely to become concentrated, and whether there is opportunity nevertheless.

The chapter begins with a review of industry analysis techniques. In addition to the standard review, we discuss how the techniques can help identify entrepreneurial entry wedges. The discussion then shifts from principles to hands-on tools for gathering and analyzing industry data. Finally, we walk through data gathering and analysis for Epigraphs—to demonstrate how industry analysis is as much art as it is science.

venture design

PRINCIPLES

One of the most useful frameworks for assessing industry attractiveness is Porter's five forces.[4] Porter's five forces takes classical Industrial Organization (IO) economics, expands it, and turns it on its head. Classical IO is interested in ensuring that industries behave competitively so that social welfare is maximized. The field enlightens most anti-trust regulation as well as litigation (for a very interesting, but very lengthy recent case, see the articles tracking the Microsoft case, where two leading economists, both at MIT, were pitted against each other as expert witnesses). The central question antitrust legislation faces is whether the behavior of the defendant(s) appears to be impeding competition. Behaviors typically viewed to be anti-competitive are pricing below marginal cost and collusion (both explicit and tacit).

Classical IO is less interested in the behaviors of firms, per se, than they are in the structure of the industry. Certain industry structures lend themselves most readily to anti-competitive behaviors. In the limit of course, economists see the ideal structure as perfect competition, where all firms make zero profits. The irony or paradox, then, is that no rational firm would enter an industry where it would make zero profits. This is the wedge that Porter exploits in developing the five forces framework.

The framework takes the basic tenets of IO and turns them upside down. Whereas IO, taking the best interest of society as a whole, is concerned with minimizing anti-competitive structures, Porter recognizes that these same structures represent durable profit opportunity for firms. One way to frame IO and Porter's work is to consider industries as being arrayed along a continuum, as shown in Exhibit 2-1, with perfect competition on the left-hand side, and monopoly on the right-hand side. Industries on the left earn zero profits; industries on the right earn monopoly profits. The vast majority of industries are oligopolies that lie somewhere between these extremes. The goal of IO is to identify those industries on the right-hand side and move them toward the left. The goal of Porter's analysis is to determine where along the continuum an industry lies, as a means to assess the opportunity for supra-normal (above cost of capital) returns. Empirical support for the utility of such an approach is given in Exhibit 2-2. The Exhibit indicates that mean return on investment (ROI) for firms is roughly 15%. The more interesting observation is that as industry size (number of firms) decreases, both market share and return on investment increase. In fact market share is the dominant predictor of firm profitability.[5]

Five Forces Framework

Let's review the basic framework. Exhibit 2-3 lays out the five forces structure. The goal in examining each element in the industry structure is to determine

Exhibit 2-1. Competitive Continuum

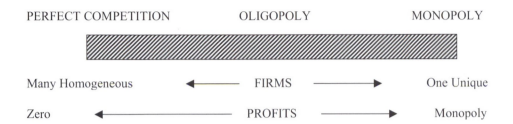

PERFECT COMPETITION   OLIGOPOLY   MONOPOLY

Many Homogeneous   ←——— FIRMS ———→   One Unique

Zero   ←———————— PROFITS ———→   Monopoly

Exhibit 2-2. Profit Impact of Marketing Study

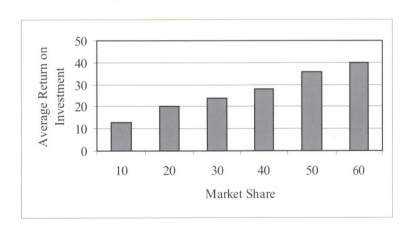

Reprinted with the permission of The Free Press, a Division of Simon & Schuster, Inc. from "The PIMS Principles: Linking Strategy to Performance" by Robert D. Buzzell and Bradley T. Gale. Copyright © 1987 by The Free Press.

Exhibit 2-3. Porter's Five Forces

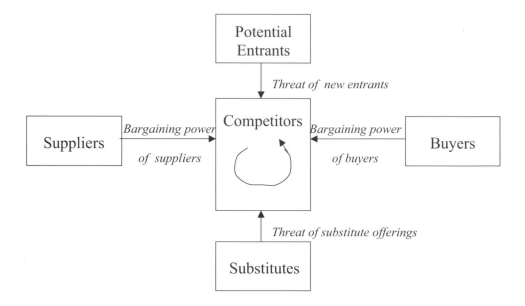

Reprinted with the permission of The Free Press, a Division of Simon & Schuster, Inc. from "Competitive Strategy: Techniques for Analyzing Industries and Competitors" by Michael Porter. Copyright © 1980,1988 by The Free Press.

the extent to which that element has the power to limit profits of firms in the focal industry. The vertical dimension of the framework considers sources of competition. The central box is direct competitors. Porter, however, expands the notion of competition to include potential entrants as well as substitutes (products/services that customers can switch to if the offerings of the focal industry are unattractive). The primary issue in this dimension is: to what extent does the expanded set of competitors approach perfect competition and thereby limit the profit potential of the focal industry. A very unattractive industry is one with a large number of competitors, close substitutes, limited growth, and no entry barriers.

The horizontal dimension of the framework examines the value chain. The primary issue here is the extent to which other elements of the value chain have the power to extract potential profits from the focal industry. This is largely an issue of relative scarcity—a sole source of supply or a sole customer (monopsony) has substantial bargaining power. In addition to the scarcity threat in the value chain, is the competitive threat—whether there is opportunity for suppliers to integrate forward, or distributors/customers to integrate backward to compete with the focal industry. A very unattractive industry from the perspective of the value chain is one in which there is scarce supply of a critical input, few distributors, and a limited number of well-informed customers.

Industry analysis of CDNow at inception would conclude that it was entering an unattractive industry, even before the emergence of other music e-tailers. This was due to factors both in the competitive dimension and in the value chain dimension. In the competitive dimension, there were few entry barriers (they themselves started in a basement),[6] and powerful substitutes including large music chains (Virgin, Sam Goody, Tower, and HMV) and record clubs (Columbia House and BMG). In the value chain dimension, there were powerful suppliers. Major record labels each had monopolies over given artists, and several had demonstrated interest and capability to vertically integrate. Virgin integrated backwards from retail sales into production, and Columbia integrated forward from production into retailing. While customers were numerous, they were well-informed as to price. In fact, one of the first Internet shop bots was for CD prices.

The Entrepreneur's Paradox

The ideal industry from this perspective, then, is one in which there is high growth, a small number of differentiated competitors, no close substitutes, high entry barriers, commodity inputs, and a mass market. The paradox from the standpoint of entrepreneurs is that a truly attractive industry is one that almost by definition you cannot enter—i.e., if you can enter, so can anyone else, and thus profits are likely to be low. Thus, an ideal industry from an entrepreneurial standpoint is one where you can close the barn-door behind you. Accordingly, we take a parallax view of industry analysis. Often this involves opening yourself to transient opportunity. While we have just demonstrated that music e-tailing was an unattractive industry, CDNow was a still a good entrepreneurial opportunity. It made money for the founders, forced adoption of Internet technology by established retailers, and changed the entire distribution of who buys music.

A Note on Complements

One important structural element of industry that is largely ignored by the Five Forces framework, is complements. Complements are products/services whose sales positively affect, and are positively affected by, those of the focal product/service. The more people buy the complementary product, they more need they will have for the focal product and vice versa. Examples of complements are: hamburger and hamburger buns, automobiles and gas stations, hardware and software, digital video discs (DVD) and DVD players, skis and bindings. Occasionally, products are their own complements. What this means is that owners derive more use from a given product as the number of other users

25

increases. This is true for fax machines and e-mail. There is not much point in having a fax machine or e-mail if no one else does.

Complements pose both opportunities and challenges to new ventures. The opportunity lies in the fact that there is a positive feedback loop by which sales of the complement increase the value of the focal product, which in turn increases focal product sales, and thereby the value of the complement. These higher sales for both the product and the complement lead to scale economies and learning that reduce the cost of the product and lead to even higher sales.

The challenge posed by complements that is particularly acute for new ventures is one of critical mass. Until adoption of the complementary product has reached a particular level, customers have limited use for the focal product. Early adopters of video cassette recorders (VCRs) had to pay $100 for pre-recorded tapes, and had few alternatives to paying the $100 because the rental market had yet to be created. The markets for both VCRs and pre-recorded tapes thus took some time to develop. Fortunately, an alternative use for VCRs, recording television programs for playback at a different time, provided some means to fuel early sales. This minimized the dependence of VCR sales on sales of pre-recorded tapes. Once VCR sales took off, then so too did sales of the pre-recorded tapes. Without the alternative use (recording television shows) for VCRs, neither market may have developed. We discuss some implications of complements in Chapter 8, Demand Forecasting, but for more comprehensive treatment of strategy in the face of complements, we recommend the book, "Co-opetition."[7]

Not all industries have complements—in fact, most do not. The main point we make here is that complements, when they exist, will be the dominant factor in the industry. If your product does have a complement, and if that product is at an early stage, you probably want to treat the two products jointly in all subsequent analyses. For CDNow, CD players would be considered a complement. However, the player market was fairly mature at the time, thus the player market posed neither an opportunity nor a challenge to the venture.

ANALYTICAL PROCESS

The analytical process for industry analysis involves rigorous mining of a wide array of secondary data. Fortunately, almost all of this data is available electronically, so there is little reason to skimp on this activity.

Defining the Industry

Industry analysis is more art than science. Perhaps the most difficult challenge is defining the industry itself. For example, an entrepreneur who develops a new technology for skis, may question whether the relevant industry is skis, ski equipment, the ski industry (including resorts and apparel, as well as equipment), or sporting goods.

A comprehensive analysis of cross-price elasticities (the percentage increase in demand for A, for each percentage increase in the price of B) of products within all these industry definitions would allow us to determine the appropriate industry boundary with a high degree of confidence. However, it is unlikely that the cost of such analysis would be justified by the improvement in boundary accuracy. If the cost were justified, then SIC code classification would likely follow such an approach. As it stands, industry definitions are rather loose.

While there is probably a value in examining each of the ski "industries" to get a sense of trends, the industry whose structure you would analyze is skis themselves. For example, ski apparel is probably outside—an increase in the price of Bogner jackets is unlikely to affect the likelihood I would buy Volkl skis. Equipment is closer—a substantial increase in the price of bindings may actually decrease the likelihood I buy skis at all. Bindings are complements to skis—I can't buy one without the other. Other skis are closest—an increase in the price of Rossignol skis makes it more likely I will buy the Volkls.

In most cases, informed intuition, like the ski example we just outlined, ought to be sufficient to choose industry boundaries. The central question to ask in choosing the boundaries is "what products/services are a part of the customers choice set when they make the purchase decision". While this is not always as simple as it sounds in industries with differentiated products, intuition is a good starting point. It can later be validated or refined by research.

In the case of the ski manufacturer, intuition would suggest that customers compare skis only to other skis in making their purchase decision—they don't compare skis to boots, skis to resorts, or skis to jackets (even though all of these are subsets of the "ski industry").

Gathering Raw Data

Most of the data needed for industry analysis should be available on-line through your university research library. If you are no longer a student, library privileges are usually available to alumni for a nominal fee.

This particular search follows Library Information Guide #8 from the SAFRA BUSINESS RESEARCH CENTER at Wharton's Lippincott Library. All commands are initiated from the library homepage (HP): www.library.upenn.edu/lippincott. Search terms are designated using quotes. Thus, if I am searching the term "wallcovering," the command will read: "wallcovering."

1) The first step is a search for relevant SIC codes. These are obtained with the following search:
   HP > Business Reference > SIC Codes > "wallcovering"

The search yields the following results:
    2679 Wallcovering: Paper
    3069 Wallcovering: Rubber
    5231 Wallcovering: Stores Retail
Rubber wallcovering sounds like special industrial use, so we ignore it in future analysis. SIC 2679 is likely our focal industry, while 5231 may be of interest in examining distribution channel characteristics.

2) The second step is to identify the firms in the idustry. These were obtained through Lexis/Nexis:

    HP > Business Databases > Lexis/Nexis Academic Universe > Company Financial Information for SIC 2679 (first for U.S. Public Companies and then for U.S. Private Companies) yields the following results:

    There are 4 major US firms engaged in wallpaper manufacturing with a total wholesale value of $870 million. The market leaders and their respective market shares are given in Exhibit 2-4.

3) The third step is to characterize the distribution channels in the industry.
    An identical search to that in step 2, for SIC 5231, found only one firm, Sherwin-Williams dedicated to paint/wallpaper. (The firm also manufactures paint). The remaining eight firms sold building products more generally. Wallpaper is sold through three channels: paint/wallpaper chains, building supply/department stores, and independent retailers (through wholesalers). Shares of distribution through each channel are summarized in Exhibit 2-5.

    In addition to identifying the major industry players, these data yield two important insights:
    a) Retail markup is roughly 100%
    b) Retail sales is a fragmented market—there are a large number of very small firms ("other" is the dominant market share followed by a handful of chains). Typically, distribution in such markets follows two channels: a direct channel to the chains, and a longer channel through wholesalers to independent retailers. At this point, we are unable to identify the wholesalers.

4) The fourth step is to characterize the buyers in the industry. Here, as in choosing industry boundaries, we need to apply some intuition. Who is likely to buy wallpaper? Ignoring firms, and making the assumption that renters are unlikely to invest in renovations, the target market is owner-

Exhibit 2-4. Market Shares of Wallpaper Manufacturers

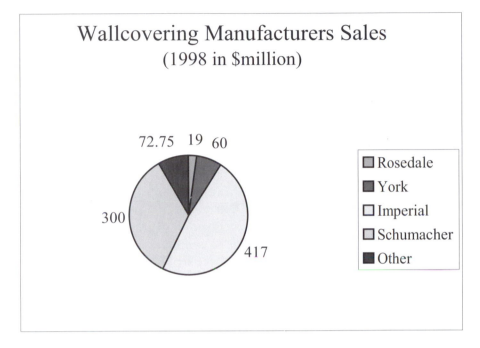

Exhibit 2-5. Retail Shares of Distribution Channels

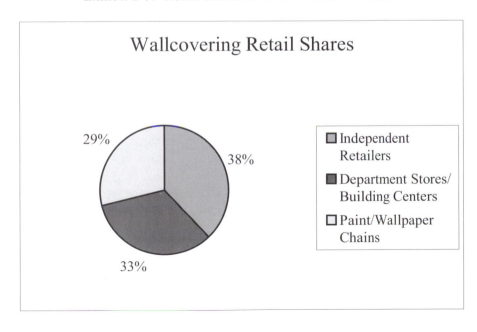

occupied households.

    HP > Statistical Universe > Statistical Abstract of U.S.> PDF Files>
    Index > Find Report 1237 Occupied Housing Units
    1995 Owner occupied households = 63,544,000
    Report 1245 Expenditures by Property owner (owner occupant)
    (there is no breakout for wallpaper. The closest category for which we
    have data is painting)

Painting:	$5192M	1989	
	$5260M	1990	Average growth =12.1%/year
	$6522M	1991	

These data are aggregate statistics of the market. Ultimately, we want to know whom to target. To help with this, we augmented the on-line data with hard-copy data published in American Marketplace.[8] American Marketplace allows us to examine buying behavior as a function of consumer demographics. This is thus a first cut at segmentation data. As with the statistical abstract, there is no specific breakout for wallcovering. There is, however, data on home textiles, which is closer to wallpaper than is paint. We can compare the two sets of data to help refine estimates for wallpaper. These American Marketplace data (summarized in Exhibit 2-6) indicate that the dominant textile buyers are middle-aged married couples in the Northeast with incomes in excess of $70,000.

Thus, we have some preliminary understanding of the forward end of the value chain. We do not have details on suppliers to the wallpaper market, but because we use different inputs from typical wallpaper manufacturers, these details would not be representative of our "industry."

Market Surveys

We refine insights gained from the raw sales data, using market surveys. In general, data characterizing the customer is expensive to collect and has a small audience. Thus, there are only three parties willing to collect such data: firms producing products for the target market, industry associations or journals, and market research companies. Producer firms are unlikely to share primary research since it has competitive value. In contrast, industry associations and market research firms are generally willing to sell their information in the form of market research reports. The challenge in obtaining market research is knowing that it exists and from whom.

Industry articles. Perhaps the best means for identifying the existence of market research reports is scanning articles pertaining to the industry. Often these articles reference reports and their source when characterizing the industry. To find articles likely to reference such reports, try any of the following data-

Exhibit 2-6. Home Textile Customer Demographics

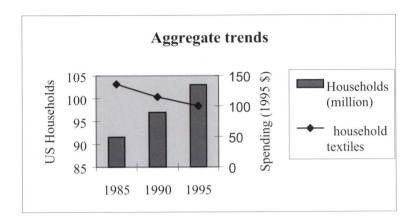

Aggregate trends

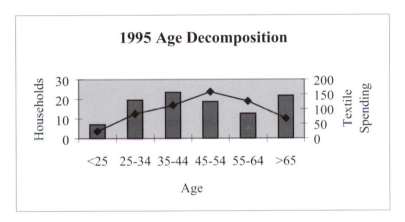

1995 Age Decomposition

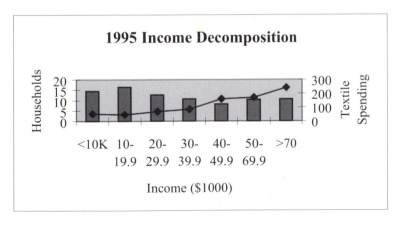

1995 Income Decomposition

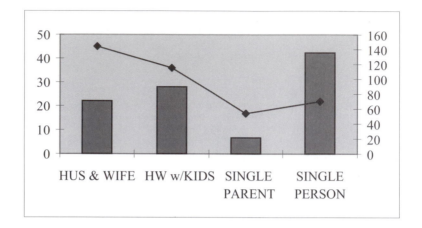

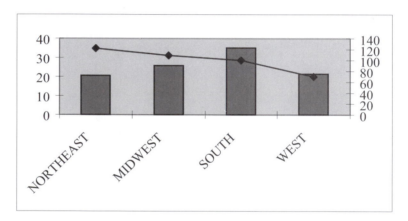

From: Heslop, Janet (Ed), " The American Marketplace:/Demographics and Spending Patterns," Ithaca, NY: New Strategist Publications, Chapter 7, Spending Trends.

bases: Business and Industry, Dow Jones Interactive, and ABI/Inform. Search on the terms "market research" with the relevant product/industry. Since the wall-covering industry is so small, searches for the terms "wallcovering market research" produced no results.

Market research companies. Some market research companies cover whole sectors of economic activity. Frost and Sullivan, Forester, Jupiter, Simmons, and Marketfull all compile reports that are generally available for a subscription fee, plus occasionally a fee for each report. Often University business libraries sub-scribe to some of these services. Fees for downloading are then proscribed by the university. A list of market research companies (with links to their reports) to which Lippincott Library subscribes is accessed from the homepage as follows:

None of these firms covered wallcovering

Industry Associations. Industry associations are valuable for a number of reasons beyond market research reports. They host annual meetings that provide information on the latest developments in the field, as well as opportunities to meet critical people. In addition, they generally produce journals or magazines with articles on trends, developments, and common problems. These articles frequently identify key participants and consultants to the industry. Even advertisements provide valuable information flagging new products and identifying sources of supply. There are several association directories. At Lippincott, the online association directory is accessed as follows:

HP > Business Reference > Associations > Unlimited > Subject: "Wallcovering"

This search yields the following organizations:
> Home Decoration Retailer's Association (Great Britain)
> International Wallcovering Manufacturers Association (Belgium)
> National Guild of Professional Paperhangers
> New York State Council of Painting and Decorating Contractors
> Paint and Decorating Retailers Association
> Paining and Decorating Contractors Association of the East Bay
> Painting and Decorating Contractors of America
> Wallcovering Manufacturers Association of Great Britain (Great Britain)
> Wallcoverings Association

Hot links to these sites indicate that Wallcoverings Association (120 members) is probably the best match to our focal industry—WA members include both manufacturers and wholesalers, but exclude decorators and paperhangers. Unfortunately their only publication appears to be a membership directory, thus they are not a source of market surveys.

One problem in identifying associations is that often the term you might use to identify the industry is not the same as that used within the industry. For example, the "National Decorating Products Association" appears to be an important source for wallcovering research, but it was not found in the above search. The best means for finding alternate designations for the industry is to review industry articles, as discussed above.

Market News and Trends

Up until now, the data we have gathered tends to be quantitative and tends to focus on the supply chain. To gain greater insight into market behavior, and to flesh out data on the broader set of competitors, we turn to Market News.

HP > Business Databases > Business and Industry > "wallcovering market" The articles from this search yield the following insights:

- Consolidation is taking place in the industry
- There is a trend toward licensing agreements with designer brands
- The industry is estimated at $1 Billion but sales have been declining over the last 3 years at the rate of 7% per year
- Imperial Home Décor Group (IHDC) has 48% share
- Wallcoverings account for 6% of UK "Do-It Yourself" (DIY) spending
- UK DIY superstores account for 56% of wallcovering sales
- Wallcovering SIC is 267952
- Wallpaper stores is 523035 (6 digits versus 4 digit SIC)
- UK customers are attracted to independent outlets because they expect it is less likely to see the same wallpaper in their neighbor's house
- 10% of purchases are ordered from pattern books; 84% are sold from stock.
- Independents share of the market is increasing at the expense of chains (US estimate at 37.9%)
- "4500 books of Royal Doullon Collection Sold" raises question: are pattern books *sold* to the retailers.
- 90% of American walls are painted (rather than papered)
- Wallcovering industry estimated at $2 Billion retail
- Attributes of wall paper that lead to preference for paint:
    Fear of hanging own paper
    Confusing instructions
    Poor merchandising
- Wallpaper designs are lagging behind other parts of home decorating industry
- Trend towards "coordinating wallpaper with other home decorating products (room in a bag) to create room themes (linens, drapes, etc.)
- High-end doing well (this may be pattern books)
- Sidewall sales (whole walls) slipping at expense of border sales
- Borders now account for 50% of wallcovering sales
- Borders are inexpensive per room ($40), and easily applied

Key Informants

In addition to providing the information above, articles also identified industry consultants who might be used as key informants. These experts are useful for clarifying remaining issues in the industry, and for validating the conclusions you have drawn from secondary data. Unfortunately, the consultants we contacted were not interested in providing information for free, since they are in the business of charging for information. We had much greater success contacting manufacturers and retailers directly. Since these sources are providing information as a courtesy, we recommend waiting to contact them until after you have developed a good understanding of the industry, and need help with details not available in public sources.

The information we needed help with was at the product level: What is the typical life cycle for a wallpaper pattern? What is the distribution of sales for wallpaper patterns?

Through these personal contacts we were able to learn the following:

- The life of a typical collection (set of coordinating patterns/colors) is three years
- The minimum life cycle is 1 year; the maximum is 10 years
- Sixty percent of a collection's lifetime sales occur in the first year
- Average lifetime sales for a collection is 7 million single rolls

Combining this information, and doing some curve-fitting, yields the sales profile in Exhibit 2-7. The Exhibit indicates sales for a new wallcovering peak in the 3rd quarter following introduction.

In addition to the product details, the interviews provided information on general trends in the industry. Many of these corroborate information we had found publicly:

Exhibit 2-7. Wallpaper Sales Profile Over the Lifecycle

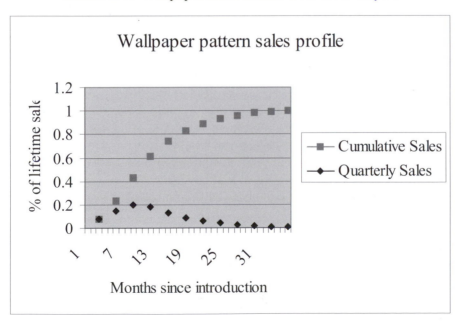

- Sales have been declining steadily over the past ten years—both wallpaper and borders are out of style
- The retail channel (bypassing wholesalers) is becoming more important to manufacturers because the margins are higher
- Manufacturers are attempting to differentiate on service and availability. Therefore, they are:
    - Providing 24-hour delivery for book orders
    - Pushing in-stock sales so the product is available when customers want it
    - Accordingly, they are offering 30% discount to retailers for stocking a 24 roll minimum inventory
- Typical payment terms: Net 30

Ratio Studies

The final piece of secondary data of interest is industry ratio studies.[9] These studies create summaries of typical accounting ratios for firms in a given industry, broken down by firm size. Again, because the wallcovering industry is so small, there were no ratio summaries of SIC 2679. As a substitute, we took the financial statements for the public firms found in step 2, and did our own ratio analysis (Exhibit 2-8). While these will be of greatest value later in informing operating decisions and generating operating economics, they are also important

Exhibit 2-8. Comparison of Wallpaper Manufacturer and Retailer Ratios

	Manufacturer	**Retailer Chain**
Income Statement Ratios		
Sales	100.0%	100.0%
Cost of Goods Sold	60.2%	56.8%
R & D	1.5%	---
Sales, General % Admin	26.5%	32.4%
Depreciation & Amort	3.2%	--
Net Income	5.5%	5.5%
Operations Metrics		
Inventory Turns	2.6	7.2
Performance Ratios		
Return on fixed assets	48.7%	38.0%
Return on Equity	13.1%	15.9%

to industry analysis. In particular, ratios provide insight into the relative importance of inputs costs (materials cost ratio), the extent to which there are entry barriers (high fixed-investment relative to marginal cost), or scale economics (significantly lower Cost of Goods Sold [CGS] as firm size increases). Finally, profit ratios validate the results of our industry analysis. If we conclude an industry is attractive, it ought to exhibit high profit margins.

The ratios indicate that input costs are moderate to high (60% of sales) for the wallcovering manufacturer. Sales, General, and Administrative Expense (S&GA) is the other major cost element (26.5% of sales). The value of Plant/Property and Equipment is low relative to Sales, indicating that sunk investments are unlikely to serve as an entry barrier. The most salient element in the ratios is the inventory turns (2.6). On average, this particular firm is holding 4.6 months inventory. This is sizable. Not only does it imply large holding costs to finance the inventory, it presents a substantial risk of write-offs from inventory obsolescence. If this ratio is truly representative, it appears that retailers are forcing manufacturers to hold inventory.

Finally, while it is probably best to do industry analysis before "checking the answer," industry profitability appears good. While return on sales is lackluster at 5.5%, the return on fixed assets is quite high at 48%. Thus, if firms can avoid high inventories, then the industry could be attractive.

EPIGRAPHS

Exhibit 2-9 fleshes out the five forces for the wallcovering industry using the secondary data we have gathered. We walk through each of these forces, discussing the data, and deriving conclusions.

Rivals

This appears be a mature industry of good size. The maturity conclusion is based on the recent steady sales decline (7% in each of the last three years), and the trend toward consolidation. Despite consolidation, behavior of rivals does not appear to be particularly competitive. If the industry were competitive we would expect to see greater advertising expenditures (currently less than 1% of sales), and greater innovation. The fact that "the product was sorely lagging behind other home textiles in terms of trends" is evidence that there isn't sufficient innovation, much less "hyper-innovation" (innovations whose aggregate industry cost exceeds resultant profits). One of the reasons rivalry is likely to be suppressed in the industry is that the product is highly differentiated. There are hundreds of patterns, no two of which are perfect substitutes.

Suppliers

We don't dwell on suppliers since the new product uses vastly different mate-

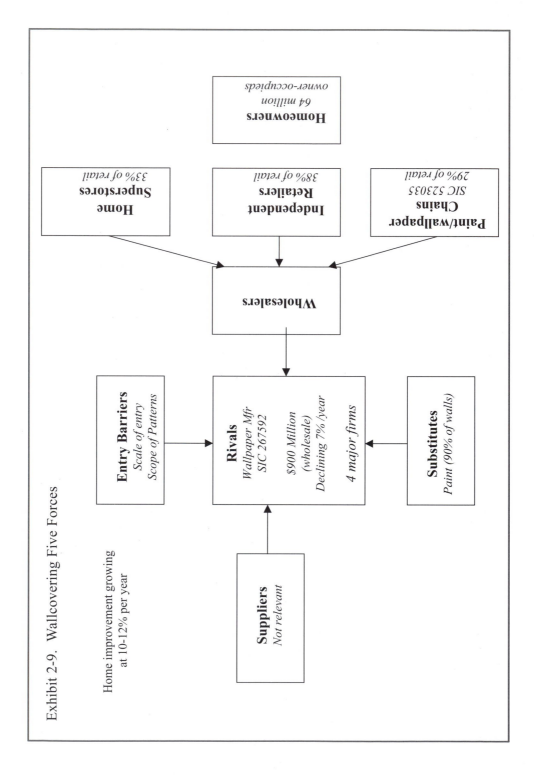

Exhibit 2-9. Wallcovering Five Forces

Home improvement growing
at 10-12% per year

Homeowners
*64 million
owner-occupieds*

**Home
Superstores**
33% of retail

**Independent
Retailers**
38% of retail

**Paint/wallpaper
Chains**
*SIC 523035
29% of retail*

Wholesalers

Entry Barriers
*Scale of entry
Scope of Patterns*

Rivals
*Wallpaper Mfr
SIC 267592*

*$900 Million
(wholesale)
Declining 7%/year*

4 major firms

Substitutes
Paint (90% of walls)

Suppliers
Not relevant

rials and technology than conventional wallcoverings. The relatively low cost of materials in the wallcovering industry tends to suggest that suppliers have little impact on industry profitability. One thing to note is that the primary input to wallcovering is paper. While paper is a commodity, its price tends to fluctuate considerably. The new venture would not be subject to those fluctuations.

Buyers

Consumers themselves have little power by virtue of sheer number (64 million households). The marginal utility of a single customer is quite low. There is, however, potentially some power in the distribution channel. The research indicates that there are roughly three channels for reaching consumers:

- Direct to paint and wallcovering chains (approximately 29% of output)
- Direct to chain department stores (including discount home centers) (approximately 33% of output)
- Through distributors to independent paint and wallcovering retailers (approximately 38% of output)

The relative balance between the various channels tends to suggest that no single channel is crucial to the success of a manufacturer. However, there are dominant players in two of the channels: Home Depot in the "department stores," and Sherwin-Williams in the paint/wallcovering chains. It is possible that there are also dominant wholesalers in the independent channel as well. The fact that retailers have to buy pattern books is some evidence of limited channel power, however this should be offset by the evidence that the manufacturer holds large inventories. Thus it is premature to draw conclusions on buyer power.

Substitutes

The trade journal articles were the only source of information on substitutes. The dominant substitute is paint, "Approximately 90% of American Walls are painted". The other substitute is borders (a subset of the wallcovering industry distinct from "sidewalls"). Currently, 50% of wallcovering sales are borders. It is unclear whether border sales have increased total wallcovering sales to enhance what would have been painted walls, or whether borders have cannibalized sidewall sales. The tone of the articles and the recent sales decline suggest the latter. Because borders are a subset of the wallcovering industry, it makes little sense to consider them here as a competitive product. We will treat them later in perceptual mapping.

The main substitute is paint. To assess the power of a substitute we need to assess cross-price elasticity—to what extent does a 10% change in the price of either paint or wallcovering lead to a shift from one product to the other? Since the prices are so widely divergent to begin with, it seems unlikely that demand for wallpaper is affected by a decrease in the price of paint (as shown in Exhibit 2-10). Paint is roughly $20 for 400 square feet of coverage (exclusive of labor). In contrast, wallcovering is approximately $200 for the same coverage (exclusive of labor). This conclusion can be evaluated via primary market research. At the current prevailing prices, paint is not a close substitute for wallcovering.

Complements

One important complement to wallcovering is installation. While some segment of the market installs its own paper, a sizable portion hires paperhangers. Paperhangers are a critical element of the industry structure for two reasons. First, without paperhangers, some sales would never materialize. Second, buyers who don't do their own installation consider the combined cost of the product and installation when they make their decisions. In most cases, the cost of installation exceeds that for the product.

Epigraphs installation is different from wallpaper. In fact, the impetus for the product was to provide a less labor-intensive alternative to wallpaper. Nevertheless, it is likely that some segments of the target market will not want to install the product themselves. Important issues for venture design then, are: how large is this group, what alternatives exist for installation, and how will these alternatives be priced.

Exhibit 2-10. Paint versus Wallpaper Substitution

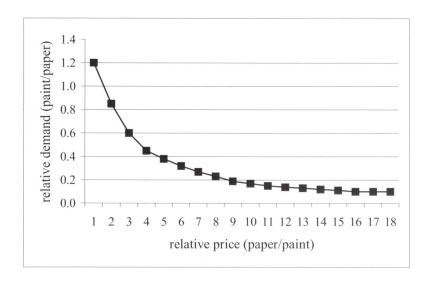

Entry Barriers

The final consideration is entry barriers. To what extent are there factors keeping the industry profitable precisely because they preclude entry? The most likely barrier candidates are generally high fixed costs, significant scale economies or learning curves, early mover advantages in building brand, or control of scarce resources. None of these seem to be present in the wallcovering industry. Fixed costs are minimal (sales/fixed assets = 1000%). Production scale economies also seem to be minimal (this makes sense given the fact that product variety is wide—if there were large scale economies we would expect to see fewer wallcovering patterns). Branding does not seem to be terribly important given that advertising expenditures are low (<1% of sales). It appears rather that consumers rely on the brand of the retailer for quality assurance.

Note, however, that there is a trend toward designer labeling of patterns—a means of "taste assurance" rather than quality assurance. Here, the wallcovering manufacturers form license agreements with prominent designers from other arenas to provide wallcovering designs that bear their name. Thus, there are Ralph Lauren patterns and Laura Ashley patterns. Customers who know their taste runs toward particular designers, can narrow their search. In some sense, the designer labeling is a substitute for using interior designers—a means for chains and box-stores to compete with independent designers.

The most scarce resource seems to be access to the distribution channels, but as mentioned previously, there are multiple channels. Since entry appears to be unimpeded, the profitability of the industry is puzzling. The main entry barrier must be a required scale and scope of entry. New entrants must provide at least a whole pattern of books (probably more), and must produce sufficient number of those books to fill the distribution channel.

Summary: Is this industry hospitable to entry?

This question faces squarely into the entrepreneurial paradox. Is this an industry that is profitable to incumbents, yet accommodating to entrants?

The preliminary conclusion to the five forces analysis is that this *is* an attractive industry. There is limited competition among existing rivals, little threat from suppliers and buyers, and no close substitutes. Ratio analysis confirms this: Return on Sales (ROS) is 5.5%; Return on fixed assets is 48%.

The paradox here is that there appear to be minimal entry barriers. Normally, the absence of barriers would tend to suppress industry profitability. The dominant entry barrier appears to be a relatively high minimum scale and scope of entry. Scope (variety of patterns) is required to make your offering attractive to retailers; scale is required to fill the distribution channels.

Thus, entry into this attractive industry is feasible for large-scale ventures (a large firm play) OR for small ventures that innovate around the distribution system. Some feasible innovations are forming an exclusive arrangement with a single chain, working through designers rather than retailers, or selling direct to consumers.

In designing the distribution system it is important to recall that 90% of sales are from stock; only 10% are from books. There is probably high correlation between the type of product, the type of sale (book versus stock), and the distribution channel. For example, high-end papers may be sold predominantly from books, which in turn are sold predominantly by independents. Thus, the product characteristics will need to be consistent with the channel chosen.

CONCLUSION

This chapter introduced you to the first stage in assessing venture feasibility: industry analysis. Industry analysis aids venture design in two ways. The primary role is to assess whether the industry will be hospitable to your particular venture. The secondary role, and the one that actually weaves through the rest of venture design, is immersion in the details of the industry. The chapter began with a review of industry analysis techniques. In addition to the standard review from strategy classes that focus on large corporations, we discussed how the techniques can help identify entrepreneurial entry wedges. The discussion then shifted from analytical principles to hands-on tools for gathering and analyzing industry data. Finally, we walked through the data gathering and analysis for Epigraphs—to demonstrate how industry analysis is as much art as it is science. The worksheet in Appendix 2-1 allows you to repeat the analysis for your own venture. The next chapter continues the data gathering and analysis but shifts from use of secondary data to the collection of primary data on customer preferences.

Appendix 2-1
Industry Analysis Worksheet

1. What industry best captures the proposed product/service?_____

2. What is its SIC code?_____

3. What were the total industry revenues in the past year?_____

4. What is the growth rate in industry revenues over the past few years?_____%
   (Revenues most recent year, y2/revenues in earlier year, y1)$^{1/(y2-y1)}$

5. How many firms compete in the industry?_____

6. Identify the five largest firms:

Firm Name	Revenues in past year	Net income in past year	Market share	Public or Private

7. Who buys the industry's product/service?
a) Are the customers consumers or businesses?_____
b) If businesses list the industries that purchase the product/service:

Industry Name	SIC code	No. Firms	Size of market for your product ($)	Share of your industry output

c) If consumers, how do sales vary over demographic segments that purchase the product/service?

Demographic segment	Size of segment (people)	Purchases of the product ($/person)	Size of market for product ($)	Share of your industry output

8. Through what channels is the product sold to customers?

Distribution Channel	SIC code	Stage in channel*	Number of firms in channel	Markup of channel	Share of your industry output

*If this channel is the only intermediary between the primary industry and the customer, then stage = 1; if product passes through one earlier intermediary, then stage =2

9. Identify the main industry associations and journals:

Association/Journal	Phone number	Membership/circulation	Main objective(s)

10. What market research companies/analysts cover the industry?

Company	Means to access reports	Key observations on the industry

11. Characterize the financials of firms in the industry:

	Focal Industry	Distributor	Customer
Income Statement Ratios			
Sales	100.0%	100.0%	100.0%
Cost of Goods Sold			
R & D			
Sales, Gen. & Admin.			
Deprec. & Amort.			
Net Income			
Operations Metrics			
Inventory Turns			
Performance Ratios			

Return on assets			
Return on Equity			

The remaining information is obtained from industry articles:

12. Distribution of product price at final customer:

Minimum:_____ Maximum:_____ Mean: _____ Std. Dev: _____ Median:_____

13. What are the closest **substitutes** to your industry's product/service?

Substitute	Average Price of substitute	Factors that favor substitute over focal product

14. Are there any **complements** to your industry's product/service?

Complement	Nature of dependence	Average price	How mature is complement industry

15. What are the main **inputs** to your industry's product/service?

Input	Input's share of your unit cost	Number of firms in supply industry	Key firms

16. Given all the above, what do you see as the main **entry barriers** to the industry?

17. Identify any **trends**, insights gained from your research that is not captured above. List source for each.

[1] See: Klepper, S., 1996. "Exit, entry, growth and innovation over the product life cycle." American Economic Review, 86, 3:562-583, and Klepper, S. 1999. "Firm survival and the evolution of oligopoly." Working Paper, Carnegie-Mellon.

[2] Lieberman, Marvin, 2001. "Did first-mover advantage survive the dot-com crash?" UCLA Working Paper.

[3] Byrne, John A, 2000. "The fall of a dot-com, Business Week, May 1, 2000, pp. 150-160.

[4] Porter, Michael, 1998. "Competitive Strategy: Techniques for Analyzing Industries and Competitors," Boston: Free Press.

[5] Buzzell, Robert D. and Bradley T. Gale, 1987. "The Pims Principles : Linking Strategy to Performance," Boston: Free Press.

[6] Grossman, John, 1996. "Nowhere Men," Inc., June 1996, pp. 62-69.

[7] Brandenburger, A. and B. Nalebuff, 1996. "Co-opetition," New York: Doubleday.

[8] Heslop, Janet (Ed.) 1997. "The American Marketplace: Demographics and Spending Patterns," 3rd ed. Ithaca, N.Y. : New Strategist Publications.

[9] See for example: Robert Morris Associates (1923-present) "RMA annual statement studies," Philadelphia: Robert Morris Associates. Also see: Dun & Bradstreet, Inc. (several years). "Dun & Bradstreet's key business ratios", New York: Dun & Bradstreet.

chapter 3

perceptual mapping

INTRODUCTION AND GOALS

Perceptual mapping is the second stage in the feasibility analysis of your new venture. Perceptual mapping is a tool to characterize the way customers view your product/service offering relative to competing or substitute products. The goal of the mapping exercise is to determine if the proposed product satisfies a clear, but currently unmet need. Thus, while industry analysis assesses whether the industry is hospitable to entry generally, perceptual mapping determines whether your particular product offering is a viable entry wedge.

Perceptual maps are important in correcting two of the most common flaws venture capitalists see in business plans: "solutions in search of a problem"—identifying an interesting idea but never assessing whether anyone has need for it, and "viewing the world through a single pair of eyes"—relying on your own intuition. Perceptual mapping corrects these flaws by forcing the entrepreneur to understand as completely as possible the customers for the intended product or service—What products will customers compare with yours? What dimensions do they use to compare products? Where does your product or service rank along each dimension? By creating a map of customers' perceptions, you can identify "position gaps" where there are customer needs or preferences, but no product satisfying them. These position gaps represent entrepreneurial opportunity. The particular opportunity you choose becomes your product's "core benefit proposition." Thus, perceptual maps can identify opportunity, or confirm that a proposed product satisfies a clear, but currently unmet need.

The chapter actually introduces two tools: the perceptual map itself, and focus groups—the technique used to gather the primary data from which the perceptual map is derived. Perceptual mapping thus begins our immersion into using primary data. Secondary data (as was used for industry analysis) are very important, and should always be the starting point for investigation, since the data are free. However, somebody else collects these data sets (usually for some general purposes), and thus the data can't answer questions specific to your venture. Secondary data will not tell you how potential customers view your particular product or service.

The chapter begins with a discussion of the principles underlying perceptual maps and focus groups. Next, it describes the processes for conducting focus groups and translating that data into perceptual maps. Finally, it discusses the application of these tools to Epigraphs, and the insights gained from that exercise.

PRINCIPLES

Perceptual Maps

Perceptual mapping is a tool characterizing the competitive space—where a particular product lies relative to competing products or substitutes. The critical elements of a perceptual map are the *dimensions*—What are they, and how many of them are there?, and the *location of competing products* along those dimensions. While the issue of proximity between products is important, probably the greatest value of perceptual maps is defining the actual dimensions along which products are compared.

You could probably derive a perceptual map using secondary data and intuition. However, doing so poses the risks that your intuition is skewed or that the secondary data exclude the dimensions providing the greatest opportunity. In fact, entrepreneurship is often the discovery of a new dimension upon which customers can evaluate a class of products. Fuel economy, for example, surfaced as a new dimension upon which automobiles were compared during the fuel crisis in the late 1970s. Frequent flier programs were introduced by American Airlines in 1981 as a new dimension along which to compare airlines (originally just airlines who had them [American] versus those who didn't). Because secondary research is likely to be constrained by extant dimensions, we strongly recommend using primary research to generate perceptual maps. In particular, we recommend using focus groups.

Focus Groups

Focus groups are a qualitative research technique comprising in-depth interviews of a small group of individuals brought together in a single location.[1] Focus groups, like most qualitative research, is an exploratory technique. The goal is to explore customer opinion by listening with an open mind. The interview itself is an "unstructured-undisguised" research format, meaning that the purpose of the study is clear, but that the responses are open-ended. This is in contrast to quantitative techniques, such as conjoint analysis, which we discuss in the next chapter. In conjoint analysis, and other quantitative techniques, the research format is structured, and the goal generally, is to confirm or refute hypotheses. While focus groups may confirm pre-conceptions, their real value, and the real fun, is in surfacing surprises.

Focus groups are an outgrowth of the group methods, such as brainstorming,[2] that became popular in the 1960s. The primary advantage of group methods over individual idea generation or opinion elicitation, is the opportunity for snow-balling—statements by one individual in the group trigger ideas in several others. In brainstorming, for example, there is an exponential increase in the number of ideas generated as a function of time. Further, the increase in quantity produces an increase in quality—the last 50 ideas are generally better than the first 50 ideas.[3] These ideas might remain latent in a one-on-one interview where individuals are more likely to remain within a single train of thought. Similarly, focus groups provide greater breadth of ideas since they are coming from individuals with different perspectives.

In addition to focus group advantages in triggering ideas, are advantages in having the triggered ideas expressed. In one-on-one interviews, often interviewees are concerned with maintaining a favorable image in the eyes of the interviewer. Thus, they may suppress ideas that could be viewed unfavorably. In a group situation, participants learn that their ideas are similar to those of peers, and thus are more forthcoming with those ideas.

There is, however, an ongoing debate on the efficacy of focus groups versus a series of one-on-one interviews. In general, the number of ideas generated by each technique is a function of the number of interviews, but there are diminishing returns to each new interview. Griffin and Hauser estimate that the first seven interviews will elicit 60% of user needs, while the next seven interviews will only elicit another 20% of user needs (Exhibit 3-1).

The issue in comparing focus groups with one-on-one interviews is whether a two-hour focus group with seven individuals is comparable to seven one-hour one-on-one interviews. On the one hand, each individual in a focus group has only 15 minutes air time (13/4 hours / 7). On the other hand, the focus group allows participants to think much of the time, and speak only when their ideas reinforce or deviate from the group. It is likely that many ideas expressed in the first 30 minutes of one-on-one interviews are redundant across interviews. Focus groups avoid this redundancy. Additionally, the interviewer takes up more air-time in a one-on-one interview than does a moderator in a focus group. While one study[4] has compared the relative efficiency of focus groups versus one-on-one interviews, and found that a 2-hour focus group equals two 1-hour interviews, this result is from a sample of one. My own experience, albeit unvalidated, is that number of people interviewed, rather than number of hours, is the main factor driving the curve in Exhibit 3-1.

Core Benefit Proposition

The main output of the perceptual mapping exercise will be your definition

Exhibit 3-1. Diminishing Returns to Interviews

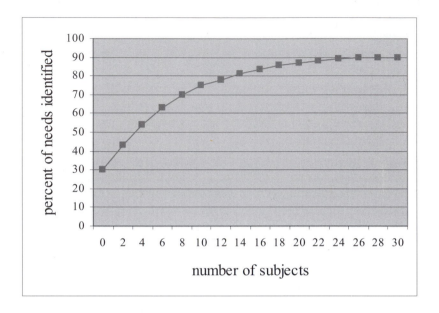

of the opportunity in the marketplace. This opportunity will be defined by the unmet needs of the target market—locations in the perceptual map where there is demand, but for which there is no existing product or service. We call this unmet need the "Core Benefit Proposition." The core benefit proposition is a concise statement of the set of dimensions that you will offer to the customer in your new product/service.

PROCESS

Designing and conducting focus groups[5]

Generally, focus groups consist of 8 to 12 recruited participants from a fairly homogeneous group. With less than 8 members, there is a greater chance that a single individual will tend to dominate the discussion; with more than 12 members, participants will have too little air-time, and will tend to become bored. The reason you want a homogeneous group is to be able to distinguish the range of perspectives within a customer segment from fundamental differences across segments.

Participants are generally selected from a sample of a particular target segment, and are typically paid a $50-$200 honorarium. While the source list from which names are identified is the first screen, a "screening phone interview" ensures that participants match desired demographics, and weeds out individuals with extensive focus group experience (who tend to be dysfunctional), and friends or relatives of other participants. See Exhibit 3-2 for a sample screening script.

The participants are brought together in a central location for 1 1/2 to 2 hours. Sessions are typically videotaped for later analysis, and often are conducted behind a one-way mirror so that other members of the venture team can observe the session. The moderator is the key to a successful session. While the moderator works from an outline, such as that in Exhibit 3-3, the real skill is in eliciting a broad range of opinions from the participants. To do so, the moderator must create a permissive attitude, yet keep discussion focused on the objective. The moderator must probe for the depth behind espoused views, "What do you mean by...?", "Describe the feeling…". The moderator must be flexible in allowing the discussion to go in unexpected directions and must secure the involvement of all participants, but do so in a non-threatening way. Finally, since the real value of focus groups over one-on-one interviews is snowballing that will elicit latent feelings, the moderator must stimulate interaction among group members, rather than conduct a series of concurrent interviews.

The session typically begins with broad open-ended inquiries such as asking the participants to describe how the product is used, describe the most recent purchase experience, enumerate likes and dislikes, or speculate about unmet needs. When using focus groups to develop a perceptual map, we also recommend use of a partially structured technique, such as "repertory grid."[6] Repertory grid is a technique aimed at developing customers' perceptual encoding schemes, through discussion of similarities and differences among products/brands. The technique consists of printing the names of all pertinent products/brands on cards. The moderator selects three cards at random and asks the participants to think of way(s) in which any two of the cards are similar and the third is dissimilar. The process is repeated with new sets of three cards until no new dimensions are elicited. Participants are then asked to rank the remaining products/brands along all the dimensions.

Appendix 3-2 is the actual transcript from Epigraphs' focus group, which included the use of repertory grid. This transcript forms the raw data from which the perceptual map is developed.

Two cautions are worth mentioning at this point. First, in some settings, particularly dispersed commercial markets, focus groups may not be feasible. Second, even when subjects are local, it takes some time to recruit them. You may need to call ten to twenty people to find one person able to participate at the

Exhibit 3-2. Epigraphs Screening Guide

Screener for Designers' Focus Group

Hi, my name is _____ and I am calling from The Wharton School at the University of Pennsylvania. We are testing a new product concept with a group of interior designers who fit a specific profile, and we were wondering if you would be willing to participate in the test. It would require you to join us and approximately 8 other designers like yourself, and to share your experiences with wallcoverings such as paint and wallpaper. The session will be held at Wharton, lasting approximately 2 hours. We will compensate you with $100 for your time. Are you interested?

Check the line: Yes_____   No_____

(If so, continue. If not, thank the person for his or her time.)

Great! As mentioned, we are looking for consumers who fit a particular profile, so I must ask you some questions to see if you qualify.

1. Do you make wallcovering decisions for your clients?   Yes_____   No_____

(If so, continue. If not, thank the person for his or her time.)

Great! The focus group will be held at _____ on _____ in Steinberg-Dietrich Hall, which is accessible from either Spruce or Walnut between 36th and 37th streets in the middle of the University campus. There are several parking lots around the campus. The most convenient one is on Walnut and 38th.

May I please have your full name and address:

_____

_____

_____

I look forward to meeting you on the _____

Exhibit 3-3. Epigraphs Moderators Guide

Moderator's Guide for Focus Group

Objectives
- Understand the attributes important to designers in selecting wallcovering for clients
- Understand the relative importance of these attributes
- Understand the level of satisfaction with current product offerings
- Assess the designer acceptance of the new product concept
- Test price point of product

Process

Brief introductions: Name, brief story about last time specified wallcovering, including what was specified, how it was selected, how it was installed, approximate price (for materials and installation), where in the client's house/facility it was installed (write onto flip charts)

Discussion of attributes: Based on stories, ask participants why they made their selections. (What was the need? What was important to them in making their purchase decisions? Why did they choose paint vs. wallpaper? Try to pull out as much information as possible unaided. When group seems to run out of ideas, go into brainstorming: dissatisfaction/satisfaction with their experience. Excursion…The client was satisfied when…)

Sort/list attributes: Have each participant rank order the attributes with 100 points.

Gap assessment: Brainstorm creative ideas to address gaps in current market: I wish…

Product concept: Introduce product concept. First in words, then show prototype. Get initial reactions.

Channel/price: Where would they learn about the product? How much do they think it should cost?

appointed time.

Given the time constraints of a semester, you may need to consider the following alternatives to conducting your own focus group:

1) Hiring a professional facility. These are listed under Market Research in the phone directory. Alternatively, you can consult www.focusvision.com for a network of 140 independent facilities that support an international video conferences

2) Conducting the focus group on-line through a chat room. While you will lose the interpersonal dynamics, these are fairly easy to facilitate. You may want to take part in someone else's before coordinating your own. To do so, consult the online focus groups at www.surveysite.com.

3) Finally, you can conduct a series of in-person or phone interviews. While you will lose snowballing, you may pick up more depth in each perspective.

Constructing Perceptual Maps

Exhibit 3-4 is a table of product attributes for small sedans. It compares 1999 models of small sedans along a number of dimensions identified in Consumer Reports. The dimensions we consider are fuel efficiency, reliability, depreciation, engine size, size of luggage compartment, and base price.[7] Note that these dimensions are actually physical attributes of the products, rather than customer perceptions, and they ignore probably the most important dimension in automobile purchasing—styling. While we are fundamentally interested in perceptions, and view physical attributes as mechanisms to shape those perceptions, these data lead to a nice exposition of perceptual mapping mechanics. In the Epigraphs example, we will deal directly with perceptions.

Exhibit 3-4 is loaded with useful information, but it does not readily facilitate comparison of models. A first step at a perceptual map then is a "snake plot"— a means to visually compare products across multiple dimensions. The simplest means to accomplish this is to merely select the entire table, and have Excel create a line plot. Because each attribute here is on a different scale, some differences would be more pronounced than others merely as an artifact of the scaling. To correct for this we recommend standardizing values. For each attribute, find the Range (Max - Min). Then, for each value of that attribute translate it into % of Range ([Value-Min]/Range). In those cases with reverse scales, such as fuel efficiency and price, where a low value is best, invert the scale by subtracting the standardized value from 1.

Exhibit 3-5 is a snake plot of the standardized values for each of the 10 models with complete data.[8] The Exhibit begins to illuminate the differences between models. The first observation is that no model dominates all others, e.g., while the Civic is at the top of the reliability, depreciation and base-price

Exhibit 3-4. Attributes of Small Sedans

Make	Model	Fuel MPG	Reliability	Depreciation % Value at 3 yrs	Engine HP	Luggage Cubic feet	Price $1,000
Chevrolet	Prism	31	0	63	120	12	12.3
Chevrolet	Cavalier	26	-35	66	115	14	11.8
Daewoo	Nubira	24	na	na	129	13	12.2
Ford	Escort	28	38	na	110	13	11.5
Honda	Civic	31	55	70	106	12	10.6
Hyundai	Elantra	25	na	63	140	12	11.5
Kia	Sephia	26	na	na	120	10	10
Mazda	Protégé	27	30	66	105	13	12
Mercury	Tracer	28	38	63	110	13	11.5
Mistubishi	Mirage	27	na	63	92	11	11.2
Pontiac	Sunfire	25	-35	66	115	12	12.7
Saturn	SL2	29	35	70	100	12	10.6
Suzuki	Esteem	29	38	63	95	12	12.2
Toyota	Corolla	30	40	66	120	12	12.2
Volkswagen	Jetta	24	0	70	115	13	16.7

scales, it rates poorly on engine size and fuel efficiency. This is not a surprise. If one model were clearly dominant on all dimensions (engine size, luggage compartment), it would either capture the entire market, or other models would lower their price to make their offering more attractive. We will tackle this issue more directly in a moment, when we discuss value maps. However, before introducing value maps, we want to consider the issue of dimensions.

Exhibit 3-5 is still quite complex. It is unlikely that customers keep track of all models on all these dimensions. Rather, the psychological literature suggests that individuals collapse attribute information into some salient dimensions. These dimensions can be derived statistically through factor analysis of customer rankings of products along several dimensions.[9] For this exercise, however, we will merely apply some intuition. If we exclude price (which makes sense, because it is instantly changed, and because we will treat it in value maps), two dimensions emerge: a lifetime cost dimension (fuel efficiency, reliability, and depreciation), and a functionality/performance dimension. If we arbitrarily weight the three cost attributes equally (add them together and divide by 3), and the two functionality dimensions equally (add them together and divide by 2), we create the simplified perceptual map in Exhibit 3-6.

Models are increasing in quality as you move up and right in the perceptual

Exhibit 3-5. Epigraphs Screening Guide

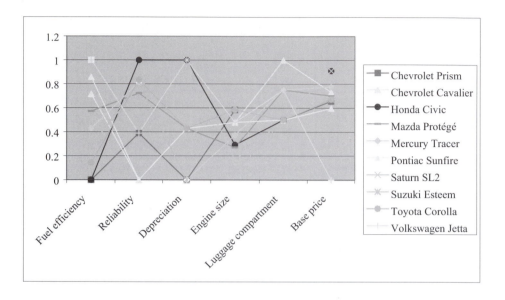

Exhibit 3-6. Perceptual Map of Small Sedans

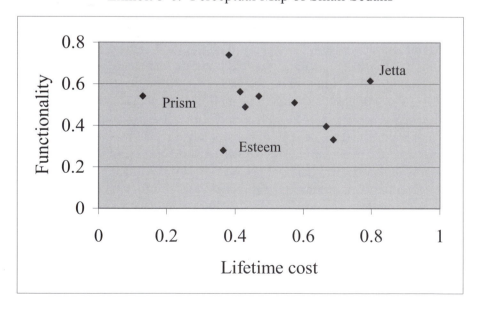

map. If we have correctly captured the important dimensions, and if customer utility has the normal concave shape in these two dimensions, then the Jetta should dominate the market. It has lower lifetime cost than all other models and greater functionality than all but one model. In contrast, the Prism and the Esteem are clearly of inferior quality. Irrespective of the shape of the consumer's utility curve, there is always a product offering more (above or to the right) utility than the Prism and the Esteem.

It is possible, however, that even if the Prism and the Esteem offer inferior quality in an absolute sense, they offer superior value. We explore the issue of value next.

Value Maps

Value pertains to the relationship between quality and price. While we recognize that a Rolls Royce is of superior quality to the cars that most of us purchase, Rolls Royce does not dominate the automobile market. The price of a Rolls Royce far exceeds most household incomes, much less the budget for automobiles. Accordingly, automobiles are compared on the basis of value rather than absolute quality—Which automobile provides me with the greatest benefit per dollar, given my budget for automobiles?

Value maps are a means to incorporate price into the product comparison. To translate a perceptual map into a value map, merely divide each dimension by price. Often, this conversion will lead to products arranging themselves along a single curve. Exhibit 3-7 converts the perceptual map in Exhibit 3-6 into a value map. Here we see that while the Jetta offered the highest quality, because of its

Exhibit 3-7. Value Map of Small Sedans

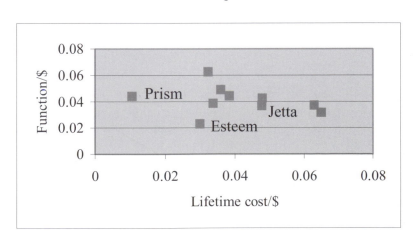

high price, it is now comparable to the other sedans. Value mapping does not substantially improve positioning of the Prism and the Esteem. (Remember, however, we fabricated the perceptual map using physical data rather than perceptual data, so we should be careful drawing conclusions).

Identifying Opportunity

Often perceptual maps will present a gap representing a new product opportunity. In our sedan example, most products lie along a curve trading functionality for lifetime cost. Volkswagon seemed to have recognized that there was an opportunity for a product with both high functionality and low lifetime cost. Because the Jetta filled an unmet need, Volkswagon was able to charge a higher price for the new sedan. Ultimately, as other firms imitate this strategy, we would expect the price of the Jetta to be more aligned with competing sedans.

Apart from the high function/low lifetime cost gap, this product space appears to be quite dense. Such density along existing dimensions suggests further differentiation requires new dimensions—styling perhaps.

The Epigraphs example is more useful than the sedan example. It uses perceptions rather than physical attributes, and the "need gap" is more pronounced. We turn to that example next.

EPIGRAPHS

Recruiting Focus Group Participants

While personal frustration with wallpaper helped identify the product need, and thus might form the basis for a perceptual map, we wanted a more thorough understanding of the wallcovering market. Originally we intended to interview two groups, an "expert" group of interior designers, and a group of wallpaper consumers. Experts, even more so than lead users, have in-depth knowledge about a given product and its associated market. Interior designers for example, have several clients, and thus can represent a whole distribution of clients. Further, because they design for a living, they have extensive experience with the industry's products, and must stay on top of all trends in products and consumer attitudes. Thus, their knowledge of the industry is very rich. The concern with relying exclusively on the opinions of experts in general, and interior designers in particular, is that they tend to work with high-end clients. Thus, the trends they perceive may never diffuse through the mass market.

Accordingly, we wanted to interview both experts and representative consumers. Ironically, it was more difficult to gather a group of consumers than professionals. Professionals were easily identified in the phone directory, whereas it was difficult to identify individuals matching desired demographic characteristics. Ultimately we were able to secure a mailing list from a wallpaper retailer. However, we found the next hurdle was consumer willingness and availability to participate. Interior design professionals seemed interested in the opportunity to meet with other professionals regarding a new product. In addition professionals had some regard for Wharton. Further, interview time at the end of the work-day was convenient—in some sense merely extending the work day. In essence the focus group fit within their definition of professional work. The consumers in contrast viewed the focus group as an inconvenience. Our response rate was less than 5%—making it unlikely we could field a group of adequate size with our mailing list of 150 names. Since we would later be surveying consumers for conjoint analysis, and would gather perceptions at that time, we felt reasonably comfortable doing a single, expert-only focus group. (The screening guide for the recruiting calls was provided earlier as Exhibit 3-2).

Conducting the Focus Group

The focus group comprised seven interior designers, a moderator and myself. The participants were served refreshments while they waited for the entire group to arrive. The actual session began at 5:30 and ended promptly at 7:00. The moderators guide in Exhibit 3-3 served as the outline for the session. The session was video-taped for later analysis. The transcript for that tape is included as Appendix 3-2.

As mentioned previously, the real value of focus groups and other exploratory techniques over quantitative techniques is the depth of information and richness of detail. While the ultimate goal of the session was construction of the perceptual map, we began with more general discussion of the industry: What wall-covering products were used and why? The group painted a slightly different picture of the industry than secondary data. For example, secondary data indicates growth of borders at the expense of sidewall sales. These designers uniformly felt borders were déclassé: "Not in vogue these days", "I just did one for an 85 year old lady at a retirement home". Since designers are lead users, this would portend a reversal in the trend toward borders.

Perceptual Map Dimensions

The group was successful in identifying a broad range of wallcovering products (broader than our own set) and identifying a set of dimensions along which they compared these products. This set came primarily from discussion of their engagement experiences rather than from direct questions about dimensions and product rankings. The complete list of dimensions and products is included as Exhibit 3-8. In addition to this unstructured approach, we conducted a repertory grid exercise, asking participants to identify ways in which two products were similar to each other, but dissimilar to a third product. In this particular case, the repertory grid exercise was redundant with the broader discussion. This is an

Exhibit 3-8. Wallcovering Products and Attributes (from focus group)

Key Attributes of Wallcoverings:	Key Attributes of New product:
Aesthetics	Inexpensive
Functionality	Accessorizes/ Offers accent to rooms (particularly children's and powder rooms)
Budget	
Durability/Ease of Maintenance	Whimsical
Ease of Installation	Customizable
Speed/Availability of Product	Functional (enhances odd spaces like hallways, elevator lobbies)
Uniqueness	
Flexibility/Customizability	
Predictability/Consistency	

indication that the broader discussion was fairly exhaustive.

Reaction to Epigraphs

The final exercise in the focus group was unveiling the new product. To prepare for the session, we had developed four prototypes of the Epigraphs product. Each prototype consisted of quotes mounted on 32" x 42" colored mat board. Quotes were taken from four different genres, produced in four colors, and in two typestyles. They were mounted on boards in either the same color (tone-on-tone), complementary colors, or contrasting colors. Prototypes were displayed along one wall of the room, and the designers were asked for their reactions. Initially the reactions were negative. The designers felt the vinyl material was inconsistent with the high-end rooms they tried to create for their clients. They also felt the product was similar to borders. (This impression was a byproduct of the prototype execution—only one quote was mounted on each board. This points to the importance of prototype execution.)

Ultimately, the mood of the reaction shifted when the designers were asked where and how this product might be used. Here they offered a number of suggestions:

"I could see doing it where you would do a big floral. I could see doing it in a powder room. It would be kind of fun"

"Media room or game room"

"I could possibly use it in a child's room"

"As a panel at the end of a long corridor"

"Church or library"

"Elevator lobbies"

"I know from personal experience that going into office buildings where there is a waiting room, I will read anything"

"You mentioned elevator lobby, what about the elevator itself?"

Sources of New Product Information

Before ending the session, we asked the designers how they found out about new products. They identified several mechanisms, most of which were personal rather than through media: trade shows, trade representative (reps) calls and visits, and luncheons in showrooms. They also receive direct mail, and review ads in design magazines.

Post-session Analysis

The real analysis took place after the session, from review of the video tape. In addition to reviewing the entire tape for emotion/timing, the tape was transcribed for content analysis. From that transcription, we derived a set of dimensions and a set of product rankings along those dimensions. This formed our preliminary perceptual map—the snake plot in Exhibit 3-9. The perceptual map confirms the need for a product with the durability, flexibility, and affordability

Exhibit 3-9. Perceptual Map for Wallcovering

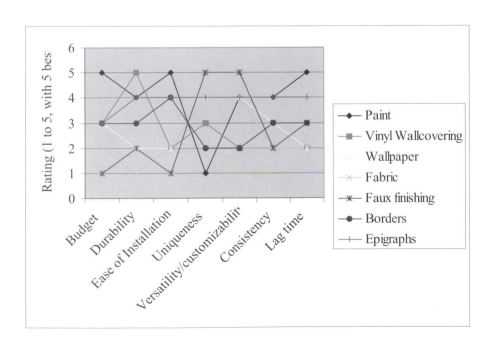

of paint, but with the uniqueness of papers and faux finishes. This forms the core benefit proposition for Epigraphs.

CONCLUSION

This chapter elicits customer perspectives using an exploratory process. Having finished this process for your venture, you should be able to answer the following questions: What is the customer's experience when using your product? Did they see value in the product? What products do customers see as competing with yours? What are the key features that distinguish your product from others? It is impossible to overestimate the value of identifying who your customers are and how they perceive your product. After completing the worksheet in Appendix 3-1, you should have enough information to realistically evaluate your venture's feasibility. In the next chapter, the final step in feasibility analysis, we use the information gathered here as the basis for characterizing demand through conjoint analysis.

Appendix 3-1
Perceptual Mapping Worksheet

1. Identifying buyers (from secondary data)

a) Are your customers consumers or businesses?_____

b) If businesses (list the industries that purchase your product/service):

Industry Name	SIC code	No. Firms	Size of market for your product ($)	Share of your industry output

c) If consumers:

Demographic segment	Size of segment (people)	Purchases of the product ($/person)	Size of market for product ($)	Share of your industry output

2. What mailing lists (or other sources) can you use to locate people/firms in your industry?

Source	Segment(s) covered	Extent of coverage (% of people in segment)	Cost per person

3. Are you conducting interviews or focus groups to gather data?_____

    Why?

4. Characterize the people you interviewed:

Name	Segment/Industry	Source of name

5. What raw dimensions were elicited in the interviews?

Raw Dimensions/Attribute	Times mentioned

6. What competing/substitute products were elicited?

Raw Dimensions/Attribute	Times mentioned

7. Summarize the rankings of each product on each dimension:

DIMENSIONS

PRODUCT	1	2	3	4	5	6	Price

8. Create Snake Diagram of above table:

RANKING (1 to 5)

DIMENSIONS	1	2	3	4	5

Legend for Products

9. Interesting comments from interviews/focus groups:

10. Where is there opportunity in perceptual map?

Attach copy of screener's guide and moderator's guide

Appendix 3-2
Epigraphs focus group transcript
October 25, 1999

Moderator: As I told all of you on the phone, the purpose of the group is to get some feedback from you guys on the current wallcovering industry, and not so much the industry, but what your experience as a designer is with wallcovering. We are defining wallcovering as anything you use to decorate a wall—whatever you put on a wall to sort of enhance its beauty or value for your clients. I'm not talking about wall sconces, those types of things. But I also do not want to use words like paint or wallpaper, because maybe there are other things that you use and we want to hear about those things as we get the group going.

The other thing that we want to do tonight is present a new wallcovering concept to you and get your reactions.

Anne Marie and I are on the research team for the person who has this idea, so we will be feeding back this information to this company. I am going to tell you that your answers will be anonymous, but we want to film you and we are going to ask if that is okay. We want to tape this so we have a record of what is going on.

While we are playing musical chairs, I want you to think about something as we do this. I am going to go around the room and ask each of you some questions about the types of wallcovering that you typically use with your clients, and those things that you think about when you are selecting a wallcovering. Does that make sense for everybody?

When you are ready, raise your pencil or finger.

Dina: I've specified all different kinds of wallcovering: zolotone paint, regular paint, vinyl wallcovering, paper, fabric, reed.

MODERATOR: What is vinyl wallcovering?

Number 7: It is durable.

Dina: Probably most widely specified in contract design, when using wallcovering more than paper more than fabric more than grass

MODERATOR: What else do you use? You use paint. Anything else? The second part of the question…what are the things that you consider when selecting a wallcovering?

Dina: Selecting a wallcovering, first of all has to do with the space that it is being specified for, whether it is in a corridor or an executive area, and that will identify whether it is a vinyl or a more high-end finish like a silk wallcovering, or something like that.

MODERATOR: So it is the space itself, but it also seems that there is a durability aspect that you are getting at.

Dina: Definitely.

MODERATOR: Anything else that you consider?

Dina: Budget.

MODERATOR: Do you have a number per square foot that you use?

Dina: No, because it depends on the project and the installation, there's a lot of facets that go into the decision-making process

MODERATOR: You mean for the budget?

Dina: No, for all..

MODERATOR: What are some of those things?

Dina: Like what the client would accept, what the style of the interior is and

MODERATOR: So taste….

Marco: Can I answer that?

MODERATOR: Oh, sure.

Dina: Yes, please!

Marco: Sometimes acoustic. I am working on a project right now, where there's a room which is going to be used somewhat like a screening room. And so we're doing fabric on the walls. Sometimes there are acoustic panels that you can put on the walls that are covered with fabric, so it is how the client using the room and to go back to vinyl… sometimes you have a client who is not really good at maintenance and really just wants something that is scrubbable or wipeable, so you would want to use something with vinyl, not grasscloth because you can't really take a damp cloth to it.

MODERATOR: Great. Maybe you can share with us, Nina, some of the wallcoverings that you've used.

Marco: Well I said fabric, paint, grasscloth, which is a type of wallpaper, vinyl wallcovering, custom screen-printed wallpaper.

MODERATOR: What do you find valuable in custom wallpaper?

Marco: You have more control over color or pattern.

MODERATOR: Great. Good. Anybody else?

Number 7: Let me springboard off of something that was mentioned about acoustics…we are doing a media room right now, where we decided because of the sound that would travel through the rest of the house, that we would cover the walls in fabric. However, the client wanted silk, but this is the main traffic pattern to the pool, so we figured with kids coming in and out with suntan lotion that it would easily get damaged, so we decided to go with a polyester/cotton blend that looked like silk but definitely durability—how it is going to be maintained, how durable the fabric is, sometimes we deal with high-end Chinese papers, that need to be handled very delicately

I know we just had one installation, an Osborne and Little paper, that required a lot of pre-work be done on the walls to make sure that it didn't stretch or bubble up over the years.

Amy: Did you use paper or fabric?

Number 7: Sometimes you have to use paper backing and the batting.

Amy: So they probably line the walls first before they put it in.

Number 7: We do a lot of encostic—hand tinted encostic, which is a wax, so we call it Venetian plaster, but I don't think that is really quite correct. It is great stuff. It really looks quite nice, but esthetics is primarily our goal in the residential end of it, but definitely cost, some clients aren't willing to spend a couple of hundred dollars a square foot. Some are. It depends on what their priorities are.

MODERATOR: Let's talk about the aesthetics a little bit. That's so hard to typify, because everyone has their own taste, but when you are working with clients, is there something that they are typically looking for or is there some issue with showing them all these different alternatives and meeting their needs or

Number 7: Well sometimes they will come right up to you with a picture they ripped out of a magazine and say "I want this look." And then you are very narrow and focused about what they want. Other clients are completely open. We just had a couple of clients come up to us and say, "Here is the layout this is the apartment, let's see what you can do"

Which is sort of like a dream, but it is also difficult because then you have nothing to start with.

MODERATOR: Good. Oscar, what about you? What types of wallcovering do you use, or have you used?

Oscar: Anything and everything, basically. In the residential end, what I have noticed is that most likely the client is interested in something unique as opposed to a more typical situation. Most of the clients who are willing to invest in a wallcovering, go for the watercolor painted paper or the silk fabric, or something that they aren't going to find just anywhere. Gold leafing is something that we have found is quite unique in the market these days. In the paper form because you can apply easily not only on vertical surfaces, but also on the horizontal surfaces and the ceilings without having to get involved in special trades to do such work, but it runs the gamut and is usually driven by cost—how much the client wants to invest, and a function of the space, without any doubt. Other items that I have used more on the commercial end are coatings, zolatone—that is something that not only serves the purpose of giving you a different aesthetic, but hides some of the imperfections in the wall and it has some other ailments you have to deal with. Another element that I have encountered very often lately is paneling something like a marbleite product that is fibreboard backed product that is wood veneered or it could be painted surface or metallic surface. That has become a very flexible material applied in modules. So it depends on the budget and a function of the space.

MODERATOR: That is good, and uniqueness—I thought that was interesting, and that gets back to I think what Nina said about certain customer controllability of material. Amy, how about you?

Amy: I do residential, and depending on the flavor of the space and the house… lately we have been doing entire homes. We work with the clients, we make a presentation, we give them sort of a choice, and they are the ones who make the final selection. But most of the papers that I select I would say ARE paper. In a certain case, the client has four children, there is a process called fibre-seal or Custom-seal. It doesn't vinylize the product, but it protects it from fingerprints. It protects it, but doesn't make it shiny, which I think adds at least a dollar a roll—no maybe more than that—not sure on the price.

Oscar: Usually by the yard.

Amy: But it is a process we do. If you want to do something for the bathroom, so it doesn't get damaged by water, but initially when I pick out a paper, its keeping with the style of the house, with what the client already has, to coordinate with something that is off of it, so that's how I make my selections, and then I make my presentation.

MODERATOR: Great. When you are making your presentations, or when you are selecting some of your samples, do you think about budget, customability, some of the things that other people are talking about?

Amy: Yes, I consider budget. Generally I don't consider custom. That is sort of a last resort. There is enough, at least for what I do, there is enough out there. There are a zillion wallpapers. I also generally go for wallpapers that are on the unusual side. Then I go more decorative with fabrics. I like sort of background papers. I do a lot of stripes—tone on tone stripes. I do simple. I use Nina Campbell, Osborne and Little. They are really beautiful, simple papers. Damasks, all the time. I don't generally do anything—sometimes in a powder room, I'll do lots of flowers, but in general, I keep my papers toned down.

MODERATOR: Great! Hey David, how about you?

David: Well I would like to explain to everyone a little bit about my business. I am more of a furnishings, I actually sell furnishings from wholesalers, and I am cutting out the furniture stores, and I am working more as a furnishings consultant. And I have dealt with wallpaper. For example, you guys may have heard of SJW Studios in Washington State. It is a wallpaper, high-end faux finish on paper—hand painted, and silk. My clients are mainly high-end client, and they demand the top-of-line in style, but they don't necessarily want to pay that price. It is $100 a yard, and a yard is very small, and I would rather—I'm not making any profits on wallpaper, and I am totally cutting out wallpaper, and I am putting it on the back burner as a last resort to use to finish off the room, because I'd rather see my profits being made on furniture. And I will pick out paint from my clients, and Ralph Lauren has textured paints. I also have for example a client that I was wanting to do some wallpaper and it was $100 a yard, and it came out to $4000. That is $4000 that I am making at 20 to 50% markup on my furniture, and I am not getting. I can't buy the wallpaper from the factories. I have to buy the wallpaper from the design center here in town, and I am not going to buy the wallpaper and make $200 on the wallpaper job.

MODERATOR: What about that for other people? I think it's an issue of profit margin. Are you able to make a decent margin on wallpaper, and is that something you consider?

Number 6: Definitely. We charge a 35% design commission on anything that we select and specify.

David: I love wallpaper. I really do. However, I would rather see them purchase the entire room from me, and then maybe if they want to do a faux finish I've got a faux finisher doing a couple of jobs for half the price. In fact I took a $100 a yard sample from SGW Studios, to the faux finisher, and he totally—two examples—he's totally copied.

Marco: Don't tell them that (LAUGHTER)

David: But I also called SGW studios, and asked them, "Can you sell me this wallpaper?" Why do I have to buy it from the Design Center? I have a tax number. I'm a business. However, they don't want to sell to me. That's fine, so I'll take it to a faux finisher. And if a client really wants that wallpaper, I'll have a faux finisher put it up. It comes down to the dollar in my case. I need to make money, and if I am not making money on wallpaper, I'm not pushing wallpaper.

MODERATOR: Good

Oscar: I have the other end of the coin which is I don't make any money on anything I specify. I am purely a specifier. I do what I do for the sake of design. I am consultant to my clients. I pass on all the discounts to my clients, because some of them have more power than I do to buy the product on discount—they have connections, they know the spreads of the dealers, so why go with the headache of the markup, so I deal strictly on consultation fees.

MODERATOR: So that is how you make your profit?

Oscar: That is how I make my profit. That is how I protect myself from the client telling me, "Oh, I was able to see the same wallpaper, the same wallcovering, the same wall treatment somewhere else and for half the price of what you are selling it to me." So I deal strictly with consultation fees.

MODERATOR: Right. Great. Marco, we skipped you.

Marco: Somehow. Well, almost everything has been covered except I think other alternatives. Oscar—was it?—mentioned things being unique. Honestly, I don't always consider paper or vinyl first. In my firm I tend to specialize in the residential, and then even specialize in kitchens and bath, and those type areas, so I think of wall finishes in a different perspective, like tiling the whole wall, or maybe panel systems, but I tend to think of wood in general as a wall finish, rather than just as a material.

MODERATOR: And why is that?

Marco: Just the kind of feeling or mode it conveys. Usually aesthetic over-powers the other factors, budget, especially in residential where you can get away with it more, I think than in the commercial work. And the unexpected, too. I think finding a surprise on the wall.

MODERATOR: Good, good. I think we heard that before with uniqueness. I want you guys to think of two things: a good experience you have had with some kind of wall covering, and a bad experience, and then let us know what made the good one, good, and the bad one, bad. It could be anything. I think David already started on that. There is some bad experience in terms of profit margin...Are you guys ready? Does somebody have their stories?

Marco: I think so much has to do with installation. Like papers in the past—there have been problems. Actually, sometimes they will blame it on the paper manufacturer—the problem sometimes is that the paper manufacturer will blame it on the installer, and the installer will blame it on the manufacturer.

(SEVERAL VOICES ALL SAY THEY HAVE ONE NOW)

MODERATOR: Before we go on you guys, I need to know more about the problems. You said there are problems, can you typify those problems?

Marco: I remember once for a sea grass, grass cloth, it did start fraying.

David: I had that happen with my best friend.

Marco: You've had that experience?—sorry.

MODERATOR: there are enough problems for everyone.

Marco: The installer said it was the paper—but the paper company said it was because of the way installed—it was the seams

MODERATOR: Like how everything had to match up?

Marco: It was ugly.

MODERATOR: Is that also because of the room? The way the room is designed? Does the seaming problem have anything to do with the shape of the room?

Number 7: That is typical of grasscloth.

Marco: Well you want it to actually look like panels (SIMULTANEOUS WITH COMMENT ABOVE).

MODERATOR: Oh, okay.

Marco: That is one condition where you want to really see the line, but this was a situation where they said that it was how it was how they were butt togeth-er is what started the fraying.

MODERATOR: Good. Amy had a burning story, so let's go to Amy.

Amy: The client from "you know where." We put this beautiful Scalamandre paper up. It is kind of like a Chinese thing with lots of people and houses and flowers. We put the paper up. There were two strips of totally different color— the dye lots were off, so that meant they had to take the paper off. But it was an inconvenience to the client. They back-ordered the paper six weeks, so by the time this whole thing was said and done, it was 3 months later. You know we had to prove… You couldn't tell until was actually up that the dye lots were different, and they were really different! They had to inspect it—Scalamandre had to send someone out to inspect it, then we had to send the bill from the paper-hanger to Scalamandre. It was like a whole production.

MODERATOR: So there seem to be a couple of things in there: 1) there is a whole timing issue—that it held everybody up, so it is safe to say you would like to have this done as quickly as possible, but there is an issue of quality— everything you sell is of good quality.

Amy: If you looked at this wallpaper, and you rolled it out on the floor, and you looked at one roll and you looked at the other roll, you would've never known until it was actually on the wall.

MODERATOR: Wow!

Amy: So it was a nightmare. So they asked, "How are you going to know that it is not going to happen again? We are going to roll it out on the table and it is going to look perfect, and it is not, when it goes up, so what do you do? Keep your fingers crossed…

MODERATOR: Predictability is in there.

Marco: Consistency…

MODERATOR: Good.

Marco: That takes away from the unique sometimes.

Amy: Oh I have another one.

MODERATOR: Go ahead, Amy

Amy: The flooring finisher makes a gouge in the wallpaper. No stock. An entire hallway—20 double rolls

Marco: Then you should call Insto-finisher.

(LAUGHTER)

Nina: I would say time is the big issue, which we have touched on. Because if it is coming from overseas and you have a client that is sort of chomping at the bit to have something installed, you are sort of a slave to when something is coming in, whereas if you did have a faux finish, you have more control over when it is going in, and the dialogue issue.

MODERATOR: Nobody has talked about borders. Does anybody do borders?

Oscar: Not in vogue these days.

MODERATOR: Borders are out?

Dina: My firm actually just started using borders, because we started doing health care and extended care facilities and so that is a big deal for them—they love borders.

(LAUGHTER)

Amy: I just did one for anz 85 year-old lady at a retirement home. It looks great.

MODERATOR: So it's a generational thing, then.

Nina: I've seen some nice borders from Europe where it would be nice if we did it, but for some reason our clients…

David: You can go to Target and buy borders.

Marco: Once Martha Stewart Everyday started doing it…

MODERATOR: Then it was over. Do what Martha Stewart doesn't do. Good. Anyone have a good story?

Marco: Well recently we had an Osborne and Little paper that the client was very hesitant to put up, and it was a wall and ceiling treatment, and actually it was finished a couple of weeks ago, and when I walked in, it totally altered the room. It was absolutely amazing, and she is absolutely in love with it.

MODERATOR: And what was it…it was just the pattern of the paper????

Marco: Well it was made to look like antique distressed plaster, but it had some ridiculous quarter drop repeat and it is this miniscule pattern, but it was a pattern, but it was made to look like it wasn't a pattern, so it was… fortunately we had a well-seasoned and expert wallhanger do it, but it just really I still think it was amazing, and she was just delighted.

MODERATOR: Right. Let's talk about that a little—the wallhanger, because that came up when Marco was talking.

Marco: It is VERY important. I mean we have had wallhangers that have botched jobs, and it is thousands of dollars which you lose out on.

MODERATOR: Is it a function of the wallpaper or the hangar

Nina: Sometimes laziness.

Marco: Laziness…cutting the corners just right. Really taking that added time to make sure everything is pressed down, and very neat. The client in this job mentioned that it didn't even seem like an inconvenience because he was so neat and cleaned up after himself as he went. I meant it really showed.

MODERATOR: What if there was a product that was incredibly easy to hang that you didn't have to worry about. Do you think there is such a thing as that?

Marco: Vinyl wallcovering, but we don't really use that.

Oscar: I think that substrate is a critical element when you are thinking of installing wallcovering. If the substrate is not perfectly finished or treated, no matter how wonderful the wallpaper is, it is still going to telegraph imperfections that are going to become very apparent.

MODERATOR: Okay, good. Any other stories?

David: I can only comment and say that it is very expensive as far as labor to have it installed, and again that is cost that I am losing. In fact, one job a month ago, I missed out on $2000 that went to a wallpaper hanger that could have been spent on services for me as far as furnishings, and I could easily have had some selected paint.

MODERATOR: Right. Okay. Now you guys have those three cards in front of you—one says paint, another says paper, another says fabric. I want you to cluster together two that sort of relate in some way to you, and keep the third one out. We are just going to go around quickly to see what comes out of that. We were going to put borders, but that is obviously a no-no, so…

Amy: You lost me—put two together...

MODERATOR: Put two together that relate to you in some way, whatever way.

Amy: Can you be more specific?

MODERATOR: I am trying to be as open-ended as possible because I don't want to direct you to say a certain thing.

Dina: I put paper and fabric together because they are in my mind-they are both goods that are produced by someone else off-site and then applied to the wall. And it seems to me paint is just a coating, it is not something that you unroll and hang up on the wall.

MODERATOR: Not many people talked about paint. It seems like paint is not a good thing these days.

(CHORUS OF DISAGREEMENT)

Dina: We use paint in probably 90% of our work.

MODERATOR: Oh, okay, because you guys haven't really brought up paint very much.

Nina: Maybe because we thought this was about wallpaper

MODERATOR: I'm sorry. I wanted to stay ambiguous. If you use paint, we need to know you use paint. So you think 90% of your work is paint?

(NODDING)

MODERATOR: And why do we use paint 90% of the time?

Dina: Because in contract, it is inexpensive.

MODERATOR: Inexpensive…Amy, why do you use paint?

Amy: Probably for budget reasons, I would use paint.

MODERATOR: Okay, David

David: Same thing. I can give them the samples, they can go down to the local Home Depot, and paint it themselves, or pay someone to paint it.

MODERATOR: Great. Oscar, why do you use paint?

Oscar: Well it is cost, definitely. The other item behind paint is that you can apply different finishes to it. It's not just paint, it can be flat, it can be eggshell, so you have a lot more flexibility.

MODERATOR: Flexibility, good.

Marco: Same reasons, and also it comes in any variety of colors, custom colors.

MODERATOR: Custom, good.

Marco: You can make decisions on-site. You can test areas easier than you can with other wall finishings.

MODERATOR: Good.

Nina: I think, too, that if we were doing a whole home, you probably just wouldn't want to do wallpaper in every single room because you want some sort of consistency throughout, and sometimes wallpaper is used as sort of a unique accent to make sort of a jewel-like space, and so sometimes it is used in specialized areas, not used widespread throughout the entire home.

MODERATOR: Okay, good. Go back to your clusterings. Dina went. Oscar went. No, Oscar told us about paint, sorry. What do your clusterings look like?

Oscar: Same.

MODERATOR: And why did you do it? Same reason?

Oscar: Same reason. The fact that Dina said—that it is applied versus coated. It just automatically differentiates two different types of applications.

MODERATOR: Is there something in your mind about a coating versus something that is applied? Do you have a preference? Would you go for something that's applied or for something that is coated, or doesn't it really matter?

GENERAL ANSWER: Depends on application.

MODERATOR: Okay, good.

Male: I have the same arrangement as they had. The one thing that I have down is that paper and fabric come in a given size, so you have to deal with a certain size factor, whereas paint just covers a wall.

MODERATOR: So the wallpaper is not always manageable…. Okay, Marco

Marco: Well, I did have it grouped the same. I feel like I should be unique…

MODERATOR: No, no.

Marco: For basically the same reasons. I think it is pretty cut and dry, unless you look at paint as a pigment, and then paint can go on paper or fabric.

Nina: You could say that paint and paper are the same in the sense that there might be less maintenance involved than with fabric—it is not as easy to clean if you get it dirty. The paint and paper you can do in such a way that it is easier to maintain for the client.

MODERATOR: Okay, good.

Amy: Okay, I'll be different. I'll put the paint and paper together. And the fabric by itself. Fabric comes first generally. Then it is a choice of paint or paper.

MODERATOR: Oh, so you always lead with the fabric in the room, so it is important that the paint or paper matches the fabric. So that is very interesting. Help me with the word for that. Everything seems to need to coordinate: the paint, the paper, and the fabric. So let's say if there was a product that was out there that didn't come in the same color scheme, it is of no use to you.

Amy: Correct.

MODERATOR: Okay, David, how about you?

David: I put fabric and paint...

MODERATOR: Okay, and why is that?

David: I always start with fabric, and paint is very simple, you just throw it on the wall. And I throw away the paper, because if I do that, they can afford the fabric of upholstery pieces. You know it is an amazing difference if you take fabric—it is expensive. In an upholstery piece you are looking at a couple thousand dollars, and then a couple more thousand for wallpaper. There is nothing left over. So which would you rather have? Upholstery or wallpaper? I have some very cheap clients—they don't want to part with their money.

(MODERATOR WRITES TRAITS ON BOARD)

MODERATOR: Am I am missing anything that you pulled out of the group in terms of any characteristics or attributes?

David: Installation

MODERATOR: I put "ease of use". Is that different from ease of use, do you think?

Oscar: Yes, because, for example, you want to separate two different traits versus paint versus paper or fabric.

MODERATOR: Anything else? I think some of the words were different, but I was trying to categorize them as we were going through. Do you think we are missing anything?

Great. Now… what I want you to do is give us the top five attributes on the board for you when you are making a decision to buy wallcovering. Write those on the back of the card.

(DELAY WHILE GROUP IS WRITING)

MODERATOR: For those of you who are done, I am going to give you 100 points, and you can divvy them up any way with the five attributes you have written down. This is a way to get at the weighting of what is more important for you. Let's say durability is your number one choice, and it is number one by a lot relative to everything else, so you may give it 70 and then divvy up the rest of the points. So you have 100 points, and this isn't scientific, so if they are all important, you can put 20-20-20-20-20, but if there's something that really sticks out as more important to you,

?: The trick is that it comes to 100 when you are done.

MODERATOR: At the Wharton School, you know we have to throw something quantitative out.

Nina: I'm sorry, are we doing percentages or just points that add up to 100?

MODERATOR: Just points.

Marco: I have a little problem—I think of function of space and acoustics as the same.

MODERATOR: No, that is good. You can actually write that on your line.

Amy: Why do you say that? A function of space and acoustics???

Marco: Well it is almost like a function includes whether acoustics are relevant.

Oscar: Well if are you are not counting not-coated wall covering in damp area.

MODERATOR: Okay, how are we doing? Pencils up when you are finished.

MODERATOR: One more thing. If I said to you guys, you've got millions of dollars, but you can't spend it personally, you can do anything you want with it to create a wallcovering business, what would it be? And it doesn't have to be…What characteristics would you address in putting this business together in terms of the product? Does that make sense?

?: Lots of options

MODERATOR: Lots of options. Good.

?: Texture.

MODERATOR: Texture. What do you mean by texture?

? Well I am always interested in something that has a texture or looks like it has a texture—that has a hand to it—something that has a luxuriant appearance or velvet on walls.

MODERATOR: Great. Oscar has a smile on his face.

Oscar: I'll go back to uniqueness. If I am going to sell something, I better sell something that nobody else can do.

MODERATOR: Great.

Amy: Choices, but within those choices, say you have 10 choices, but within A only have 5 colors to choose from—don't go crazy. Don't make it…

MODERATOR: Too confusing…

Amy: Um hum.

MODERATOR: Wallpaper seems to be confusing—all these options.

Amy: Too may choices…

MODERATOR: Good. David…

David: I picked cost and style. Cost, number one, and of course having the top of the line in style.

MODERATOR: Good.

Dina: Durability, with flexibility

MODERATOR: Good, and what do you mean by flexibility?

Dina: If you are able to change something in the field during installation.

MODERATOR: Help me understand that some more.

Dina: The process that I can equate to it really is application of a coating-like zolatone, where you can change the size of the spots while they are spraying it on.

MODERATOR: Oh, so you have flexibility while you are actually doing the treatment?

Dina: Yeah, but I would want to have that still be a permanent coating, so I need both of those at the same time.

MODERATOR: Right. Okay, good. Oscar. Joshua.

Nina: I think I would go with either with style or uniqueness. I said before that I probably would stay away from lots of options and maybe go toward a specific niche that there is not a lot of, because I still think that specifically in wallpaper that there are tons of options. Sometimes there still seems to be not enough, yet maybe in a clean modern sophisticated sort of vein. There are tons of florals and printed patterns and stuff like that.

MODERATOR: We know Amy stays away from florals.

Marco: Except for bathrooms (SIMULTANEOUSLY WITH MODERATOR)

MODERATOR: Good. You guys talked a lot about options and uniqueness. Is there something behind that? Something you are thinking about? Why uniqueness? Is it just so you differentiate your product, or are your clients looking for something unique, or there is something out there that is not there that you are looking for?

Marco: We look at it at our firm that the client is spending so much money that they don't want something that they could flip through Better Homes and Gardens and say, "Oh, look, there is my living room"—something about a custom approach to things, like "this is mine," this is unique, no one else has this, no one else will have this.

MODERATOR: Okay. Excellent ideas. Now is the unveiling. I am going to first read to you what this product concept is, and you guys think about it and we will get some reactions from you.

"This product is a wallcovering intended to be applied over paint. The original concept is quotes, but available in a palette of colors, and can be applied with any spacing, so it is easy to maneuver within spaces, and you can use any phrases or characters in the quotes that we are talking about"

Does that make sense?

Nina: Are you asking us to fill in the blanks like MadLibs?

(LAUGHTER)

MODERATOR: I'm not doing this very well.

Amy: Is this like lettering on the wall?

MODERATOR: Yes, thank you. Lettering on the wall.

Joshua and Marco: So, Graphics…

MODERATOR: Yes, graphics.

Joshua: So we are becoming graphic designers as well as interior designers?

MODERATOR: Well, yes.

Joshua: So we have the option of the font and the phrase?

MODERATOR: Yes, so you can basically customize the lettering, the quote, or you could even do a poem. If you have someone who is addicted to baseball scores, you could even put up baseball scores all over the wall.

Marco: What would be the advantage of using this system over having an artist paint it? My first thought if I wanted something graphic on the wall would be to hire an artist… or stencils

(LOTS OF AGREEMENT)

MODERATOR: okay, what do other people think?

David: I think it is a wonderful idea. However, as a designer, I would probably rather see something like that in Target where everyone can customize maybe a kid's room. I think it is a great idea. In fact I know a furniture store that just opened that spent a lot of money on quotes and phrases out in West Chester, so as you tour the showroom, in each vignette, you see on the wall a nice quote or phrase that had to be hand done, and if there were something that someone could easily stencil up there… Is that what you are saying?

MODERATOR: Yeah, exactly. I didn't get a reaction from you, Dina.

Dina: Can you say it again?

MODERATOR: Basically, it is something you apply over paint. It would come to you almost like wallpaper, but it would be the letters cut out in a clear material.

Dina: The only way I can see the application in contract design is to use it for company logos.

Marco: Like signage.

Dina: Yeah.

David: I can honestly say I would probably never use it.

Dina: Our clients NEVER ask for verbiage on the walls.

MODERATOR: Okay, what if we got back to the idea of faux finishing and stenciling that it would be considerably cheaper than doing that.

Marco: The other thing that comes to mind to me at least, and you mentioned this before, is border. I've done an application in a library where we had a Ralph Waldo Emerson quote. That is the only thing I could ever see using it for. I mean it is sort of reminiscent of a French textile that has sort of a script on it, but it is sort of non-descript.

MODERATOR: Script, but non-descript???

Joshua: It looks like the Declaration of Independence.

Marco: Right. I don't know the name of it, but it is not meant to be read.

David: I think it would be a good catalog order piece—say Pottery Barn.

Amy: Oh, I think that is a good idea.

MODERATOR: Pottery Barn.

David: Pottery Barn, if that was in one of their catalogs, that would be great.

Nina: Ballard

(LOTS OF AGREEMENT)

David: Not as a designer, but as an average person. Yeah, I would order something like that.

(MORE AGREEMENT)

MODERATOR: (UNVEILING THE PROTOTYPES): this is to give you an idea of what it looks like.

Marco: Well, you can have that done at Kinko's.

(LAUGHTER)

Marco: My gut reaction is when I used to be in visual merchandising, and we would use that kind of thing for retail all the time, with like a stick back and available in a million different finishes, and we would put it on walls or glass. That is what it kind of reminds me of.

MODERATOR: So you did it more for commercial?

David: I know where this could work well: in Staples or Office Max.

MODERATOR: You mean selling it or putting it up on the wall?

Nina: My immediate reaction was, we do a lot of restaurants too, I could see certain signage that happens at the very end, like men's or women's bathrooms or when we wanted to do it in different languages.

Marco: But signage and wall finishes are two different things

Oscar: Galleries. How galleries change exhibits on a regular basis. That is what it reminds me of. Vinyl lettering that is done for gallery spaces.

Marco: Maybe if it were exquisitely done, like a silver or gold leaf I could see it as a panel at the end of a long corridor, but for an all-over wall treatment, for me, it would give me a headache. It would be too much of a distraction.

David: Some businesses have mission statements,

(LOTS OF AGREEMENT)

…and if I owned a business and I, for example, shop in Office Max or Home Depot, and I saw where this was available, I would say, "Well that's cute." I would pay probably 50 bucks to have my, and put it up myself. I can't see as a designer EVER using this.

Nina: At the same time, I could see someone ordering it out of a catalog.
(LOTS OF AGREEMENT)

MODERATOR: So, let's sum this up, 1) I think everyone in this room agrees they probably wouldn't use it.

Amy: I could possibly could use it in a child's room.

MODERATOR: Child's room.

Amy: Yeah. If you had a wall or a border.

(LOTS OF TALKING AT THE SAME TIME)

Amy: I just had three boys: one was 3, 6, and 7. We did a whole wall of tack board for them, so they could put their stuff up—their posters, their pictures, or whatever they wanted. They could do whatever they wanted and stick pins in it. So they might want to take a wall, and…

MODERATOR: Okay, would you do a whole wall?

Amy: No, I would just do part of it.

MODERATOR: Okay, part of the wall. Would it be a border?

Amy: No. I also see the bathroom thing going.

MODERATOR: Oscar…

Oscar: Beside that application, it would be as a border, perhaps in the library, in church…

MODERATOR: But it doesn't seem like anyone would cover the whole wall.

Marco: Now that I was thinking about it, where you would do a big floral, something like a powder room. I could see doing it in a powder room.

Amy: Yeah, definitely.

Marco: It would be kind of fun.

MODERATOR: So we see it in children's rooms. Let's just talk residential for a minute, because we also had some good commercial uses… Child's room, powder room…

Marco: Media room or game room.

MODERATOR: Media room or game room.

Joshua: A room that you are not going to spend a lot of time in.

MODERATOR: Sort of a more whimsical feel. Okay, does everyone agree that we don't see quotes all over the wall. Oscar said, "border." Amy said, "part of a wall."

Amy: Well maybe one wall, just one wall or part of one wall.

MODERATOR: Okay, and would you put one quote or one poem, or does it depend on the space.

Amy: It depends on the space. Are there characters that go with this, like elves and mice?

MODERATOR: We can probably get you elves and mice. Right now we have the letters, we don't know about the characters.

Somebody said a hallway.

Joshua: As like a panel at the end of a long corridor. If you had something that didn't have a door at the end of a blank wall, I could see doing that.

MODERATOR: The other thing I heard earlier, people like maybe a gold leaf..

Marco: It depends on how it is applied to, and how durable it is. We talked about that too. We don't really know anything about it. Is this like vinyl letters where a little kid can sit there and start there and start picking at the corner and peel it all off?

Nina: And also how easy is it to install? You want to have it straight.

Marco: And how easy is it to remove? You don't want someone to paint over it and have that impression forever.

MODERATOR: Sure.

Amy: Oh, yeah. Removal is important.

Nina: Who would install it?

MODERATOR: It would probably be your paper hanger or whomever.

Marco: You specify the quote and it comes in a sheet. Is that what you are saying?

MODERATOR: Yeah, yeah.

David: I can honestly tell you, if this has to be applied by a professional, no one would ever buy it, unless they could put it up themselves. I would never pay anyone to hang it on my wall. Is that what you are saying?

MODERATOR: Because I am talking to designers, I would say paper hanger, but it is actually to be very easy to put up. And any consumer, including myself, could do it.

Marco: You mentioned it would be a clear coat applied over paint, so basically you could do whatever background you wanted.

MODERATOR: Actually I was wrong because I hadn't really seen it. There is no clear. The letters come right off .

Marco: So it is just like vinyl lettering if it peels right off. So what is the advantage of this over going to Kinko's?

MODERATOR: We'll do your whole quote.

(LAUGHTER)

Marco: Because we will write out the whole Declaration of Independence
(LOTS OF SIMULTANEOUS COMMENTS)

Nina: You have to have more sophisticated finishes.

MODERATOR: Okay, to make it unique from going to Kinko's... We heard some commercial uses: restaurants.

Nina: Any time we do a restaurant there is always some last minute signage.

MODERATOR: Like "All employees have to wash their hands before leaving."

Marco: That just happened actually.

(LAUGHTER)

I had to have something done that was nicer than you find anywhere, cause there's not anything that nice that you can find that says that. Not everyone wants mens and womens, we have done latin.

Oscar: However, there has to be code in those circumstances.

MODERATOR: Okay, good. Whatever commercial uses can we think of?

Joshua: Retail

MODERATOR: Retail, okay. Oscar said, "church."

Nina: We've done lettering in elevator lobbies.

Dina: That would be nice if it was flexible enough in removal and redoing it.

(AGREEMENT)

Marco: I know from personal experience that going into office buildings where there is a waiting room, I will read anything. You mentioned elevator lobby, what about the elevator itself? Just something to look at, to do, but I wouldn't do it someplace where you had to look at it for a long time.

David: I see this as being 90% commercial and 10% residential.

MODERATOR: What do others feel about that?

Joshua: If I were to use words or phrases in a residential application it would have to look so knock-out spectacular—you were talking about that Emerson quote—I would only see an artist…it would have to be so special, and I don't see that as looking special.

MODERATOR: Okay. What if this were sold in Target or Home Depot, would you guys use it?

David: I would recommend it to someone.

MODERATOR: You would recommend it, you would tell them to go get it.

David: Sure.

Oscar: But then they would have their own focus group.

MODERATOR: I know, I'm just testing.

David: I know if I were doing a family room, this would be great in a family room or a kids room, and I would say, "Oh, by the way, after you do the room package, go down to Home Depot and do a phrase" and then explain a little bit about it as being a cute idea, and that's it.

Dina: It's something the consumer can do.

David: To be honest with you, I don't really want to waste a lot of time on something like that.

Nina: My first thought too is how open would an installer be to putting it up, because it is a lot more than just matching a pattern. It seems that if you are installing each letter you have to make sure that the letters are level and evenly spaced.

(AGREEMENT)

83

MODERATOR: So it looks difficult to install.

Nina: I don't know if it comes letter by letter or if it is installed by sheet. If somebody is ordering custom phrases, it needs to come on sheets so it is easier to install.

MODERATOR: Let's pretend that we really like the idea, and we are going to put it up in Amy's children's rooms

Amy: Bathroom. I'll do the bathroom.

MODERATOR: How big would you have this lettering?

Dina: It depends on where it is. If it is in a larger space, and it were up high, it would need to be larger than if it were in a powder room.

Marco: Yeah, if it is in a powder room do it much smaller scale.

MODERATOR: So you would like the flexibility to be able to adjust the size?

(AGREEMENT)

MODERATOR: Okay, great. Does everyone feel that way pretty much?

Marco: I wouldn't even consider it unless it was totally flexible.

MODERATOR: Okay. What if there were different types of poems, the romantic poem package, and someone had selected the top ten romantic poems of western civilization, and you could buy this package and put them all over your powder room. Amy doesn't like that idea.

(LAUGHTER)

Dina: I think that would be nice to help me specify it, but I do not think that would make me want to buy it.

David: As a retailer, I could never see stocking something like that. Maybe ordering, yes.

MODERATOR: Yeah, you wouldn't stock it, you would order it. You would call me up and say, Kyle, order me the romantic package.

David: Then that is great.

(LAUGHTER)

Amy: How long is it going to take?

MODERATOR: And that is the beauty of this. This could be brought to you in a week.

Marco: Again, Kinko's can do this in about a day, so what is the advantage of this?

Joshua: If it were gold leaf you might consider it, but again it's like you mentioned, but if were an idea to consider, I would definitely go to a painter or an artisan. I don't think I would do something like that.

MODERATOR: How much would you pay for this?

David: Oh, wow.

Dina: I keep equating it with vinyl lettering, so…

(AGREEMENT)

Marco: It doesn't look any better than vinyl lettering to me.

David: It looks like $20 wholesale phrase.

Marco: Even the gold one looks like gold vinyl.

David: I am sure it didn't cost $20. It probably cost $1.

MODERATOR: Well, I don't know how much it cost, but... How would you want to buy it? Would you want to buy it by the word?

David: By the poem.

MODERATOR: By the poem.

Amy: By the word. I would say by the word.

MODERATOR: By the word, because you would want the flexibility I would think.

David: Well if there was a poem, it would be easy to say, "that's a cute poem" rather than trying to think of one, maybe a favorite

Nina: That goes back to the package thing. I could honestly see this as being sold in a catalog.

David: Definitely. Pottery Barn.

Nina: It is the kind of thing where people are flipping through and for some reason a particular poem touches someone, but maybe it's not for everyone, but I could see people ordering it, because it is already sort of done for them.

Oscar: However, although I see this as being packaged, I think you have too many variables to deal: size, spacing, size of wall, location, background, material. A person trying to make a selection on this is going to have to consider so many things, by the time they are ready to order they are going to have to reconsider are they making the right decision.

Nina: That's why I see it as being like a pillow that people somebody buys with like a needlepoint poem on it, or a...

MODERATOR: So you wouldn't give the consumer all these choices, you would say, "here's the poem" or "here's the phrase"—"take it or leave it."

David: Choices in color. The number one color you would probably get orders for is black, because white you can't read very well.

Oscar: But you may not want to read.

(LOTS OF SIMULTANEOUS COMMENTS)

David: Any time I have ever seen these type of things it's been done in black, and I can also see gold and silver leaf, and maybe one or two other colors, and that's all the options I think that you would really need.

Marco: I think that if you were marketing this directly to designers, I would have a lot of choices, but when you are dealing with clients and the consumer at large, a limited number of choices I think is better because...

David: Less confusion.

Marco: Right. For us it's like it would be easy for us to have a client come over and peruse our fabric samples and pick out whatever colors you like, but we are never going to do that because we narrow it down for them.

Nina: You know what it sort of reminds me of—t-shirts. There are some people who love to buy t-shirts that have quotes on them, and I can see certain people will go through a catalog...

David: I have to tell you that none of my clients would ever spend more than 3 minutes looking through a catalog that is a $20 item. I am not going to waste my 20 and 30 minutes on a $20 item, when I can channel that for maybe a $3000 sofa, or something like that. I don't want to be bothered with the little stuff, and that I consider very little.

MODERATOR: How do others feel about that? This is kind of like a minor piece.

Marco: It doesn't have to be a minor piece. If that clear, subtle behind you...

David: As far as flipping through a catalog..

Marco: It goes back to who you market to. Are you marketing to designers, or are you marketing to the general public.

Nina: I think most designers also look to accessorize. It goes beyond finishes and furniture too. If you are really working on an entire room or house, and you are trying to also tap into what your client's personal tastes are, working with the kids room, you might want to do something really whimsical on the wall... You might not always be focusing in on a sofa. You want to personalize things.

David: Well I prioritize things, and a $20 item on the wall is last on the list.

Joshua: But if you are charging hourly, it doesn't matter.

(AGREEMENT)

David: If I left the house, and was charging them $100 an hour to show them little things to go on the wall that cost $20, they would be complaining I was wasting their time.

Marco: This tone on tone is an interesting idea. It is like a subtle effect for a hallway or something that you don't see right away, but maybe later when you are walking with a candle you may pick it up... or maybe something whimsical.

Dina: I just happened to think of the Paramount in New York, and you would use that kind of thing.

Joshua: That's the most sophisticated idea of all.

Joshua: It is subtle, but I don't really think there is a market for it. I think it is a very specific job oriented product.

David: It is definitely more retail oriented.

Amy: Possibly on a children's wing in a hospital.

Oscar: Borders.

(LAUGHTER)

Oscar: Borders is the only application I can see. It will be easy to install, just strip after strip. I have trouble seeing everything lined up. How does it come? You may have to have skilled labor to line up all these things. It is a different skill altogether.

MODERATOR: Okay.

Nina: And also, I don't think any of us here would say we would use it on every single job.

(AGREEMENT)

Nina: I mean it would be once in—

Oscar: If I were to use letters in something like this in a space, I would do it two ways: with dimensions; second with sophisticated light fixture with acetate, and project onto the wall and that way I could change it every so often, and that is something much more unique

MODERATOR: What if a client of yours says they want a poem on the wall, would you do this, or would you go to a faux finisher?

Marco: I would go to a faux finisher. With the kind of clients I have, if I were to propose something like this, they would laugh.

MODERATOR: One last comment. When a new product comes out on the design market, how do you guys usually find out about it?

Joshua: A luncheon

Nina: Or a trade show

Oscar: Magazines

Nina: Reps

Joshua: Calls

Marco: Right now there are a lot of new things coming out it seems

David: Mail is another

Marco: But I think a trade show or a luncheon at a showroom is nice because you really get to see everything. I know Coach just came out with their line of furnishings.

David: I can't imagine going to a luncheon for this.

(AGREEMENT)

David: This is not Coach or some big line.

Oscar: No, but it could be tied in to a multiple line rep, that brings in several products, and you tie in the product with that face. I think this product to make it really identifiable would have to have a person behind it. We rely on reps.

MODERATOR: That is how you would buy it is through a rep

Oscar: You would become aware of it through a rep.

Marco: Well if it was of designer quality…if we were talking about the high-end finishes and options…

MODERATOR: So that seems to be coming up over and over again. You don't feel it is designer quality?

Not in this state

<u>Dina:</u> it feels more like in corporate—like a signage package.

<u>MODERATOR:</u> Okay, well it is 7:00. Thank you very much for your time. I know you guys have a lot to do, so it was nice of you to do this.

1   For discussions of focus groups in the context of marketing research see Urban, Glen L. and John R. Hauser, 1993. "Design and Marketing of New Products," New York: Prentice-Hall; Churchill, Gilbert A. and Gilbert A. Churchill Jr., 1999. "Marketing Research Method Foundations 7e," Harcourt College Publishers. For more general discussions of focus group technique, see Calder, "Focus Groups and the Nature of Qualitative Marketing Research," Journal of Marketing Research, 14, August 1977, pp. 353-64. Templeton, Jane Farley, 1994. "The Focus Group: A Strategic Guide to Organizing, Conducting and Analyzing the Focus Group Interview," New York: McGraw-Hill.

2   For discussion of brainstorming see: Osborn, Alex F., 1963. "Applied Imagination," New York: Scribner.

3   ibid.

4   Silver and Thompson, 1991.

5   See Templeton for greater discussion of each of these design issues, and samples for each stage. Note also that professional focus group firms will perform all of these functions for a fee. A typical fee includes $500 facility fee, $100 per participant recruiting fee, $1000 moderator fee. This is in addition to the costs you would incur conducting the focus group yourself for honoraria and materials (video tape and food).

6   For original development of repertory grid, see Kelly, G.A., 1955. "Psychology of Personal Constructs," New York: Norton.

7   While Consumer Reports also forms an overall rating, we are more interested in the multi-dimensionality of automobiles. Data for this section comes from Consumer Reports, November 1999, several articles.

8   The normalized scale would ordinarily have models at 0 and 1 values for each attribute. The reason this does not happen for some attributes in the Figure is that the normalization is done for the full set of models, and the figure only includes those for which all data are available.

9   For discussions of factor analysis, see, Harman, Harry H., 1976. "Modern Factor Analysis," University of Chicago Press. For discussions of factor analysis in the context of Marketing Research, see Urban & Hauser (op cit) or Churchill (op cit).

chapter 4

characterizing demand

INTRODUCTION AND GOALS

Conjoint analysis is the centerpiece of the venture design process. Its use marks the transition from feasibility analysis to venture design. The previous chapter helped us reveal the perceptual dimensions customers use to distinguish one product from another. In this chapter, we convert those perceptual dimensions into physical attributes of the product. We then gather primary survey data and apply conjoint analysis to characterize demand for each of those attributes. From these demand curves, we can choose the optimal product configuration and price under any assumption about market structure. The goals of chapter then, are to close feasibility analysis by defining whether the unmet need identified in the perceptual map has sufficient demand at a profitable price, and to begin venture design by gathering the information necessary to define the optimal price and configuration.

Conjoint analysis is important for two reasons. At the most simple level-carefully gathered survey data is the foundation for a reliable estimate of product demand. Since almost all venture decisions rely upon the demand forecast, moving forward without a good estimate of demand is similar to beginning a trek without knowing your destination, yet trying to make decisions about what equipment and supplies to bring. The real power of conjoint analysis, however, lies not in knowing the extent of demand, but in knowing the nuances of the demand—how much of one attribute are customers willing to give up to get more of another? What price will they pay for more of a given attribute? This information allows you to pinpoint the most lucrative market segments with the most profitable product.

The chapter proceeds as follows. First, we discuss the principles underlying conjoint analysis. Then, we walk through each of the steps in the analysis: identifying attributes and attribute levels (how to measure or categorize the attributes); designing a survey that elicits customer preferences for different configurations of attributes; and using the survey data to derive demand curves (or price schedules) for each attribute as well as for the product as a whole. In addition to gathering data for the conjoint analysis, the survey design we recommend gathers ancillary data about customer characteristics to inform decisions beyond price and product configuration. In particular, the survey data will help determine if the target market you envision exists and if the market has segments. Additionally, it will define the media habits of that target. It will test the effectiveness of the preliminary core benefit proposition and corresponding ad copy. Finally, the survey gathers qualitative comments to augment those from the focus group, and confirm them on a wider scale.

PRINCIPLES

Conjoint analysis is a technique that allows a researcher to decompose an individual's judgment into its underlying structure.[1] The foundational premise that necessitates conjoint analysis is that individuals don't know their underlying decision structure. Thus, self-reports of that structure are unreliable.

This self-reporting problem manifests itself in mismatches between the set of attributes individuals claim are important in their decisions, and the actual attributes that are evident in their ultimate decisions. In a really nice illustration of this mismatch, one study asked venture capitalists what criteria they use in choosing which business plans to fund.[2] The study compared these reports with attributes of the portfolio of ventures that the same venture capitalists had actually funded or rejected. The research team found that while the venture capitalists reported that the management team was the most important criterion, in practice, the structure of the proposed industry was the most important factor in their decisions.

While conjoint analysis can be applied to any complex decision, we are interested in it here for characterizing consumer preferences and product demand. In a marketing context the problem of mismatches is one between stated preferences and ultimate purchases. Say, for example, that I believe (and tell a realtor) that what I am looking for in a house is a fireplace, a grand stairway, a new kitchen, and a garage. The realtor shows me several houses with those characteristics and finds that none of the houses appeal to me. Ultimately, he expands the search to include several houses, and finds that what really appeals to me are ostentatious exteriors. He would have saved a great deal of time (both mine and his) if I hadn't misled him. (Note that the misleading is not intentional—I am actually specifying what I truly believe matters to me.)

The cost of fallacious understanding of customer decision structures in the house search problem is fairly trivial. Ultimately, the realtor solves the problem by expanding the search to include more houses. It is likely that people want to look at several houses even if they fall in love with the first one, so they can convince themselves they have made the best choice. The problem is far more severe in the case of mass markets. Here, firms make product design decisions based on market surveys. If customers innocently, yet incorrectly, report that they care about x when they really make their decisions based on y, then the cost to the company is the entire product development, product launch, and the amount of production that occurs until the problem is discovered. With long distribution channels, it could take several months of production before the problem is even discovered.

A better way to solve the product design problem is for the firm to do something comparable to what the realtor does. Rather than ask customers what matters to them, ask them to evaluate a whole series of products (actual houses), all of which are feasible configurations of the ultimate product. This is essentially what conjoint analysis does. Each "product" is characterized by a product description or a real physical prototype, comprising a specific bundle of attributes. Statistical analysis allows the researcher to decompose the ratings of the set of products into customer utilities for each of the attributes. This decomposition can be done for each individual, aggregated for the market as a whole, or aggregated for any segment of the market. In fact, the analysis allows the researcher to determine if the market is naturally segmented or if it is homogeneous.

In essence, conjoint analysis creates utility curves for each individual and each product attribute. These utility curves are then aggregated to create the demand curves for any group of individuals, combination of attributes, or both. These demand curves in turn, can be combined with internal cost data (marginal cost curves) to find the optimal product configuration. This is exactly what we plan to do. We will execute conjoint analysis in this chapter to find attribute demand curves. In Chapter 5 we will combine these demand curves with cost data to derive optimal price and product configuration under a variety of market structures.

One point worth making here is the distinction between dimensions and attributes. When we discussed dimensions in the last chapter, we were referring to perceptual dimensions—intangible aspects of products that buyers use to discriminate them from one another. In contrast, the attributes we will be discussing in this chapter and the next are physical attributes—physical characteristics of the product that can be specified and costed. One challenge in product design is converting perceptual dimensions to physical attributes. In the case of Epigraphs, examples of these perceptual dimensions were durability, uniqueness, and ease of installation. There are a number of physical means to make a wall-covering more durable: it could be coated with polymers to make it washable, or the actual paper could be made thicker, so that it didn't tear when being applied. Conjoint analysis in essence is a means of determining the extent to which these physical attributes satisfy customer desires along intangible dimensions.

Before beginning the analytical process discussion, you may want to actually see a conjoint survey. Websurveyor.com maintains a nice "Conjoint Analysis Demo" that you can access from its home page.

ANALYTICAL PROCESS

The conjoint analysis procedure involves a number of steps: 1) Identifying the various physical attributes of the product/service together with "levels" for each of these attributes, 2) Creating potential product configuration descriptions that combine each level of an attribute with each level of every other attribute (full-factorial design), 3) Designing and administering a survey that probes customer preferences for each potential product configuration, 4) Analyzing survey data to create demand curves for each attribute, and5) Combining that information analytically to choose optimal product configurations and prices for each segment. We discuss steps 1 through 4 in this chapter, and leave step 5 to the next chapter.

Attribute Matrix

One of the outputs of the focus group should be a set of dimensions characterizing the consumer's choice map—what dimensions they use to compare/rank competing products. In the case of automobiles, these may be fuel efficiency, acceleration, comfort, etc. In the case of cellular phone service, these may be size of network, clarity of calls, customer service. Note that for established products and services, *Consumer Reports* does a nice job of defining these attributes/dimensions and ranking products against them—thus, this may be a good starting point for the focus group. Be careful not to confine yourself to *Consumer Reports'* characterizations, however. As noted in the previous chapter, often the real value in creating a new product is identifying and exploiting a new dimension.

Once the attributes have been identified, the next step is choosing levels for each attribute. The levels for attributes can be either discrete or continuous (ordinal scale). Returning to the automobile example for example, transmission is generally a discrete choice: either automatic or manual, whereas fuel efficiency is continuous (any value from 8 mpg for the Ferrari 550 to 68 mpg for the Honda Insight[3]). In the case of discrete attributes, choice of levels is simple—merely include each of the discrete options. In the case of continuous variables, three levels are recommended. Three levels is the minimum required to define a curve, but the refinement gained by having more than three levels generally does not justify the added complexity of the survey task. (Unless this is a key dimension along which the industry's products are differentiated—i.e., each point along the curve corresponds to a different customer segment.)

The choice of the specific three levels for ordinal scale attributes is governed by the desire to capture the "optimal" level with the range of the levels. Thus, if current automobiles offer fuel efficiency of 15 miles per gallon (mpg) to 45 mpg, you might want to offer 10mpg, 30mpg, and 50mpg (go slightly beyond the existing performance range). Summary statistics of existing products might be helpful here. If available, you might choose the mean value and the $\pm 2\sigma$ values. Unfortunately for most new ventures, these data are not available at the outset. Don't forget that one of the most important ordinal scale attributes is price.

This process of choosing levels for each attribute should yield a table like that in Exhibit 4-1. The total product configurations implied by this table is 162 = 3 fuel efficiencies x 3 transmissions x 3 accelerations x 2 brakes x 3 prices. The reliability of the conjoint responses is an inverse function of the survey complexity. You can see that even a simple matrix like the one above involves 162 products, so generally fewer attributes are better. Thus, you should only include in your matrix those attributes that either you control, or that interact with other attributes. It is probably easiest to explain this by discussing what attributes to exclude:

1) Exclude any attribute that is expected as part of the industry standard. In the case of automobiles, this set is infinite, but a recent example is driver-side airbags. Since you know you have to include airbags, there is no reason to estimate their value. Sometimes these attributes are referred to as "Table Stakes." They are the ante you need merely to enter the game.

2) Exclude choices like color, which do not interact with other attributes and for which the choice can be made in the absence of a demand curve (for which the marginal cost is zero). If you know you can only offer one color, you can merely ask what color respondents prefer, and choose the most popular color. If you can offer multiple colors, you can ask for color rankings, and then attempt to offer those colors that span the most "first choices".

Conversely, some items not typically considered part of the product bundle, may be best treated as such. Location and distribution channel are examples of important decisions linked to other product attributes that we might ordinarily consider to be outside the normal definition of "product configuration."

Exhibit 4-1. Automobile Attribute Matrix

ATTRIBUTES

Fuel Efficiency (mpg)	Transmission	Acceleration (sec to 60 mph)	ABS Brakes	Price
15	Automatic	5.0	No	$12,000
30	4-speed	7.5	Yes	$15,000
45	5-speed	10.0		$18,000
3	3	3	2	3

Reducing the Size of the Attribute Matrix

We saw that the full factorial design of the simple automobile matrix above yields 162 potential product configurations. Any respondent faced with choices between 162 products will be completely overwhelmed—producing more or less useless responses. Generally the recommended number of configurations is 18. This number balances a desire for statistically significant observations with the companion goal of reliable responses. Fortunately, we can take advantage of simple sample statistics to reduce the full set of potential products to a more manageable set. We create a "fractional factorial" design of the matrix.

The goal of fractional factorial design is to preserve a balance across all attributes and the paired interactions. This is important, because if we arbitrarily tried to reduce the set of "products" it is likely we would introduce interdependence between attributes that doesn't exist naturally. The result is that we may overstate or understate demand for the affected attributes. As an example, assume that we manually tried to create 18 products. One thing that could inadvertently happen without the aid of a fractional factorial matrix, is that all configurations having manual transmission might also have low fuel efficiency. Our expectation would be that low fuel efficiency increases demand, while manual transmission decreases demand. However, because our configuration choices would always combine the two, we would likely obtain results that neither fuel efficiency nor transmission has any effect on demand. Thus, unless you are using a full factorial design, we strongly recommend use of the fractional factorial matrix in Exhibit 4-2.

Exhibit 4-2 lays out the basic conversion from a full factorial design to a fractional factorial design.[4] To use the table:

1) Designate each of your attributes by a letter, A through F.
   (In the auto example of Exhibit 1, fuel efficiency would be attribute A, transmission B, etc.)
2) Next, assign a number 0 to 2 for each level of each attribute.
   (In the auto example, 15 mpg would be level 0 for attribute A, 30 mpg would be level 1, etc.)
3) Highlight the relevant columns of the fractional factorial matrix for your product options depending on whether they have two or three levels. (In the auto example, you would highlight Column A3 because there are three levels of fuel efficiency [attribute A]; you would also highlight B3 and C3 and E3 because there are three levels of transmission, acceleration and price; but you would highlight D2, because there are only 2 levels of brakes)
4) Specify your 18 products, by merely reading across each row to identify the respective level for each attribute (the highlighted columns).

Exhibit 4-2.   REDUCING FACTORIAL DESIGNS

This table allows you to reduce a full factorial design to a manageable set of 18 product configurations. The designs in this table will allow you up to 7 attributes with up to three levels per attribute. This only allows estimation of main effects.

Product	A3	B3	C3	D3	E3	F3	G3		A2	B2	C2	D2	E2	F2	G2
	Attributes with 3 levels								Attributes with 2 levels						
1	0	0	0	0	0	0	0		0	0	0	0	0	0	0
2	0	1	1	2	1	1	1		0	1	1	0	1	1	1
3	0	2	2	1	2	2	2		0	0	0	1	0	0	0
4	1	0	1	1	1	2	0		1	0	1	1	1	0	0
5	1	1	2	0	2	0	1		1	1	0	0	0	0	1
6	1	2	0	2	0	1	2		1	0	0	0	0	1	0
7	2	0	2	2	1	0	2		0	0	0	0	1	0	0
8	2	1	0	1	2	1	0		0	1	0	1	0	1	0
9	2	2	1	0	0	2	1		0	0	1	0	0	0	1
10	0	0	2	1	0	1	1		0	0	0	1	0	1	1
11	0	1	0	0	1	2	2		0	1	0	0	1	0	0
12	0	2	1	2	2	0	0		0	0	1	0	0	0	0
13	1	0	0	2	2	2	1		1	0	0	0	0	0	1
14	1	1	1	1	0	0	2		1	1	1	1	0	0	0
15	1	2	2	0	1	1	0		1	0	0	0	1	1	0
16	2	0	1	0	2	1	2		0	0	1	0	0	1	0
17	2	1	2	2	0	2	0		0	1	0	0	0	0	0
18	2	2	0	1	1	0	1		0	0	0	1	1	0	1

Source: Addleman, "Orthogonal Main-Effect Plans for Asymmetrical Factorial Experiments," Technometrics 4, February 1962, p. 21-46.

To use the table:
1) Designate each of your attributes A-F.
2) Next, assign a number 0-2 for each level of each attribute.
3) Highlight the relevant columns for your product options. (Thus if you have a product with 3 levels of attribute A, 3 levels of attribute B, 3 levels of attribute C, and only 2 levels of attribute D, you would highlight: A3, B3, C3 and D2).
4) Identify your 18 products, by merely reading across each row to identify the respective level for each attribute (the highlighted columns)
   For the case of A3,B3,C3,D2 just mentioned:
   Product 1 has 0 level for each of the four attributes
   Product 2 has level 0 for attribute A, level 1 for B, level 1 for C and level 0 for D
5) Because these products are organized in a structured manner, respondents might have a tendency to recognize the pattern and simply anticipate questions. To avoid that, we randomize the order of products. (You can pull 18 numbers out of a hat).

For the auto example, we read across row 1 to find the highlighted columns (A3,B3,C3,D2,E3) just mentioned:

–Product 1 has 0 level for each of the five attributes (Row 1-column A3, Row 1-column B3, Row 1-column C3, Row 1-column D2, Row 1-column E3). Translating this code back into the actual levels of the auto attributes means that the first product gets 15 mpg, is an automatic that reaches 60mph in 5 seconds, has no ABS and sells for $12,000.

–Product 2 has level 0 for attribute A, level 1 for B, level 1 for C, level 0 for D, and level 1 for E (Row 2-column A3, Row 2-column B3, Row 2-column C3, Row 2-column D2). Again translating back into the auto attributes, the second product gets 15 mpg, has a 4-speed, that reaches 60mph in 7.5 seconds, has no ABS and sells for $15,000.

–Continue in this manner for all 18 products in the matrix.

5) Because these products are organized in a structured manner, respondents might have a tendency to recognize the pattern and simply anticipate questions, thus biasing results. To avoid that, we randomize the order of products. You can simply pull 18 numbers out of a hat to determine the order in which you present the product configurations.

Exhibit 4-3 steps through the entire process of creating the 18 products for the Epigraphs survey, randomizing them, and then restructuring their coding to support statistical analysis.

Designing the Survey

Survey design involves six elements: 1) choosing the method of administration, 2) specifying/obtaining the sample, 3) designing the cover letter or contact script, 4) writing the instructions, 5) designing the template for the product configuration questions, and 6) writing the ancillary questions regarding demographics (to assess segmenting), distribution channel (if not part of the product configuration), and media exposure.

Generally, response rates to mail surveys are quite low (modal response is about 20-40%). Thus, the goal in all elements of survey design is to induce the subject to respond reliably—you want both a high rate of response, and high reliability of those responses. Techniques commonly recommended to achieve these goals are:

- Preliminary contact (so respondents anticipate the survey)
- Monetary (or other) inducements
- Follow up contact (since the response rate increases from 10% for a single contact to 24% for 5 contacts)

Exhibit 4-3. Epigraphs product configurations

6) Reorder the products according to column 6 to create the order for questions. Thus the first question is now product 18 (random# 1), the second question is product 7 (random# 2), etc (Table 4-3b).

Table 4-3b. Random Order Product Configurations.

Product	C3	D3	A2	B2	Random#
18	chain	60	std	Std	1
7	Internet	100.	std	Std	2
15	Internet	35	custom	Std	3
10	Internet	60	std	Std	4
14	superstore	60	custom	custom	5
1	chain	35	std	Std	6
5	Internet	35	custom	custom	7
16	superstore	35	std	Std	8
6	chain	100.	custom	Std	9
11	chain	35	std	custom	10
12	superstore	100.	std	Std	11
8	chain	60	std	custom	12
3	Internet	60	std	Std	13
9	superstore	35	std	Std	14
13	chain	100.	custom	Std	15
4	superstore	60	custom	Std	16
2	superstore	100.	std	custom	17
17	Internet	100.	std	custom	18

Reconfiguring the Matrix for statistical analysis

While the above database is sufficient to generate the 18 product configurations for the survey, the configurations need to be characterized as binary choices for the conjoint data base. Table 4-3c below converts the product configuration table into binary variables. To make the conversion, first create a column for each level of each attribute. In the case of Epigraphs there are 10 total levels: 3 distribution channels + 3 prices + 2 color levels + 2 genre levels. Next create 18 rows (one for each of the 18 product configurations). Start by putting zeroes in each cell of the matrix. This essentially creates a matrix of 18 identical products consisting of the first level of each attribute. To characterize each of the 18 products, assign "1" to a cell whenever the corresponding product (row) uses that level of an attribute. For example, Table 4-3b above indicates that the first product is distributed through *chains*, at a price of *$60*, with *standard* colors and *standard* themes. We therefore put "1" in each of those four cells of the first row, and leave the remaining cells in the row "0". Repeat this process for the remaining 17 products. Note number of "1"s in each row will always equal the number of attributes.

6) Reorder the products according to column 6 to create the order for questions. Thus the first question is now product 18 (random# 1), the second question is product 7 (random# 2), etc (Table 4-3b).

Table 4-3b. Random Order Product Configurations.

Product	C3	D3	A2	B2	Random#
18	chain	60	std	Std	1
7	Internet	100.	std	Std	2
15	Internet	35	custom	Std	3
10	Internet	60	std	Std	4
14	superstore	60	custom	custom	5
1	chain	35	std	Std	6
5	Internet	35	custom	custom	7
16	superstore	35	std	Std	8
6	chain	100.	custom	Std	9
11	chain	35	std	custom	10
12	superstore	100.	std	Std	11
8	chain	60	std	custom	12
3	Internet	60	std	Std	13
9	superstore	35	std	Std	14
13	chain	100.	custom	Std	15
4	superstore	60	custom	Std	16
2	superstore	100.	std	custom	17
17	Internet	100.	std	custom	18

Reconfiguring the Matrix for statistical analysis

While the above database is sufficient to generate the 18 product configurations for the survey, the configurations need to be characterized as binary choices for the conjoint data base. Table 4-3c below converts the product configuration table into binary variables. To make the conversion, first create a column for each level of each attribute. In the case of Epigraphs there are 10 total levels: 3 distribution channels + 3 prices + 2 color levels + 2 genre levels. Next create 18 rows (one for each of the 18 product configurations). Start by putting zeroes in each cell of the matrix. This essentially creates a matrix of 18 identical products consisting of the first level of each attribute. To characterize each of the 18 products, assign "1" to a cell whenever the corresponding product (row) uses that level of an attribute. For example, Table 4-3b above indicates that the first product is distributed through *chains*, at a price of *$60*, with *standard* colors and *standard* themes. We therefore put "1" in each of those four cells of the first row, and leave the remaining cells in the row "0". Repeat this process for the remaining 17 products. Note number of "1"s in each row will always equal the number of attributes, since each product has to designate a distribution channel, a price, a color level and a theme level.

Table 4-3c. Table of binary variables for the product configurations, needed for the conjoint data base.

Prod-uct	chain	super	web	$35	$60	$100	Std color	Cust color	Std theme	Cust theme
18	1	0	0	0	1	0	1	0	1	0
7	0	0	1	0	0	1	1	0	1	0
15	0	0	1	1	0	0	0	1	1	0
10	0	0	1	0	1	0	1	0	1	0
14	0	1	0	0	1	0	0	1	0	1
1	1	0	0	1	0	0	1	0	1	0
5	0	0	1	1	0	0	0	1	0	1
16	0	1	0	1	0	0	1	0	1	0
6	1	0	0	0	0	1	0	1	1	0
11	1	0	0	1	0	0	1	0	0	1
12	0	1	0	0	0	1	1	0	1	0
8	1	0	0	0	1	0	1	0	0	1
3	0	0	1	0	1	0	1	0	1	0
9	0	1	0	1	0	0	1	0	1	0
13	1	0	0	0	0	1	0	1	1	0
4	0	1	0	0	1	0	0	1	1	0
2	0	1	0	0	0	1	1	0	0	1
17	0	0	1	0	0	1	1	0	0	1

Finally, because the product attributes with levels now have 3 columns to describe them, those columns are now linearly dependent, i.e.,if I sum any two columns, I obtain the third column by merely subtracting the sum from 1. Accordingly the data matrix is not positive definite, and I cannot do a regression. Thus the final step in refining the data base for statistical analysis is ensuring that all the variables are linearly independent. You do this by defining one level of each attribute as the default, and then deleting that column. This default level of the attribute will be part of the "default product configuration" that will be captured in the intercept demand in the regression. Intuition suggests choosing the lowest level of each attribute. Note for binary variables, you have implicitly chosen a default. By labeling the gender column, "male," and coding "1" for male and "0" otherwise, you have made "female" the default. If you have three prices ($35,$60,$100) you would set $35 as the default, and retain columns for $60 and $100. This approach to choosing a default is only a suggestion. You may want to play with changing the defaults. Table 4-3d makes this conversion from Table 4-3c.

Table 4-3d. Table of linearly independent attribute variables for the product configurations, needed for the regression.

super	web	$60	$100	colors	Themes
0	0	1	0	0	0
0	1	0	1	0	0
0	1	0	0	1	0
0	1	1	0	0	0
1	0	1	0	1	1
0	0	0	0	0	0
0	1	0	0	1	1
1	0	0	0	0	0
0	0	0	1	1	0
0	0	0	0	0	1
1	0	0	1	0	0
0	0	1	0	0	1
0	1	1	0	0	0
1	0	0	0	0	0
0	0	0	1	1	0
1	0	1	0	1	0
1	0	0	1	0	1
0	1	0	1	0	1

- An efficient questionnaire length and format (shorter, simpler surveys reduce the perceived time commitment for participation)
- Survey sponsorship by a reputable institution (adds credibility to the study)
- Type of postage (hand applied first class stamps convey personalization, and, accordingly, the importance the sponsor affords the study)
- Personalization (as discussed for type of postage)
- Confidentiality/Anonymity of responses (increases likelihood people will provide sensitive information)

Note for the Epigraphs survey we followed all these suggestions other than preliminary and follow-up contact, and survey brevity. We included a dollar with the survey (as much to instill guilt as to offer an incentive), and included a contest for those who returned responses quickly. We had a reasonably lengthy questionnaire, Wharton sponsorship, 1st class metered postage, and personalization (mail merging the mailing list with the basic letter). This approach yielded a 25% response rate. Interestingly, another 10% of the addressees returned the dollar even though they didn't respond to the survey (an alternative approach to resolving guilt).

Method of administration. The major distinction between methods of administration is interview versus written survey. Of these, interviews are the most costly because they require approximately 30 minutes to 1 hour of interviewer time per respondent. Their primary advantage is that the interviewer can clear up any ambiguity about the questions. Of course, most question ambiguity should be revealed and corrected during a survey pretest. Thus interviews are warranted primarily when the subject matter is inherently complex, and you want to ensure respondent understanding. In most other instances, a written survey is preferable. Not only is it less expensive, but the inherent anonymity of the survey makes it more likely that the respondent will respond to questions truthfully. This is a similar argument to the one expressed earlier for using focus groups rather than independent interviews.

Sample. The choice of sample is usually made jointly with the choice of administration method. Sample choice is an art as much as a science. The problem with almost any sampling technique is that it introduces sample bias. Thus the best sample is one in which the attendant bias is least likely to affect you. Most samples will be based on mailing lists, but we also discuss an interesting sampling approach for interviews: malls.

Internet. A recent innovation in survey administration is Internet surveys. There are several advantages to Internet surveys. In fact, there are so many advantages that unless you will be affected by sampling bias, I strongly encourage this method. The advantages include: *immediate response* (avoiding lags both directions when using mail), *flexibility*—if you discover that subjects are misinterpreting something, you can change it for all subsequent subjects, *reliability*—data is collected electronically, thereby avoiding the time and errors associated with coding, *novelty*— which may induce higher response rates, and *simplicity*—their page configuration makes surveys appear shorter and easier to complete. Better still, a number of websites will host your survey for free.[5]

The disadvantage of Internet surveys is that they may introduce sampling bias. By definition, responses are only collected from people who have Internet access (more affluent segments). This is the modern day equivalent of using the phone book to sample voters prior to the Dewey-Truman election (and having high confidence that Dewey would win). Of course, if you are distributing your product or service exclusively over the Internet, this bias is irrelevant. Similarly, if you are targeting affluent segments, its impact may be minimal.

While you can contact potential Internet subjects by mail or phone, a more logical means to contact them is by e-mail. PostmasterDirect.com maintains 12 million e-mail addresses that you can rent for 10 to 35 cents per name.

Malls. Another fairly recent survey innovation is to sample respondents in malls. In fact, Heakin Research was created explicitly to take advantage of the inherent attractiveness of mall samples. Malls maintain demographic information on their customers, and generally any demographic distribution is likely to be matched to that of some mall. Local malls offer the advantage of expediency—there is some positive probability you could collect the requisite number of responses in a single Saturday. Necessarily, malls introduce regional bias. If regional effects appear to be insignificant based on preliminary information from American Marketplace, then malls may be an appropriate administration method.

Mail Lists. Mailing lists are "rented" on a per use basis for a cost of $0.10 or more per name, subject to minimums of 1000 to 5000 names. Lists are available in a variety of formats, including electronic files, hard copy lists, and mailing labels. The vehicle from which you rent the list will want a copy of your mailing for advance approval. To verify that the approved copy is the actual mailer sent, and that each name is used only once, list sources generally include themselves in the mailing list under bogus names.

A good place to start your search for a mailing list is InfoUSA.com. This site rents downloadable (or hard copy) mailing lists for both businesses and consumers. It allows you to sort on a wide range of criteria to help target your list. Before deciding to use their list, investigate their sources. A search on interior designers elicited less than 300 names. This compares to 30,000 members in the American Society of Interior Designers (ASID).

In the past, the best source of mailing lists both for consumer and commercial customers was advertising media. Most media target particular segments of the market and thus exclude large portions of the population. Newspapers are possible exceptions, but like malls they are prone to regional bias. If you choose to administer a survey by mail using a media mailing list, you should choose a vehicle with broader distribution than your target market. This allows you to confirm your assumptions about who is in the target market. Each media vehicle (particular magazine, show, etc.) distributes a "media kit" with demographic information on its audience, primarily for use by advertisers. Media kits, as well as mailing lists, are obtained by contacting each vehicle's advertising offices. General information on a wide range of media audiences is available from a number of sources.[6]

Another good source for mailing lists is the industry associations and trade journals you discovered during industry analysis in Chapter 2.

The Cover Letter. The goal of the cover letter or e-mail is to capture the attention of the potential respondents, and to provide them with a compelling reason to participate in the study. (Note if the survey is done in person, a script serves the same purpose as a cover letter). Think of the cover letter as an advertisement for your study. People are most interested in participating in a study if they feel it is important or interesting, and if they feel that their participation is highly valued. Many of the techniques listed above are efforts to convey these messages. Exhibit 4-4 is the electronic version of the cover letter for the Epigraphs survey. The letter was printed on Wharton letterhead, and signed personally[7].

Instructions. The instructions restate the project goals, provide a general description of the product, and include an example which interprets the question as well as the response. Additionally, the instructions clarify all assumptions respondents should make, such as what product attributes are included in all products (even when those attributes are not mentioned specifically in the configuration questions). See Section A of the Epigraphs questionnaire (Exhibit 4-5). This instruction section is written AFTER the survey body is designed. Instructions should explain that each product should be treated separately. For example: "If Product 1 is attractive to you, and you compare it with all existing products and feel you are likely to purchase it, then you would mark 'X' for likelihood you would purchase this product. When you get to question 2, *ignore* your answer to question 1. Assume only Product 2 and all existing products are available in the market."

Product literature sheet. One very important component of the instructions is the product literature sheet. A product literature sheet is a detailed version of the ultimate ad copy. Including a product literature sheet with the survey increases the clarity of the offering, reduces the perceived complexity of the instructions, and adds interest to the survey "package". Because the product literature sheet serves the same role for your survey as advertising will for ultimate product sales, you should devote some effort to its design. The goal of the product literature sheet is to accurately convey the core benefit proposition in a compelling manner. If you aren't confident in your ability to write compelling ad copy, consider enlisting an ad agency. In essence, the survey will be pre-testing your copy as much as it is testing potential product demand. You don't want the copy to be the weak link (causing people to report that they are uninterested in your product when in fact they would be interested if you conveyed its value properly). Exhibit 4-6 is the product literature sheet included with the Epigraphs survey.

Product Configuration Question Template. The most important issue in designing the configuration questions is the respondent's rating method. There are a number of options and a good deal of disagreement about the best option.

One approach has respondents make direct comparisons among all 18 configurations and then rank order them. A variation on this approach, acknowledging the cognitive complexity of this task, simplifies it by making a series of paired comparisons. The problem is that a full set of pairs involves 162 comparisons.

Exhibit 4-4. Epigraphs Cover Letter

November 8, 1999

«Title» «First_name» «Last_name»
«Address»
«City», «State» «Zip»

Dear «Title» «Last_name»,

I am leading a research team at The Wharton School to help a new firm design and market its first product for the home decorating market. We would like to ask for your help in designing this product.

In order to help us, we will ask you to read the enclosed "advertisement". This ad is in very rough form, but imagine that it would appear in more professional form in a home decorating magazine some time in the future.

Once you have read the ad, we would like you to complete the attached survey, which asks your opinions about the new product. Your opinions will help in creating the final design for the product and will also help determine where and how it should be sold.

Since it is a new firm, there is not much of a budget (we are offering our services for free). However, we are able to offer a very small token ($1.00) of thanks. In addition, all people who respond by November 15 may enter a contest to win $100. Since we are only sending the survey to 150 people, and not all of them will respond, there is a decent chance of actually winning. Details on the contest are at the end of the survey.

If you are willing to help us, please return the survey in the enclosed envelope by November 12, and keep the $1.00 as a token of our thanks. If you are unable to help us, we ask that you return the $1.00 in the enclosed envelope, so that we can find another opinion to replace yours.

We sincerely appreciate your help!

Sincerely

Anne Marie Knott

Exhibit 4-5. Epigraphs Survey

PROPOSED WALLCOVERING SURVEY

We would like you to evaluate the product described in the attached "advertisement".
As you consider the product keep in mind the following assumptions:

a) Assume that product is **packaged in 50 foot sets**. Each set will fill 50 square feet of wall space. This is comparable to a double roll of wallpaper. (A good size 10' X 15' room has 400 square feet of wallspace)

b) Assume that the product comes packaged with **fully-illustrated instructions**, and that it can be installed by a "do-it-yourselfer" with more effort than paint, but less effort than wallpaper.

c) Assume that the **only special tool needed to install the product is a squeegee, that comes packaged** with the product. The only other tools you will require are a ruler and a level.

d) Assume that when you purchase the product, we will provide **suggestions for coordinating paint**. These suggestions will include two to three "looks" (tone-on-tone, complements, contrasts) that you can choose from. For each look, we will identify a specific manufacturer's paint name and color number.

e) Assume that for standard options, your **purchase will be shipped within 2 weeks**, and for custom options, the product will be shipped in 4-6 weeks.

PRODUCT FEATURES: *We need your help in determining the best possible design for this product. The following descriptions will aid you in evaluating possible designs.*

Colors:
Standard colors : the basic product will come in a variety of 7 standard colors, including gold, silver, hunter, burgundy, sapphire, black and white
Custom colors: for a premium, the product can be made in a variety of 100 colors

Quote Themes
Standard themes: the basic product will come in a variety of 5 standard themes, including literary, humorous , inspirational, sports, movies
Custom themes: for a premium, you can specify a custom set of quotes/graphics that you would like to have produced. We would provide you with information on how many words you would need given your space requirements.

Place Sold
Paint/wallpaper chain (such as Sherwin-Williams or Wallpapers to Go)
Home superstore (such as Home Depot)
Internet

Price per 50 foot set *(see note a)*
$35.00
$60.00
$100.00

DIRECTIONS:
- You will be presented with a series of potential product designs (set of the above features).
- For each product, estimate how many sets (50 feet each) of the product you would purchase in the next 12 months, given the choice between that product an all available wallcovering options.
- Mark an X by the amount of that product you would likely purchase

EXAMPLE:
If you believe that in the next 12 months, you would buy *8 sets* of a product that had *standard quotes*, in *standard colors*, offered over the *Internet* for *$30.00* per set, then you would place an X over the number 8

| COLORS: | Standard (choice of 7) | PLACE SOLD: | Internet |
| THEMES: | Standard (choice of 5) | PRICE: | $30.00 (per 50 feet set) |

Number of sets purchased in next 12 months: _____ X _____

| | 0 | 2 | 4 | 6 | 8 | 10 | 12+ |

Do not choose from among the product designs. Answer each question as a standalone question. Assume that each product is the *only* option available for the new product. However, all existing wallcoverings are still available. For each question mark the number of sets you are likely to buy, given the choice between the new product and all currently available wallcoverings.

1) COLORS: Standard (choice of 7)   PLACE SOLD: Paint/paper chain
    THEMES: Standard (choice of 5)   PRICE: $60.00 (per 50 feet set)
Number of sets purchased in next 12 months: _____
                                            0   2   4   6   8   10   12+

2) COLORS: Standard (choice of 7)   PLACE SOLD: Internet
    THEMES: Standard (choice of 5)   PRICE: $100.00 (per 50 feet set)
Number of sets purchased in next 12 months: _____
                                            0   2   4   6   8   10   12+

3) COLORS: Custom   PLACE SOLD: Internet
    THEMES: Standard (choice of 5)   PRICE: $35.00 (per 50 feet set)
Number of sets purchased in next 12 months: _____
                                            0   2   4   6   8   10   12+

4) COLORS: Standard (choice of 7)   PLACE SOLD: Internet
    THEMES: Standard (choice of 5)   PRICE: $60.00 (per 50 feet set)
Number of sets purchased in next 12 months: _____
                                            0   2   4   6   8   10   12+

5) COLORS: Custom   PLACE SOLD: Home superstore
    THEMES: Custom   PRICE: $60.00 (per 50 feet set)
Number of sets purchased in next 12 months: _____
                                            0   2   4   6   8   10   12+

6) COLORS: Standard (choice of 7)   PLACE SOLD: Paint/paper chain
    THEMES: Standard (choice of 5)   PRICE: $35.00 (per 50 feet set)
Number of sets purchased in next 12 months: _____
                                            0   2   4   6   8   10   12+

7) COLORS: Custom   PLACE SOLD: Internet
    THEMES: Custom   PRICE: $35.00 (per 50 feet set)
Number of sets purchased in next 12 months: _____
                                            0   2   4   6   8   10   12+

8) COLORS: Standard (choice of 7)   PLACE SOLD: Home superstore
    THEMES: Standard (choice of 5)   PRICE: $35.00 (per 50 feet set)
Number of sets purchased in next 12 months: _____
                                            0   2   4   6   8   10   12+

9) COLORS: Custom   PLACE SOLD: Paint/paper chain
    THEMES: Standard (choice of 5)   PRICE: $100.00 (per 50 feet set)
Number of sets purchased in next 12 months: _____
                                            0   2   4   6   8   10   12+

10) COLORS: Standard (choice of 7)   PLACE SOLD: Paint/paper chain
    THEMES: Custom   PRICE: $35.00 (per 50 feet set)
Number of sets purchased in next 12 months: _____
                                            0   2   4   6   8   10   12+

11) COLORS: Standard (choice of 7)   PLACE SOLD: Home superstore
     THEMES: Standard (choice of 5)   PRICE: $100.00 (per 50 feet set)
Number of sets purchased in next 12 months: _____
                                    0   2   4   6   8   10   12+

12) COLORS: Standard (choice of 7)   PLACE SOLD: Paint/paper chain
     THEMES: Custom   PRICE: $60.00 (per 50 feet set)
Number of sets purchased in next 12 months: _____
                                    0   2   4   6   8   10   12+

13) COLORS: Standard (choice of 7)   PLACE SOLD: Internet
     THEMES: Standard (choice of 5)   PRICE: $60.00 (per 50 feet set)
Number of sets purchased in next 12 months: _____
                                    0   2   4   6   8   10   12+

14) COLORS: Standard (choice of 7)   PLACE SOLD: Home superstore
     THEMES: Standard (choice of 5)   PRICE: $35.00 (per 50 feet set)
Number of sets purchased in next 12 months: _____
                                    0   2   4   6   8   10   12+

15) COLORS: Custom   PLACE SOLD: Paint/paper chain
     THEMES: Standard (choice of 5)   PRICE: $100.00 (per 50 feet set)
Number of sets purchased in next 12 months: _____
                                    0   2   4   6   8   10   12+

16) COLORS: Custom   PLACE SOLD: Home superstore
     THEMES: Standard (choice of 5)   PRICE: $60.00 (per 50 feet set)
Number of sets purchased in next 12 months: _____
                                    0   2   4   6   8   10   12+

17) COLORS: Standard (choice of 7)   PLACE SOLD: Home superstore
     THEMES: Custom   PRICE: $100.00 (per 50 feet set)
Number of sets purchased in next 12 months: _____
                                    0   2   4   6   8   10   12+

18) COLORS: Standard (choice of 7)   PLACE SOLD: Internet
     THEMES: Custom   PRICE: $100.00 (per 50 feet set)
Number of sets purchased in next 12 months: _____
                                    0   2   4   6   8   10   12+

Now, we'd like to ask you a few questions about your reactions to this product.
Which color(s) are you most likely to be interested in? (please circle)
     Gold   Silver   Hunter Green   Burgundy   Sapphire Blue   Black   White   Other _____

Which theme(s) are you most likely to be interested in? (please circle)
     Literary   Humorous   Inspirational   Sports   Movies   Other _____

If you purchased this product, how likely is it that you would install it yourself? (please circle)
     Definitely would   Somewhat likely   Not sure   Unlikely   Definitely would not

What type of room or rooms do you think the product is best suited for?

What do you like most about the product?

What do you like least about the product?

Now, we'd like to ask you a few questions about your experiences with wallpaper.
What percentage of wallpaper have you purchased from each of the following sources:
Designer___%   Independents___%   Paint/paper chain___%   Home superstore___%   Mail/phone order___%

What percentage of wallpaper do you purchase from books_____%, from store stock_____%

Have you ever installed your own wallpaper? (please circle) Yes   No
      If so, how long ago?____years ago
      If so, what bothers you most about the installation process (list as many things as you would like):

Where do you typically get your decorating ideas (please rank order, with 1 as the highest):
      Interior designers   _____
      Magazines   _____   Please list your favorites:
      Store displays   _____   Please list your favorites:
      Design houses/home show _____   Please list your favorites:
      Television shows   _____   Please list your favorites:

Approximately how much money did you spend on home improvements in the past 12 months? (please circle)
      $0   <$100 $100-$500 $500-$1000 $1000-2500 $ 2500-5000   >$5000

Approximately how many of these home improvement purchases did you make by mail or phone order?
(please circle)
      $0   <$100 $100-$500 $500-$1000 $1000-2500 $ 2500-5000   >$5000

Do you have Internet access? (Please circle)   Yes   No

Approximately how many purchases did you make via Internet in past 12 months?
      $0   <$100 $100-$500 $500-$1000 $1000-2500 $ 2500-5000   >$5000

Finally, we'd like to ask you a few questions about yourself.
1.   Sex: (Please circle)   Male Female

2.   Marital status: (Please circle)   Single Married Partnered Other (widowed or divorced)

3.   Number of people in household: _____ Adults   _____ Children

4.   Finally, please check your approximate total household income (please circle).

   < $25,000 $25,000-50,000 $50,000-75,000 $75,000-100,000 $100,000-150,000   >$150,000

We are running a contest to help identify fresh quotes. There is a $100 award for the best quote mailed before November 15. If you would like to enter, please write your quote below. Then make sure to include your name and address (in case you win). Note, if you are not entering the contest, and prefer to remain anonymous, we do not need your name and address.

Quote:
Source for quote:

Your name   _____
Your address   _____
                        _____
                        _____

Thank you, we really appreciate your help!

Exhibit 4-6. Epigraphs product literature sheet

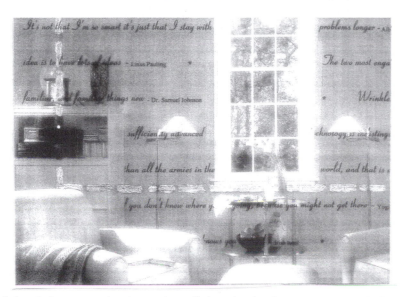

Epigraphs is a new product that can be applied to painted walls to create a custom look. Epigraphs have the look of stencils, but with less repetition, and far less work. Single lines of epigraphs can be used as an accent, or several lines can be used in lieu of wallpaper to create a whimsical room.

Epigraphs come in strips of self-stick graphics ready for installation. The product is applied dry, so it has none of the mess of stencils, borders or wallpaper, nor any of the rush to apply the product before it dries. Further, because there is space between words, epigraphs do not have the alignment and abutment problems of wallpaper. This leads to two advantages over wallpaper: 1) Epigraphs tolerate minor installation problems that wallpaper won't, and 2) there is no need to buy 20% extra epigraphs to compensate for matching problems, and waste around doors and windows. Experience indicates that an entire 10' X 15' room (400 square feet of wall) can be installed in less than 8 hours.

Epigraphs come in 7 standard colors (including gold, silver, hunter, burgundy, sapphire, black and white), and 5 standard themes (including literary, humorous, inspirational, sports, movies). For each of the standard colors, Epigraphs has identified coordinating paints for three different looks: tone-on-one (a very subtle look), complementary (a subdued look), and contrasting. These combinations create 105 different patterns. While this is a good deal of variety, there is also an option for you to create your own unique look with custom colors and graphics.

Literary: *A classic is something that everybody wants to have read and nobody has read* — Mark Twain

Humorous: *We're not lost. We're locationally challenged-* John C Ford

Inspirational: *It's not that I'm so smart it's just that I stay with problems longer—* Albert Einstein

Sports: *One man can be a crucial ingredient on a team, but one man cannot make a team* -Kareem Abdul-Jabbar

Movies: *Frankly my dear, I don't give a damn* — Scarlet O'Harat

Quote shown actual size:

Even if the complexity issue can be resolved, rankings yield only relative utilities. I would know, for example, that the subject prefers configuration 1 to configuration 2, but I won't know if it likes 1 twice as much as 2, or only slightly prefer it. This leaves the challenge of converting relative utilities to absolute demand, and ultimately dollar value.

Accordingly, I advocate asking the demand question directly: either likelihood of purchase, expected frequency of purchase, or expected units purchased. While purchase intentions are known to be optimistic, they can be rescaled. Rescaling can take advantage of historical estimates of response optimism. Exhibit 4-7 is a comparison of actual purchases versus stated intentions that can be used to rescale responses. Note that only about 40% of those saying they "definitely will" buy the product, actually do so. Perhaps more interesting is the fact that 10% of those saying they will "definitely not" purchase the product, will do so. This is an indication of how powerful the social effect of diffusion is.

For durable goods that consumers purchase infrequently, the best response frame is likelihood of purchase: respondents can be asked to mark on a scale of 1-5, how likely it is that they will purchase products in next 6 months. For calibration, they can be asked when they last purchased that product and what brand they purchased. This can be compared to aggregate statistics. For repeat goods, like shampoo, consumers would be asked how frequently they would purchase this product within the next 6 months or how many they would purchase in that period.

Ancillary Questions. The most important ancillary questions are demographics. If there is much variance in the reported demand for your product, this is an indication that your market is segmented. Demographic questions will allow you to characterize the segments. In designing an urban shuttle service for example, you might find that there is a large variance in the number of stops respondents are willing to tolerate. If you have demographic data, you may be able to determine that women prefer more stops (under the assumption that more stops means more passengers and greater safety in number) whereas men prefer fewer stops (indicating little concern with safety, but a premium on convenience). With such a result you could choose to offer two services, or serve the more lucrative segment. Without such data, you would be forced to design a compromise service unlikely to be attractive to either group.

Another important set of ancillary questions deal with product attributes excluded from the configuration matrix for reasons specified earlier. For example, if you are trying to decide how many and which colors to offer, here you would ask respondents to rank a set of colors.

If distribution channel is not part of product configuration, you would now ask where respondents are likely to look for (or last searched for/purchased) the product. You would identify candidate channels and ask them to rank or choose.

Exhibit 4-7. Rescaling survey responses for optimism

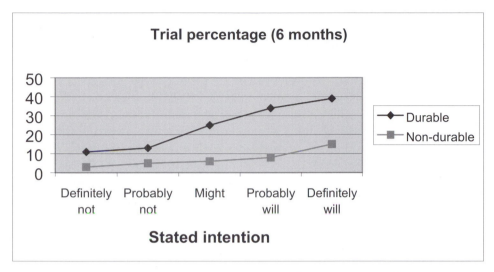

Reprinted with permission from The Journal of Marketing Research, published by the American Marketing Association, Jamieson, L. and F. Bass, 1986 26(3): 336-345.

You might also include an "other _____" choice to surface channels you had not considered.

Finally, an equivalent question to the distribution channel asks respondents what media they have greatest exposure to. This may merely confirm what you know from secondary data, but to the extent you find segments, it will help you target advertising to those segments.

Raw Date Base

The first step in analyzing the survey data is creating a database of the raw data. If you use a hosted Internet survey, this step is done for you automatically. The site will allow you to download the entire database and will also generate summary graphics. If not, then you will need to create a database and enter the data manually.

In the raw database, each survey is one observation (row), and each question is one variable (column). The first column you create identifies each survey. This may just be the order in which the surveys were received, e.g., the first returned survey is ID number 1, the second is number 2, etc. If this is how you plan to identify the surveys, just number them as they arrive. After creating the ID column, add one column for each question in the survey (excluding open-ended questions).

After the structure has been created, you will begin entering data for each question (column). For continuous scale variables, such as number of purchases, entries are straightforward. For dichotomous (two) choice variables such as gender, choose one of the choices as the variable name, then code each entry "1" if the response matches the variable name, and "0" otherwise. For example, if you choose to name your gender variable "male", then code all males as 1 and all females as 0. For multi-chotomous choice variables, such as color, create a variable (column) for each color, then enter "1" if that color is chosen and "0" otherwise. For the product questions you want a continuous variable. If you phrased the question as likelihood of purchase with a 5-point scale, then translate the rating into the numerical purchase probabilities from Exhibit 4-7. If you have a durable good, enter 0.39 for all "definitely will", enter .34 for all "probably", enter .25 for all "might", enter .13 for "probably not", and enter .11 for "definitely not". Exhibit 4-8 shows the raw data base of Epigraphs survey responses.

It is usually interesting at this point to create summary statistics for the data. To do this, merely create a new row below the raw data. Title the first row "mean", and set the formula in the first cell: "=average (first observation in column: last observation in column)". Title the second row, "standard deviation", and set the formula in the first cell: "=stdev (first observation in column: last observation in column)". Copy these formulas across all the variable columns. You can use these two rows to create bar charts that graphically depict the summary statistics. Exhibit 4-8 includes means and standard deviations for data used in the regression analysis. Exhibit 4-9 shows the summary statistics for the Epigraphs ancillary data.

Conjoint Data Base

In order to execute the conjoint analysis, the raw database needs to be manipulated. This is the most tedious and non-intuitive part of conjoint analysis. In the near future there should be software that does this for you, but in the meantime, follow the step-by-step instructions and refer to the Epigraphs example (Exhibit 4-8 for the raw database, and Exhibit 4-10 for the converted conjoint data base).

The raw database has n observations (rows) on p questions (columns), where "n" is the number of surveys and "p" is the number of product questions. The basic conjoint database has "n x p" observations (rows) and one column (demand),[8] where each observation in the conjoint analysis is a person-product.

To expand the raw data base into a conjoint data base, you need to do the following:

1) First copy each observation 17 times (to make 18 total rows for each

Exhibit 4-8. Raw data base

ID#	1	2	3	4	5	6	7	8	9	10	11	12	13	14	15	16	17	18	Fem	Marr	Adul	Kids	<25	25-5	50-7	75-1	100-	>150
1	0	0	0	0	0	0	0	0	0	0	0	0	0	0	0	0	0	0	1	0	1	0	0	0	0	0	0	0
2	0	0	0	0	2	4	0	4	0	0	2	0	0	4	4	4	0	0	1	1	3	2	0	0	0	1	1	0
3	2	0	0	2	0	4	0	8	0	0	0	0	2	8	0	0	0	0	0	1	2	2	0	0	1	0	0	0
4	6	0	0	0	6	6	0	8	6	12	4	8	0	8	2	8	0	0	0	0	2	2	0	0	0	0	0	1
5	0	0	0	0	0	10	2	8	0	8	0	6	0	8	6	0	8	0	0	1	2	0	0	0	0	0	0	0
6	8	4	8	4	10	10	10	10	4	8	4	6	10	10	6	10	8	0	1	1	2	6	0	0	0	0	1	0
7	4	0	0	0	4	6	0	6	0	6	2	6	0	6	0	6	0	0	0	0	2	0	0	0	0	0	0	0
8	0	0	0	0	0	2	0	2	2	2	0	0	0	2	0	0	1	0	1	1	2	2	0	0	0	0	0	0
9	0	0	0	0	2	2	0	2	0	2	0	0	0	0	0	2	0	0	0	0	2	3	0	0	0	0	0	0
10	6	0	0	0	0	4	0	0	6	2	2	2	0	0	4	4	0	0	0	1	2	0	1	0	0	0	0	0
11	4	2	8	4	4	8	2	8	2	4	0	4	2	6	2	2	0	0	0	0	2	1	0	0	0	0	0	0
12	0	0	0	0	0	0	8	0	0	0	0	0	0	8	0	4	0	0	0	0	2	0	0	0	0	0	0	0
13	2	0	6	0	0	6	8	6	2	8	0	0	8	8	0	0	0	0	0	1	3	1	0	1	0	0	0	0
14	0	0	0	0	0	2	0	2	2	4	0	0	0	0	0	0	0	0	0	0	2	2	0	0	0	0	0	0
15	0	0	0	0	0	4	0	6	0	4	0	2	8	8	0	2	2	0	0	1	1	0	0	1	0	0	0	0
16	1	0	0	0	4	4	0	4	0	6	0	0	0	4	0	0	1	0	0	0	4	2	0	0	0	0	0	0
17	0	0	2	0	0	2	0	6	2	2	2	2	8	2	4	2	0	0	1	1	4	2	0	0	0	0	0	0
18	2	0	0	0	0	8	0	0	0	8	0	0	0	8	0	0	0	0	1	0	3	2	0	0	1	0	0	0
19	10	0	0	0	10	6	8	8	0	10	0	0	8	6	0	6	0	80	0	1	4	3	0	0	0	0	0	0
20	6	0	0	0	6	6	0	8	0	8	6	0	8	8	8	0	4	6	1	1	3	0	0	0	0	0	1	0
21	0	0	0	0	0	8	0	8	0	4	0	0	0	0	0	2	0	0	0	0	3	2	0	0	1	0	0	0
22	2	0	0	0	2	4	0	4	1	2	0	4	0	4	0	0	8	0	0	1	3	0	0	1	0	0	0	0
23	0	0	8	0	0	2	8	2	0	8	0	0	0	2	8	4	4	0	1	1	2	1	0	0	0	1	0	0
24	8	0	8	8	4	0	8	8	0	8	8	8	8	8	8	8	8	0	1	1	3	3	0	0	0	0	0	0
25	8	8	10	8	8	8	8	10	4	8	6	6	2	2	8	8	0	0	0	1	3	0	0	0	0	1	0	0
26	6	0	0	0	0	10	0	10	0	2	6	0	0	0	8	0	0	0	1	0	2	0	0	0	0	0	1	0
27	0	0	2	0	0	2	0	0	0	8	0	4	2	2	8	2	0	0	0	1	3	2	0	0	0	0	0	0
28	0	0	0	0	12	0	0	0	0	0	0	0	0	0	0	0	0	0	1	0	2	0	1	0	0	0	0	0
29	0	0	0	0	0	6	0	6	0	6	0	0	0	6	0	0	0	0	0	1	2	3	0	0	0	0	0	0
30	0	0	0	0	0	6	10	6	0	10	0	0	0	0	0	0	0	0	0	0	2	2	0	0	0	0	0	0
31	0	0	0	0	0	0	0	0	0	0	0	0	0	0	0	0	0	0	0	1	0	0	0	0	0	0	0	0
32	4	0	6	4	6	6	0	6	0	0	0	0	0	0	0	2	0	0	1	0	2	0	0	0	0	0	0	0
33	4	0	0	0	0	6	8	6	0	6	0	0	0	0	0	0	0	0	0	1	0	0	0	0	0	0	0	0
34	0	0	0	0	0	6	10	6	0	10	0	0	0	6	0	0	0	0	0	1	2	1	0	0	0	0	0	0
mean	2.15	0.67	2.00	0.75	2.91	4.06	2.18	4.12	1.06	4.00	0.79	1.82	0.91	4.24	1.06	2.12	0.97	2.97	0.76	0.79	2.12	1.00	0.07	0.18	0.25	0.32	0.11	0.04
sd	2.98	2.04	3.39	1.81	3.54	3.14	3.69	3.43	2.12	3.74	1.93	2.71	2.24	3.46	2.29	3.00	2.23	###	0.44	0.42	0.74	1.35	0.26	0.39	0.44	0.48	0.31	0.19

Yes / no questions: 0=no; 1=yes

Male / female: 0=male; 1=female

Exhibit 4-9. Summaries of ancillary data

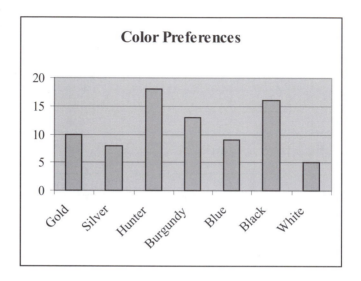

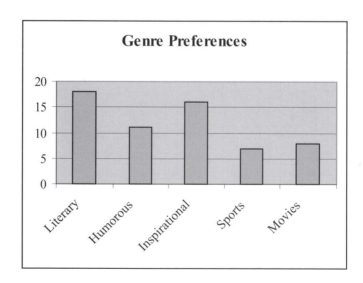

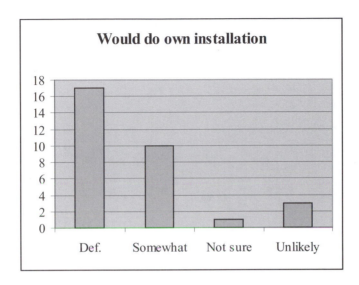

Would do own installation

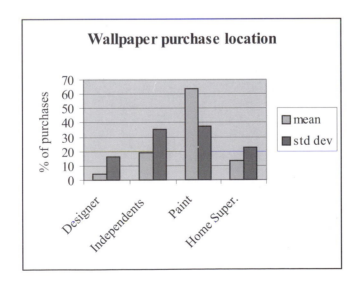

Wallpaper purchase location

venture design

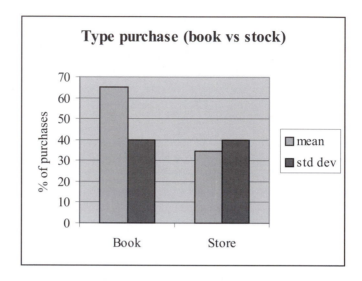

Type purchase (book vs stock)

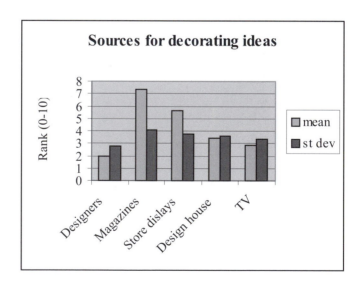

Sources for decorating ideas

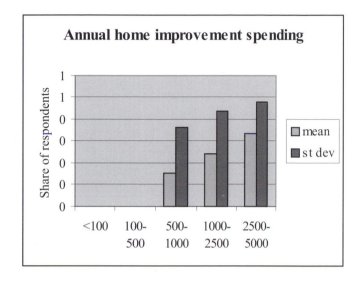

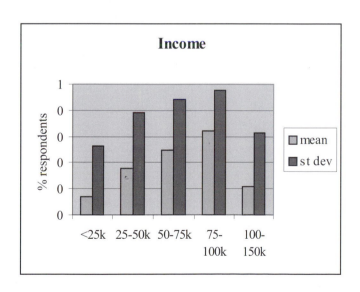

respondent), keeping all observations by the same respondent together. The reason we need 18 rows per respondent is that we need one row for each product. If you have done this step correctly, you should have. 18 (x # surveys) rows (plus the header).

2) Transpose all *product responses* for each respondent, but keep all the demographic information as is. In the raw database, the responses to the product questions are in rows, one row for each product. You want to convert these into a single column that you re-label "demand." (To transpose in Excel, copy the **18 product responses only** for survey 1, in "edit" → Paste Special; select "transpose," then click on the first product cell.

3) Repeat step 2 for all your responses.

4) Delete the remaining 17 "product columns."

5) Next you will insert the product configuration matrix you originally used to design the survey (Table 4-3c). To ensure you don't overwrite other survey data, you should probably insert the appropriate number of columns into your data base. For Epigraphs, there are 10 total attribute-levels, so we insert 10 columns. (There is no need to insert the product number, column 1 in Table 4-3c.)

6) Copy the product matrix from its original file and paste it *with headers* into the inserted columns "observation 1". Next, copy the product matrix *without headers*, and paste it n-1 times into the remaining "person observations." (Note each person now has 18 rows, whereas before, each person was only a single row.)

Table 4-10 is the first 37 observations in the final database used to support Epigraphs' conjoint analysis. The complete database has 612 observations (18 products x 34 respondents).

Regression analysis

Our primary analysis is characterizing demand as a function of the product configuration. This gives us a set of demand curves that we can evaluate in the next chapter to find optimal price and product configuration. To characterize demand, we execute regression analysis using the general equation:

$\text{Demand}_{ij} = \beta_0 + \Sigma \, \beta_K \, (\text{product attribute})_k + e_{ij}$
Where: i is an individual (number of respondent)
            j is a product configuration (1 to 18)

You don't need this equation to do the analysis—all you need to do to execute this regression in Excel is choose:

Exhibit 4-10. Epigraphs Conjoint Data Base

ID#	Dem	Sup	Web	Chai	35	60	100	Cold	Ther	Fem	100s	100-	500-	1000	2500	>500	mari	kids	25-5	50-7	75-1	100-	>150
1	0	0	0	1	0	1	0	0	0	1	0	0	0	1	0	0	0	0	0	0	0	0	0
1	0	0	1	0	0	0	1	0	0	1	0	0	0	1	0	0	0	0	0	0	0	0	0
1	0	0	1	0	1	0	0	1	0	1	0	0	0	1	0	0	0	0	0	0	0	0	0
1	0	0	1	0	0	1	0	0	0	1	0	0	0	1	0	0	0	0	0	0	0	0	0
1	0	1	0	0	0	1	0	1	1	1	0	0	0	1	0	0	0	0	0	0	0	0	0
1	0	0	0	1	1	0	0	0	0	1	0	0	0	1	0	0	0	0	0	0	0	0	0
1	0	0	1	0	1	0	0	1	1	1	0	0	0	1	0	0	0	0	0	0	0	0	0
1	0	1	0	0	1	0	0	0	0	1	0	0	0	1	0	0	0	0	0	0	0	0	0
1	0	0	0	1	0	0	1	1	0	1	0	0	0	1	0	0	0	0	0	0	0	0	0
1	0	0	0	1	1	0	0	1	0	1	0	0	0	1	0	0	0	0	0	0	0	0	0
1	0	1	0	0	0	0	1	0	0	1	0	0	0	1	0	0	0	0	0	0	0	0	0
1	0	0	0	1	0	1	0	0	1	1	0	0	0	1	0	0	0	0	0	0	0	0	0
1	0	0	1	0	0	1	0	0	0	1	0	0	0	1	0	0	0	0	0	0	0	0	0
1	0	1	0	0	1	0	0	0	0	1	0	0	0	1	0	0	0	0	0	0	0	0	0
1	0	0	0	1	0	0	1	1	0	1	0	0	0	1	0	0	0	0	0	0	0	0	0
1	0	1	0	0	0	1	0	1	0	1	0	0	0	1	0	0	0	0	0	0	0	0	0
1	0	1	0	0	0	0	1	0	1	1	0	0	0	1	0	0	0	0	0	0	0	0	0
1	0	0	1	0	0	1	0	1	1	1	0	0	0	1	0	0	0	0	0	0	0	0	0
2	0	0	0	1	0	1	0	0	0	1	0	0	0	0	0	1	1	0	0	0	1	0	0
2	0	0	1	0	0	0	1	0	0	1	0	0	0	0	0	1	1	0	0	0	1	0	0
2	0	0	1	0	1	0	0	1	0	1	0	0	0	0	0	1	1	0	0	0	1	0	0
2	0	0	1	0	0	1	0	0	0	1	0	0	0	0	0	1	1	0	0	0	1	0	0
2	2	1	0	0	0	1	0	1	1	1	0	0	0	0	0	1	1	0	0	0	1	0	0
2	4	0	0	1	1	0	0	0	0	1	0	0	0	0	0	1	1	0	0	0	1	0	0
2	0	0	1	0	1	0	0	1	1	1	0	0	0	0	0	1	1	0	0	0	1	0	0
2	4	1	0	0	0	0	0	0	0	1	0	0	0	0	0	1	1	0	0	0	1	0	0
2	0	0	0	1	0	0	1	1	0	1	0	0	0	0	0	1	1	0	0	0	1	0	0
2	0	0	0	1	1	0	0	0	1	1	0	0	0	0	0	1	1	0	0	0	1	0	0
2	2	1	0	0	0	1	0	0	1	1	0	0	0	0	0	1	1	0	0	0	1	0	0
2	0	0	0	1	0	1	0	0	1	1	0	0	0	0	0	1	1	0	0	0	1	0	0
2	0	0	1	0	0	1	0	0	0	1	0	0	0	0	0	1	1	0	0	0	1	0	0
2	4	1	0	0	1	0	0	0	0	1	0	0	0	0	0	1	1	0	0	0	1	0	0
2	4	0	0	1	0	0	1	1	0	1	0	0	0	0	0	1	1	0	0	0	1	0	0
2	4	1	0	0	0	1	0	1	0	1	0	0	0	0	0	1	1	0	0	0	1	0	0
2	0	1	0	0	0	0	1	0	1	1	0	0	0	0	0	1	1	0	0	0	1	0	0
2	0	0	1	0	0	1	0	1	1	1	0	0	0	0	0	1	1	0	0	0	1	0	0
3	2	0	0	1	0	1	0	0	0	0	0	0	0	0	0	1	0	1	1	0	0	1	0

Tools $\rightarrow$ Data Analysis[9] $\rightarrow$ Regression

Then select the entire "demand" column for the *dependent variable,* and select all the product attribute levels as the *independent variables*[x].

Segment Analysis

It is likely that the target market is not homogeneous—that different segments of the market favor different product configurations. Large standard errors in the primary regression are a good indication that the market is segmented. To confirm this is the case, and to characterize those segments, add demographic variables to the demand regression:

$$\text{Demand}_{ij} = \beta_0 + \Sigma \, \beta_k \, (\text{product attribute})_k + \Sigma \, \beta_l \, (\text{demographic variables})_l + e_{ij}$$

Again, you don't need this equation to execute this regression in Excel. Just select the entire "demand" column for the *dependent variable,* and select all the product attribute levels and all the demographic variables as the *independent variables*.

EPIGRAPHS ANALYSIS

For Epigraphs, we chose \$35.00 as the default price, "independent retailers" as the default distribution channel, and "standard" as the default level in the two binary variables, themes and colors. When we say we chose attribute levels as the defaults, it means we omitted those columns in the product configuration matrix when we were correcting for linear dependence (going from Table 4-3c to 4-3d). The resulting regression equation is:

$$\text{Rolls purchased}_{ij} = \beta_0 + \beta_1 \, (\$60 \text{ price}) + \beta_2 \, (\$100 \text{ price}) + \beta_3 \, (\text{superstore}) + \beta_4 \, (\text{Internet}) + \beta_6 \, (\text{custom colors}) + \beta_7 \, (\text{custom themes}) + e_{ij}$$

Exhibit 4-11 presents the regression results from the Epigraphs demand equation. The intercept of 4.03 is interpreted as follows: If a product with standard themes and colors is sold through paint/wallpaper chains at a price of \$35.00 (the default product configuration), then on average, each person in the target market will purchase 4.03 rolls. This assumes that the sample is representative of the target market and that respondents have responded truthfully (subject to optimism bias). If the estimate is correct, total demand for the product is 4.03 rolls times the target market (15,000,000 households that purchase household textiles each year), or 60 million rolls.

This estimate is an average over those who like the product and would need 8 or more rolls, and those who dislike the product and would not purchase any rolls. It is likely that this estimate overstates true demand, thus we will want to do some rescaling. We will defer that rescaling to Chapter 8, Demand Forecasting. We focus here on sensitivity of demand to changes in the product configuration.

Price. If we increase price to \$60, demand drops roughly in half to 2.07 rolls. We obtain this result by adding the coefficient on \$60 price (-1.96) to the intercept of 4.03. If we further increase the price to \$100, demand drops by 2.82 to 1.21 rolls. This is illustrated in the raw demand curve in Exhibit 4-12. Each of the price coefficients are highly significant, suggesting we can have some confi-

Exhibit 4-11. Regression results

PRODUCT CONFIGURATION WITHOUT DEMOGRAPHICS ($35 & CHAINS)

Response: Demand
Summary of Fit

RSquare	0.168419
RSquare Adj	0.160158
Root Mean Square Error	2.937564
Mean of Response	2.09329
Observations (or Sum Wgts)	611

Lack of Fit

Source	DF	Sum of Squares	Mean Square	F Ratio
Lack of Fit	8	82.9330	10.3666	1.2046
Pure Error	596	5129.1541	8.6060	Prob>F
Total Error	604	5212.0870		0.2937
Max RSq				
0.1817				

Parameter Estimates

Term	Estimate	Std Error	t Ratio	Prob>|t|
Intercept	4.0343137	0.290862	13.87	<.0001
Super	0.1617647	0.290862	0.56	0.5783
Web	-1.108013	0.291222	-3.80	0.0002
60	-1.960954	0.291222	-6.73	<.0001
100	-2.823529	0.290862	-9.71	<.0001
colors	-0.210699	0.251998	-0.84	0.4034
themes	0.11283	0.251998	0.45	0.6545

Effect Test

Source	Nparm	DF	Sum of Squares	F Ratio	Prob>F
Super	1	1	2.66912	0.3093	0.5783
Web	1	1	124.91547	14.4758	0.0002
60	1	1	391.25636	45.3405	<.0001
100	1	1	813.17647	94.2345	<.0001
colors	1	1	6.03264	0.6991	0.4034
themes	1	1	1.72994	0.2005	0.6545

Whole-Model Test

dence in the resultant demand curve. Note that this curve assumes the default values for all other elements of the product configuration: distribution through chain retailers, and standard themes and colors.

Distribution Channel. We offered three distribution channels: paint/wallpaper chains (the default), home superstores, and the Internet. The price curve we just developed is for chains, because that is the default channel. The coefficient

Exhibit 4-12. Demand curve

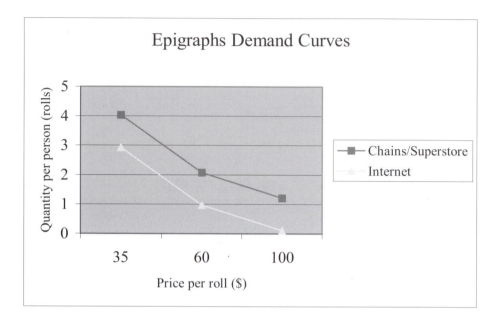

on superstores is small (0.16) and not significant (t-ratio=0.56). Thus it appears that chains and superstores are interchangeable. The Internet however, has a significant negative impact on demand. At each price, demand on the Internet is 1.11 fewer rolls than it would be in chains. We add the demand curve for the Internet channel to Exhibit 4-12.

Product configuration. Neither "colors" nor "themes" is significant. This indicates that there is little demand for customization, and accordingly there is no price premium for customization. This is consistent with comments in the focus group, that the product offered to customers needs to be simple—already, customers have an implicit choice among 35 configurations (7 colors x 5 themes). Choice from among infinite alternatives requires considerable work on their part.

Segment Analysis

The small standard errors (t-ratios) in the prior regression suggest that the market is fairly homogeneous, and therefore free of natural segments. We examine that more thoroughly by including demographic data in the regression. The results in Exhibit 4-13 preserve those in the preceding regression. While the intercept is lower (1.41 versus 4.03), if we restrict attention to married couples

Exhibit 4-13. Regression with demographic data

PRODUCT CONFIGURATION WITH DEMOGRAPHICS ($35 & CHAINS & <$25k income)
Key: sex=female; marital status=married; kids=has kids

Response: Demand
Summary of Fit

RSquare	0.251948
RSquare Adj	0.230487
Root Mean Square Error	2.835218
Mean of Response	2.077535
Observations (or Sum Wgts)	503

Lack of Fit

Source	DF	Sum of Squares	Mean Square	F Ratio
Lack of Fit	255	1971.2354	7.73033	0.9230
Pure Error	233	1951.5333	8.37568	Prob>F
Total Error	488	3922.7687		0.7347
Max RSq				
0.6279				

Parameter Estimates

Term	Estimate	Std Error	t Ratio	Prob>|t|
Intercept	1.4062687	0.698182	2.01	0.0445
Super	0.1964286	0.309348	0.63	0.5257
Web	-0.862442	0.309817	-2.78	0.0056
60	-2.041013	0.309817	-6.59	<.0001
100	-2.767857	0.309348	-8.95	<.0001
colors	-0.113422	0.268039	-0.42	0.6724
themes	0.0026496	0.268039	0.01	0.9921
sex	1.4341819	0.3643	3.94	<.0001
marital s?	2.1751794	0.394055	5.52	<.0001
kids	0.9317585	0.29652	3.14	0.0018
25-50k	-0.727283	0.648036	-1.12	0.2623
50-75k	-0.861834	0.603335	-1.43	0.1538
75-100k	-1.002432	0.657434	-1.52	0.1280
100-150k	0.3398396	0.676197	0.50	0.6155
>150k	-3.042633	0.920457	-3.31	0.0010

Effect Test

Source	Nparm	DF	Sum of Squares	F Ratio	Prob>F
Super	1	1	3.24107	0.4032	0.5257
Web	1	1	62.29038	7.7490	0.0056
60	1	1	348.86138	43.3990	<.0001
100	1	1	643.52679	80.0560	<.0001
colors	1	1	1.43937	0.1791	0.6724
themes	1	1	0.00079	0.0001	0.9921
sex	1	1	124.58438	15.4985	<.0001
marital s?	1	1	244.93451	30.4703	<.0001
kids	1	1	79.37268	9.8741	0.0018
25-50k	1	1	10.12467	1.2595	0.2623
50-75k	1	1	16.40226	2.0405	0.1538
75-100k	1	1	18.68866	2.3249	0.1280
100-150k	1	1	2.03036	0.2526	0.6155
>150k	1	1	87.83458	10.9268	0.0010

(the majority of owner-occupied households), then we add the 2.17 coefficient for "married", and demand becomes 1.41 + 2.17 =3.58.

Children. Demand increases in households with children by 0.9 rolls. This is an interesting result, since it runs counter to the trends in American Marketplace (Exhibit 2-5). Associating this quantitative result with comments from the focus group provides some insight. Children pose problems for many wallcoverings—fingerprints, tearing, etc. The Epigraphs product is less susceptible to these problems and thus may be tapping latent demand for wallcovering. That demand may be suppressed by the characteristic fragility of existing wallcovering. An alternative explanation is that this product is somehow matched to children (suitable for children's rooms). We can test these two hypotheses by reviewing the summary of open-ended responses in Exhibit 4-14. These data indicate that a child's room is in fact the third most popular room for the product—suggesting support for the latter explanation.

Gender. Demand is significantly higher for females. The coefficient on females is 1.43. This is consistent with conventional wisdom suggesting that women do most of the home design (they comprise 85% of subscribers to "shelter" magazines).

Income. The final result pertains to income. Here we see that demand peaks at incomes of $100,000 to $150,000. This too is consistent with the focus group results. The designers in the focus group tended to respond negatively to use of the product for their clients, but said they could envision its attraction to the mass market. Negative coefficients below incomes of $100,000 are consistent with patterns of aggregate home textile expenditure (Exhibit 2-5). This likely reflects a budget constraint—as income decreases, households are more likely to choose paint over wallpaper.

Thus, the target market for Epigraphs does not appear to be segmented. Rather it appears to match the general distribution of home decorating that we found from industry analysis. Accordingly, we can take advantage of cumulative industry wisdom regarding access to the wallcovering target market—both distribution channels and media vehicles.

Having generated the demand curves from primary data, we now combine the demand curves with cost data to analyze optimal price and product configuration. Note that there is a good deal of data from the survey that we have not discussed as part of the regression analysis. These data are captured in charts of summary statistics (Exhibit 4-9), and summary of open-ended responses (Exhibit 4-14). While not germane here, these data become important in subsequent analyses.

Exhibit 4-14. Open-ended responses

#	Additional colors	Additional themes	Den/Family	Rec	Study	Baby	Child's	Card	Bedroom	Bath	Library	Kitchen	Guest Bath	Guest Room	Living Room	Dining Room	Basement	Laundry	Waiting	Classroom	Office	Positive aspects	Negative aspects	Last Project	Problems with installation
1	NA	NA	1	1																		Not much	Cost is high	6	Pasting and soaking
2	NA	Nursery rhymes	1			1		1														Novelty	NA	12	Time consuming; messy; wrinkles; hard to work
3	NA	Cartoons			1											1					1	Unique; constant inspiration; conversation piece	Too busy for the whole wall. Would use as a border or on a small area of a room.	30	Getting glue on paper when installing a border.
4	NA	NA	1																			Originality and creative possibilities	Would like to customize.	12	Having to buy a double roll and only needing a small piece.
5	NA	NA								1												Whimsical	Too much would be overpowering	NA	NA
6	NA	NA	1	1						1												A new idea in decorating	Only 7 standard colors	48	Stripping walls and preparation
7	NA	NA										1	1									It's a do it yourself project	Nothing	6	Water mess
8	NA	NA				1											1					Different idea; good for rooms with special themes	Would not want entire wall covered but might be good as border or single quote	NA	NA
9	NA	Nursery rhymes	1			1																Unique	NA	24	NA
10	NA	Custom						1														Unique idea	I need to see it	12	Surface conditions
11	NA	NA													1	1					1	Ease of installation; choices	Product sounds great	12	Matching seams

#	Color	Type	Marks	Like	Concern	No.	Dislike
12	NA	NA	1 ... 1	No mess; easily installed	Should have 25 and 100 ft. rolls	12	Mess, prep of the walls
13	NA	NA		It is not my taste		6	Edges rolling
14	NA	NA	1	Innovative	Graffiti related	12	Corners
15	NA	NA	1 1 1 1	Adds personal touch, unique, subtle yet noticeable	May be complicated to install. 2 person job.	6	Tedious. Would like to be able to buy a video with instructions
16	NA	Custom	1 ... 1 1	Can express yourself	Price	12	NA
17	NA	NA	1 ... 1	Interesting, easy to install	Would like choice of 5 quotes per theme	10	Difficult to match patterns and cut lines. Quality seems to be getting cheaper.
18	NA	Custom	1 ... 1	Could replace border	Don't think I would like a full room of it	6	Wall paper is too thin and tears
19	NA	NA	1 ... 1	New idea	NA	24	Matching seams
20	NA	Music	1 ... 1 1 1	No messy cleanup	NA	NA	NA
21	Tan, beige, oyster white, yellow	NA	1	NA	Matching?	36	Matching, waste, paste, clean up
22	NA	NA	1 ... 1	Don't like it		12	Cutting and measuring
23	Plum	NA	1 ... 1 ... 1	Tool is packaged with product; directions included		10	Lining up paper
24	NA	NA	1 ... 1	Different; can express yourself	Would like product to include designs	12	
25	Pas-tels	NA	1 ... 1	Original idea	Perhaps a bit too quirky	NA	NA
26	NA	NA	1	Uniqueness	Limited rooms to decorate	6	Cutting wallpaper around doors, windows
27	NA	NA		Easy installation	Don't like it	2	Matching

28	NA	NA	1							1										1	Easy to install	Not crazy about words on wall	36	Pasting
29	NA	NA				1														1	Self application	Price	NA	NA
30	NA	NA	1																		Not appealing		NA	NA
31	NA	NA						1													Easy to install	Words on wall	10	messy
32	NA	NA			1				1				1	1							Unique idea	NA	12	Difficult to align patterns
33	NA	NA		1		1															Originality	Not functional	12	Mess, matching, alignment, plumb line
34	NA	NA	1			1														1	Easy to install; not expensive; different	May get tired looking at the same quote	NA	NA
35	NA	NA	1																		Quality and price	Installation cost	NA	NA
To-tals			19	4	2	3	5	1	4	4	4	3	1	2	2	2	4	1	1	1	8				

CONCLUSION

This chapter gathers primary survey data, and applies conjoint analysis to characterize demand for the new venture. Conjoint analysis allows consumers to compare products comprising different combinations of attributes. Keys to this process include defining attributes, determining the attributes' levels, limiting the set of possible product configurations so as to not overwhelm the consumer with choices, and deriving a demand curve for the product configurations and the individual attributes. This requires significant effort. Yet, this market research can save entrepreneurs significant amounts of time and money by carefully developing a product that consumers will want and be happy to pay for. The next chapter continues by analyzing this chapter's demand data to develop the venture's competitive strategy.

Appendix 4-1
Conjoint Analysis Worksheet

1. Matching dimensions to attributes:
   What physical attributes of the product can you create to capture the perceptual dimensions elicited from the focus group/interviews:

Perceptual dimension	Physical attribute

2. a) Some of the attributes above may be "table stakes"—meaning you would offer these attributes no matter what. Some of these attributes don't require demand data for decision making (see discussion page 4-4.). In the table above, designate whether attributes are "table stakes" or "demand independent".
   b) Develop the attribute matrix using the remaining attributes. For each important physical attribute, identify "levels" at which the attribute could be offered. For continuous scale attributes (e.g., price) choose 3 levels that bound the likely optimum.

Levels	Attribute 1	Attribute 2	Attribute 3	Attribute 4	Price
1					
2					
3					

3. All combinations of all levels of each attribute with all levels of every other attribute (full factorial design) will likely produce excess product configurations. Reduce the full design to a set of 18 "products" using the instructions in Exhibit 4-2. (You can refer to the Epigraphs example (Table 4-3a)

Product	Level of Attribute 1	Level of Attribute 2	Level of Attribute 3	Level of Attribute 4	Price
1					
2					
3					
4					
5					
6					
7					
8					

9				
10				
11				
12				
13				
14				
15				
16				
17				
18				

4. Create the template question. See page 4-9 for issues to consider. You can refer to the example question in Exhibit 4-5 (page 4-22).

5. Create ancillary questions:

    a) For those attributes that were demand independent in Question 2

    b) For demographic information to help identify market segments

    c) For media habits, to help identify advertising channels

    d) Anything else that is important to understanding the customer

5. How are you going to administer the survey, and why? (see pg 4-7 for thoughts)

6. What mailing lists (or other sources) can you use to locate people/firms in your industry?

Source	Segment(s) covered	Extent of coverage (% of people in segment)	Cost per person

6. Which of the above sources will you use, and why? (see pg 4-7 for thoughts)

Attach copy of cover letter, survey, and any product literature sheet

notes

1. Green, Paul and Vithala R. Rao, 1971. "Conjoint Measurement for Quantifying Judgmental Data," Journal of Marketing Research, 8, pp. 355-363.

2. Shepherd, Dean A. and Andrew Zacharakis, 1997. "Conjoint Analysis: A Window of Opportunity for Entrepreneurship Research," in Katz, Jerome A. (Ed) "Advances in Entrepreneurship, Firm Emergence, and Growth," London: JAI Press.

3. Values obtained from www.fueleconomy.gov.

4. Addleman, "Orthogonal Main-Effect Plans for A Symmetrical Factorial Experiments, "Technometrics 4, (February 1962) pp. 21-46.

5. See for example, formsite.com.

6. Burnett, Leo (annual), "Worldwide Advertising and Media Factbook," Chicago: Triumph Books Adweek. (Semi-annual), "Marketer's guide to media". New York, NY : Adweek, Inc., Simmons Market Research Bureau (annual). "Simmons Study of Media and Markets", Tampa, FL: Simmons Market Research Bureau; Audit Bureau of Circulations, "News Bulletin," Schaumburg, Ill. : The Audit Bureau of Circulations

7. Don't merely copy this letter and change the names as several students did. The contest—coming up with a quote—was specifically linked to the product in the Epigraphs. It makes less sense for other products. Have fun with the letter and the incentive/contests—if you have fun, you will likely create something that interests the readers and makes them more likely to respond.

8. Note that the expanded analysis includes additional columns for demographic data.

9. If you have not used Excel for data analysis before, you may have to add the Data Analysis Tool Pak. This is done using the drop-down menu from Tools → Add Ins → Analysis Tool Pak

10. Note that if you have not omitted a default level for each attribute in the product matrix, eg., if you omitted the step demonstrated in Table 4-3d, then you will not be able to run your regression since the data matrix will not be positive definite. You can still fix the problem at this stage by following the instructions in the Exhibit.

133

designing the venture

competitive strategy

INTRODUCTION AND GOALS

This is the first chapter where we make strategic decisions regarding the venture design. Up until now we have been characterizing the industry, the competitive space, and the customers to determine if there is a viable venture. Here forward we assume the venture is viable, and will focus on how to optimize it. The price and product configuration decisions (competitive strategy) are the first step in that process.

The goal of this chapter is to utilize the demand curves derived from conjoint analysis to develop a competitive strategy. What we mean by competitive strategy is the choice of price and product configuration that maximizes venture profits. We examine the price and configuration choices jointly over a range of industry conditions. We then determine which choices will best shape the industry conditions as well as position the venture optimally within those conditions. The basic assumption underlying the analysis, is that as a new venture, you will have some market power, and that you can take advantage of that power to maximize current profits, or to limit entry, and thereby maximize lifetime profits.

Very few firms actually do conjoint analysis, and therefore lack the information to optimize the product configuration and price. Thus it is clearly possible to begin a venture without doing so. This is a mistake. Sales may fail to materialize because of a mismatch between the bundle of attributes you offer and the bundle of attributes that the customers prefer. Accordingly, you may attract entry by a competitor who learns from your mistakes to offer a product better matched to customer preferences. This is the classic phenomenon of first movers as market losers.[1] A strong entry with the "optimal product" not only generates short-term profits (to fuel growth), but also constrains the opportunity for later entrants, thereby maximizing lifetime profits.

We begin the chapter by reviewing the principles of pricing and product differentiation under a wide range of industry conditions. We examine why the competitive structures we discussed in Chapter 2 emerge and behave the way they do. The reason we do this is that entrepreneurs creating new industries have some power to shape the industry structure.

After reviewing the principles, we derive the demand curves for each of the Epigraphs attributes, and then use those demand curves to define the optimal price and product configuration under various industry conditions. We conclude by comparing the profits under each industry condition, to make a decision about whether to use market power to extract current profits, or to shape future industry conditions.

PRINCIPLES

We treat economic pricing principles in order of increasing market complexity. The simplest conditions also provide the pricing extremes: perfect competition (no market power) and monopoly (complete market power). While these are the extremes, they are relatively rare. Most industries are oligopolies falling somewhere between the extremes.

For purposes of comparing prices and profits across the market structures, let's assume a specific aggregate demand curve (and also assume marginal cost, c, is $0):

$$p = \$120 - q \tag{1}$$

and the standard firm profit equation:

$$\Pi_i = q_i * (p_i - c_i) = q_i * p_i \tag{2}$$

where:

Π_i is profits for firm i

q_i is output for firm i

p_i is price

Perfect Competition

A perfectly competitive, or competitive, industry is one exhibiting the following characteristics:

- A large number of firms, each producing the same homogenous product.
- Each firm attempts to maximize profits.
- Each firm is a price taker: its actions have no effect on market price
- A large number of consumers—each attempting to utility maximize
- Each consumer is also a price taker: its actions have no effect on market price
- Prices are assumed to be known to all market participants—information is perfect
- Transactions are costless: buyers and sellers incur no costs in making exchanges

This, then, is a condition where firms have no market power, and thus the pricing decision is superfluous. The profit maximization assumption requires that firms set marginal revenue equal to marginal cost. Since marginal revenue equals price (in a price taking setting), price equals marginal cost (p=c=0). Thus by substituting price and cost in equation 2, we obtain zero profits [q*(p-c) = q(0) = 0].

Because firms have no discretion in setting price or product configuration (due to the homogenous product assumption), we are interested in perfect competition only insofar as it establishes the pricing floor. We turn next to the opposite extreme—monopoly.

Monopoly

A monopoly market is one in which a single producer faces the entire demand curve. The monopolist may choose to produce at any quantity along the market demand curve, and that output decision will determine the good's price. We assume the law of one price, i.e., we ignore opportunities for price discrimination—charging different prices to different buyers in separated markets.

Firms in monopoly markets set price in the same manner as those in competitive industries—they profit maximize by setting marginal revenue equal to marginal cost. The distinction between the two outcomes is that for competitive firms, marginal revenue equals price, whereas for monopolists, marginal revenue is less than price (since to sell an additional unit, the firm must lower its price).

Profits are still defined by q*(p-c), and c is still $0, thus profits in this case are:

$$\Pi_t = q_t*(\$120 - q) \tag{3}$$

Profit maximization for the monopolist occurs at:

$$d\Pi/dq[q*(\$120-q)] = 0 \tag{4}$$
$$d\Pi/dq[(\$120q-q^2)] = 0$$
$$120-2q=0$$

Thus the monopolist sets output at 60 units. By equation 1, monopoly price =120-q, and monopoly profits are (60 units * $60) = $3600

Oligopoly

In both perfect competition and monopoly, pricing and output are perfectly circumscribed by the demand curve and the marginal cost curve. Profit maximization in both conditions is trivial. However, perfect competition and monopoly are the exception rather than the rule. Most industries are characterized as oligopolies, falling between the two extremes of perfect competition and monopoly. Here optimal pricing and product configuration decisions depend not only on the demand curve and production function, but on assumptions regarding the behavior of other firms. We treat these in order of increasing complexity. In the first condition, we assume non-strategic interaction. In the latter conditions, we introduce competitive interaction, and address it via game theory.

Game theory is a tool to examine the decisions of firms in interactive games where outcomes depend not only on your decision but also on the decisions of other firms. What differs among the various games we examine are the rules of behavior. The outcomes of these games are dictated by their Nash equilibria. A Nash equilibrium is a pair of strategies (a*, b*) such that each firm's strategy is the optimal response taking the other firm's strategy as given.[2] For simplicity we treat competition between two firms (duopoly) rather than n firms as we examine the various interpretations of oligopoly. The intuition from the duopoly holds as the number of firms increases.

Cartel. A cartel is collusion among a group of producers to maximize industry profits, by restricting output. The producers sell at monopoly price ($60) and split monopoly outputs and profits. If there are n firms who share equally, the output of each firm is $q_t = 60/n$, and the profits of each firm are $\Pi_i = \$3600/n$. Thus if there are two firms, price = $60, $q_i = 30$ units, and $\Pi_i = \$1800$. The problem with cartels in the United States is that they violate antitrust legislation. Even in instances where cartels are lawful, they are generally unstable, since each firm has an incentive to reduce price to capture the entire market.

Betrand Duopoly.[3] In Bertrand competition firms produce identical products and can't commit in advance to a level of output. Under these circumstances, the sales distribution of the product is determined exclusively by its price. If one firm has a lower price than the other firm, then it captures the entire market. If both firms price identically, then the market is split evenly. This type of game is characteristic of industries in which each firm has made substantial investments in capacity, and has relatively low marginal cost, e.g., airlines serving identical markets with comparable schedules.

In a Bertrand game, the Nash equilibrium has both firms price at marginal cost: $p_a = p_b = c$ and split the market. To demonstrate that this is the equilibrium, consider a situation in which *firm a* has price of $40, while *firm b* has a price of $41. All customers prefer to buy from *firm a*, thus a has profits of pq = p(120-p) = $3200, while *firm b* has 0 profits. Thus b has an incentive to drop price to $39 leaving it with profits of $3159, and a with 0 profits. This continues until neither firm has any incentive to lower price further: at $p = c = 0$. Thus a Bertrand game results in perfect competition, even if there are only two competitors.

Cournot Duopoly.[4] A Cournot game is one in which firms can commit in advance to an output level. This is the case, for example, if firms build manufacturing plants with fixed capacity (and it is costly to have excess capacity). The structure of the game assumes firms move simultaneously to choose output (set capacity), and the sum of their output choices determines market price. Each firm recognizes that its profits depend not only upon its choice of output, but also on that of the competitor. Thus it takes into account conjectures about rival output in determining its own output. In particular, the profit function confronting *firm a* is:

$$\Pi a = qa(120 - (qa + qb)) = 120qa - qa2 - qaqb \qquad (5)$$

This payoff function implies a derivative "reaction function", which is a's best strategy against b, for each output choice of *firm b*, q_b. This reaction function is defined by:

$$d\Pi/dqa \ [120qa - qa2 - qaqb] = 0 \qquad (6)$$
$$120 - 2qa - qb = 0$$
$$qa = (120 - qb)/2$$

We assume that firms a and b are identical. Thus they have the same payoff function and symmetric reaction functions. Accordingly, $q_b = (120 - q_a)/2$.

The Nash equilibrium is the pair of strategies at which each firm is responding optimally taking the other firm's strategy as given. This occurs where the two reaction functions intersect. Thus we solve the two reaction functions simultaneously:

$$qa = qb$$
$$qa = (120 - qa)/2$$

Thus each firm chooses output, q = 40. This results in market price of $40, and profits for each firm of $1600. These profits are lower than monopoly profits of $3600 and profits for the two-firm cartel of $1800.

Stackelberg Duopoly.[5] In the Cournot game we assumed that both firms move simultaneously in choosing industry output. This leads to parity in the solution strategies. In the Stackelberg game, one firm moves first in choosing quantity, and the other firm responds. To aid intuition in distinguishing between the two games, a Cournot game might be one in which two firms are racing to introduce identical products to market. In contrast, a Stackelberg game is one where a leader introduces a product, another follower firm then recognizes the value of the corresponding market, and enters with an identical product. The Stackelberg game allows us to examine the potential for first mover advantage.

Firm a enters first and anticipates that *firm b* will follow. Furthermore, *firm a* assumes that *firm b* will choose the optimal strategy defined by the Cournot reaction function above. Here the reaction function is indeed a *reaction* function, since *firm b* moves second and thus *reacts* to *firm a*'s strategy. In the Cournot game, the reaction functions served more as *anticipation* functions. In the Stackelberg game, *firm a* incorporates *firm b*'s reaction function into its anticipation function to find the optimal first mover strategy:

d Π/dq_a $[120q_a - q_a{}^2 - q_a((120 - q_a)/2)] = 0$. Thus $q_a = 60$. *Firm b's* best response to *firm a's* output choice is thus: $q_b = (120-60)/2 = 30$. The market price is: $120 - (60+30) = \$30$.

A few things are interesting here. The first observation is the tremendous advantage to moving first—*firm a* captures twice the output of *firm b*, and thus enjoys twice the profits. The second, and possibly more interesting, observation is that Stackelberg output is the same as monopoly output. *Firm a's* optimal strategy under a monopoly is identical to its optimal preemptive strategy limiting the market of later entrants. Under this particular set of rules, there is no penalty for behaving like a monopolist. The only thing changing for *firm a* post-entry is that profits drop from \$60 under monopoly to \$30 under Stackelberg duopoly.

Bertrand Differentiation. In all the games so far, the product is assumed to be homogeneous and customers' tastes are also assumed to be homogeneous. Here we introduce non-homogeneous (differentiated) products, but keep the assumption of homogeneous customers. The simplest way to examine the impact of product differentiation is to modify the Bertrand game of price competition.

One way to model differentiation is through an assumption of customer loyalty. Think of two products that are essentially undifferentiated. Customers randomly choose which of the two products to try first, but once they have tried a product, they slightly prefer the known product to the unknown product. (People tend to behave this way toward their utility suppliers, since they don't want to risk having their service interrupted.) To capture customer loyalty, we modify the demand function, so that customers trade-off the price of the preferred product to that of the alternative product, i.e., there is cross-price elasticity. Because we have customer loyalty, the coefficients on the prices differ:

$$q_a = \$120 - 2p_a + p_b$$
$$q_b = \$120 - 2p_b + p_a$$

We find each firm's reaction function as we did for the Cournot game, except that here we are using pricing strategy rather than output strategy, so we maximize each firm's profit function with respect to price:

$$d\Pi_a/dp_a \, [p_a \, (120 - 2p_a + p_b)] = 0 = 120 - 4p_a + p_b$$
$$d\Pi_b/dp_b \, [p_b \, (120 - 2p_b + p_a)] = 0 = 120 - 4p_b + p_a$$

The Nash equilibrium is the pair of strategies at which each firm is responding optimally taking the other firm's strategy as given. This occurs where the two reaction functions intersect. Thus we solve the two reaction functions simultaneously:

$$120 - 4p_a + p_b = 120 - 4p_b + p_a$$
$$p_a = p_a = \$40$$

Thus each firm chooses price, p = \$40. This results in output for each firm of 80 units, and profits for each firm of \$3200—far better than the \$0 profits of Bertrand competition without differentiation.

Summary. We could continue to gradually expand the complexity of these games. The next most logical step would be to introduce heterogeneous customers through a model of spatial competition.[6] However, most of the insights we wish to draw are already evident. The main conclusion we draw from consideration of pricing and product configuration under various industry structures, are that in most markets, output, price and, product configuration decisions are interdependent. Moreover, the equilibrium values for firm output, market price, and firm profits vary substantially as assumptions about the rules of competition change. These differences are summarized in Exhibit 5-1.

The main insights are:

1) Industries with undifferentiated products, where capacity can be expanded quickly and inexpensively, are likely to produce price competition and zero profits.
2) Having capacity constraints actually supports higher prices.
3) Product differentiation evades price competition.
4) Moving first in settings with either capacity constraints or product differentiation can produce permanent advantage.
5) In some cases the monopoly choices or price, configuration and output are also the best pre-emptive choices. In those cases there is no cost to behaving "strategically."

Exhibit 5-1. Equilibrium Outcomes in Industries with
Homogeneous Goods

Demand: $q = 120 - p$
$c = 0$

	Driving Function	Firm a			Firm b		
		p_A	q_A	Π_A	p_B	q_B	Π_B
Monopoly	$\Pi_A = 120q - q^2$	60	60	3600	--	--	--
Perfect Competition	$p = c$	0	60	0	0	60	0
Cartel	$\Pi_A = (120q - q^2)/n$	60	30	1800	60	30	1800
Cournot Competition	$\Pi_A = 120q_a - qa^2 - q_a q_b$	40	40	1600	40	40	1600
Bertrand Competition	$q_a = 120$ if $p_a < p_b$, else 0	0	60	0	0	60	0
Stackelberg Competition	$\Pi_A = 120q_a - qa^2 - q_a((120-q_a)/2)$	30	60	1800	30	30	900

These games are quite stylized, and provide us with general insights. However, we now apply the game theoretic tools to real demand curves in real settings to develop competitive strategies for new ventures. Because the process is fairly complex, we use the Epigraphs example throughout the analytical process section, rather than discussing the process in one section and then applying it to Epigraphs in the following section.

ANALYTICAL PROCESS

Ideally, you will be able to maintain a monopoly for your new product. In all likelihood however, if your market appears lucrative, you will attract entry. While you will form your real response strategy, if and when an entrant has executed its entry strategy, the goal at this stage is to determine whether anything you do can do now will affect the likelihood of another firm entering the market, and the strategy that firm will employ if it does enter. In other words, is there a strategy you could employ now, other than monopoly price and product configuration that might increase lifetime profitability? Often it is the case that the monopoly strategy is also the best preemptive strategy.

Determining Monopoly Price and Product Configuration

The demand curve. The first step in the analysis of price and product configuration under any of the industry structures is to transform the three price points from conjoint analysis into a differentiable function—a curve. In Exhibit 4-12, Epigraphs demand was characterized as a piece-wise linear function (two-line segments). It is more likely that demand is actually characterized by a single, higher-order function. You can find the best fitting function through regression analysis of the three data points. Typically, the best fit for demand data is either a 2nd order polynomial (quadratic): $q=ap^2 + bp +c$, or a power curve: $q=cp^b$.[7] To assess best fit, check the R-squared for both regressions. In all cases, be wary of values outside the range of the data. For Epigraphs, the best fit through the demand data for chains was a polynomial:

$$q_{chains}=0.000875p^2 - 0.1616p + 8.612 \tag{1}$$

To obtain demand for internet sales we merely added the internet coefficient (-1.1) to the intercept (8.612).

$$q_{internet}=0.000875p^2 - 0.1616p + 7.512 \tag{2}$$

These functions are shown in Exhibit 5-2.

We now have demand functions that we can combine with cost data to assess optimal price and product configuration.

Cost function. While we will discuss cost in greater detail in Chapters 9 through 11, we need a preliminary estimate of unit cost. The preliminary esti-

Exhibit 5-2. Exhibit 5-2 Epigraphs Demand Curve

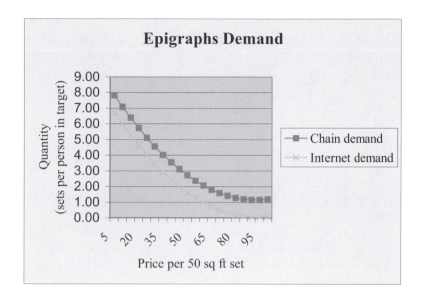

Epigraphs Demand

mate assumes that we produce the product in-house using Gerber equipment and materials. This configuration yields a unit cost per roll of $10.73 (materials and labor). Because there is a glut of used Gerber equipment, we can obtain all necessary equipment for approximately $10,000.   Since this amount can be expensed rather than capitalized, we assume that recurring fixed costs are $0.

Monopoly price. To obtain optimal price for a monopolist under the baseline product configuration of chain distribution, with standard genres and colors, we maximize profits. The most straightforward means to do this is to form the profit equation, take the first derivative and set it equal to zero.[8]   If the calculus is rusty, we can merely create a spreadsheet of prices and associated profits, and then visually examine where profits are greatest. In either case, we need the profit equation. The general form of the profit equation is:

$$\Pi = q*(p-c) - F \tag{3}$$

where:
	Π	is profits
	q	is the quantity sold
	p	is unit price
	c	is unit cost
	F	is fixed cost

Because q is actually a function of p, and because demand is characterized for retail price rather than wholesale price, we need to expand the basic equation for

Epigraphs. We express q as a function of p_{retail}: $q=q(p_{retail})$. One thing we need to account for is the difference between retail price (which defines the demand curve) and wholesale price (which defines profits). The two are related through the channel mark-up. We therefore express $p_{wholesale}$ as a function of p_{retail} and the channel markup, m: $p_{wholesale} = (p_{retail})/(1+m)$. We then make the substitutions for q and $p_{wholesale}$:

$$\Pi_{chains} = q(p_{retail}) * [p_{retail}/(1+m) - c] - F \qquad (4)$$

where: $q(p_{retail})$ is the quantity sold as a function of retail price

p_{retail} is retail price

m   is channel markup over wholesale price

Substituting equation (1) for $q(p_{retail})$, and inserting Epigraphs' values for m, c and F yields:

$$\Pi_{chains} = 0.000875p^2 - 0.1616p + 8.612*[p/(1.4) - 10.73] - 0 \qquad (5)$$
$$\Pi_{chains} = 0.000625p^3 - 0.1244p^2 + 7.8854p - 92.4068 \qquad (6)$$

To find the profit-maximizing price, we take the derivative of profits with respect to price and set it equal to zero:

$$d\,\Pi/dp = 0.001875p^2 - 0.2488p + 7.8854 = 0 \qquad (7)$$

This yields two solutions, the one for which d^2P/dp^2 is negative (indicating a maximum, rather than a minimum) is:

$$p_{retail} = \$51.55 \qquad (8)$$

This price yields demand:

$$Q_{chains} = 0.000875p^2 - 0.1616p + 8.612 = 2.61 \text{ rolls per person} \qquad (9)$$

and corresponding profits (gross margin) per person:

$$\Pi_{chains} = q * (p_{wholesale} - c) = 2.61 * ((51.55/1.4) - 10.73) = \$68.01 \qquad (10)$$

We obtain the same optimal price without calculus by creating a spreadsheet of profits versus price using equation (6). This spreadsheet and the corresponding graph is given in Exhibit 5-3. What the Exhibit adds to the calculus is the observation that profits through chain distribution are relatively inelastic at prices above \$35. This is not the case for sales through the internet. There, profits decline rapidly at prices above the optimal price.

Optimal Product Configuration. The prior analysis treats optimal price for the baseline configuration. To determine whether the baseline configuration is in fact the optimal product configuration, we find the optimal price for each con-

Exhibit 5-3. Epigraphs Optimal Price

Price	Chain Quantity	Chain Gross margin per customer	Internet Quantity	Internet Gross margin per customer
5	7.83	-56.02	6.73	-38.54
10	7.08	-25.41	5.98	-4.37
15	6.38	-0.10	5.28	22.57
20	5.73	20.37	4.63	42.92
25	5.12	36.48	4.02	57.35
30	4.55	48.69	3.45	66.51
35	4.03	57.48	2.93	71.06
40	3.55	63.30	2.45	71.65
45	3.11	66.63	2.01	68.95
50	2.72	67.94	1.62	63.60
55	2.37	67.70	1.27	56.26
60	2.07	66.37	0.97	47.59
65	1.80	64.43	0.70	38.25
70	1.59	62.34	0.49	28.89
75	1.41	60.57	0.31	20.17
80	1.28	59.59	0.18	12.75
85	1.20	59.87	0.10	7.27
90	1.16	61.88	0.06	4.40
95	1.16	66.09	0.06	4.79
100	1.20	72.96	0.10	9.11

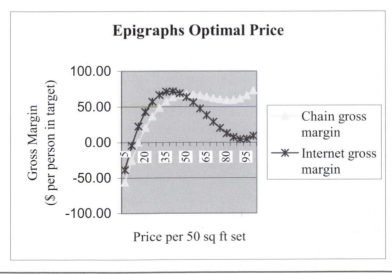

Epigraphs Optimal Price

figuration, then compare profits across those configurations. To find the optimal price we change the intercept in equation 5 to incorporate the coefficient for the configuration change (as we did going from equation 1 to equation 2 for distribution channel). We then repeat the steps captured in equations 6 through 10. Exhibit 5-4 is a summary of optimal price and corresponding demand and profits for each single dimension change to the baseline.

Since price and distribution channel were the only significant attributes in Epigraphs conjoint analysis, the configuration decision is primarily one of distribution channel. However, the channel decision involves additional considerations such as access, awareness, and opportunities for personal selling. We treat these in detail in Chapter 6.

In the absence of detailed channel analysis, the optimal product configuration appears to be sales of standard genres and colors through the Internet at a price of $38.06. This results in profits of $71.88 per person in the target market. The Internet generates higher profits despite lower price, because it is a zero-stage channel. Thus wholesale price equals retail price. The revenue to the firm for each roll sold is the optimal retail price of $38.06. In contrast, the revenue to the firm for each roll sold through chains is $36.82 (the wholesale price corresponding to a retail price of $51.55 given a 40% markup).

Custom genres and custom colors yield lower profits than do standard genres and colors. This stems from the fact that they are more costly to produce, yet are no more attractive to customers than are the standard genres and colors. This is consistent with the focus group comment that too many options overwhelm customers.

Marginal value of attributes. A more straightforward approach to choosing the optimal product configuration looks at attributes one at a time, rather than whole bundles. What we want for each attribute is an estimate of its marginal value to compare to its marginal cost. We would then include all attributes for which marginal value is greater than marginal cost.

To estimate the marginal value for each attribute we need the demand curve for the product with the base features (preferably expressed as an equation), and the set of demand coefficients for each attribute.

In the case of Epigraphs, the basic demand curve is equation 1:

$$q_{chains} = 0.000875p^2 - 0.1616p + 8.612 \tag{11}$$

This is the "basic" demand curve because it is for the default product configuration. (We could use the Internet demand curve, but then would need to take precautions when we looked at the signs of coefficients.)

A change in the product configuration (by adding and deleting an attribute) shifts the demand curve up or down by the amount of the attribute's coefficient.

Exhibit 5-4. Comparison of Epigraphs profits across configurations

Configuration	Demand Curve	Optimal Price, p*	Quantity Q(p*)	Profits Π(p*)	Comments
Baseline	$.000875p^2 - .1616p + 8.612$	$51.55	2.61	$68.01	
Internet	$.000875p^2 - .1616p + 7.512$	$38.06	2.63	$71.88	Retail price = wholesale price
Superstore	Same as baseline			$=\Pi(p^*)$	Coefficient not significant Markup same as baseline
Custom genres				$<\Pi(p^*)$	Coefficient not significant; Unit cost higher
Custom colors				$<\Pi(p^*)$	Coefficient not significant; Unit cost higher

**Note all values of q and Π are expressed per person in the target market

For example, adding custom themes (coefficient of 0.11) changes the intercept in the equation above from 8.612 to 8.722.

We have two strategies with respect to product attributes. We can preserve price for the default product configuration (throw in the attribute for free), and enjoy higher demand. Alternatively, we can preserve demand, and charge a higher price. These options are shown graphically in the Exhibit 5-5 for a notional attribute with a coefficient of 2.00. Assume that the optimal price for the basic configuration is $35.00. The corresponding demand is 4 units. By introducing the new attribute I have a choice of preserving the $35.00, and enjoying demand of 6 units (moving vertically to the new demand curve). Alternatively, I can preserve demand, and charge a price of $65.00 (moving horizontally to the new demand curve.).

The analytical process for both approaches begins with the new demand curve. For Epigraphs, the new demand curve for each attribute is merely the equation above plus the coefficient for the attribute. So for example, the demand curve for custom colors is:

$$q_{chains} = 0.000875p^2 - 0.1616p + 8.612 - 0.21$$
$$= 0.000875p^2 - 0.1616p + 8.402 \tag{12}$$

If I want to preserve the price of the basic configuration, I merely substitute $35.00 for p in equation 2, and solve for q. This yields demand of 3.82 units. If

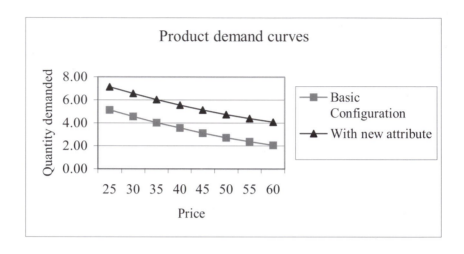

Exhibit 5-5. Demand curve shift from addition of attribute

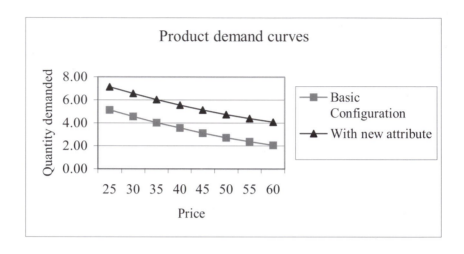

instead, I want to preserve demand for the basic configuration (4.03 units), then I merely substitute 4.03 for q, and solve for the new price. This is slightly more complex, since it involves solving a quadratic, but the new price is $32.96.

Finally, the best approach to making the decision of whether to include an attribute is to compare its marginal value to its marginal cost. The marginal value is the price premium over the basic configuration. In our example for custom colors, the price of the basic configuration is $35.00. The demand preserving price for the product with custom colors is $32.96. Thus the marginal value of custom colors is -$2.04, so we would never offer them.

Exhibit 5-6 summarizes the marginal value analysis for each of the Epigraphs attributes. Column 2 is the attribute coefficient from conjoint regression. Column 3 is the new intercept (constant) in the demand equation, (obtained by adding the coefficient to the intercept in equation 1). Column 4 is the demand at the base price, (obtained by solving for q in the equation with the new intercept). Column 5 is just an aid to solving the quadratic for new price (obtained by subtracting basic configuration demand of 4.03 from the intercept in column 4). Column 6 is the demand-preserving price (obtained by solving the new demand equation for p). Column 7 is the marginal value of the attribute (obtained by subtracting base price of $35.00 from price in column 6).

The two attributes that seem to add value are superstores and custom themes (though remember these weren't significant). If the marginal cost of selling

Exhibit 5-6. Worksheet to determine implicit attribute price
(also called hedonic price)

Attribute	Coefficient	Intercept in demand eqn	Demand at base price	Value of c in quadratic	Price to preserve q	Marginal value
Intercept	4.03	8.612	4.03	4.582	35.02	---
Superstore	0.16	8.772	4.19	4.742	36.64	1.62
Web	-1.11	7.502	2.92	3.472	24.86	-10.16
Custom Colors	-0.21	8.402	3.82	4.372	32.96	-2.06
Custom Themes	0.11	8.722	4.14	4.692	36.13	1.11

through superstores (relative to chains) is less than $1.62, it is probably worth-while to do so. Similarly, if the marginal cost to offer custom themes (relative to standard themes), is less than $1.11, Epigraphs should do so.

Ancillary data. A final piece of the optimal product configuration considers *which* standard colors and genres to offer. While we could offer all 5 genres in all 7 colors, this involves inventorying 35 (5 x 7) versions of the product. This implies considerable inventory costs, and higher obsolescence write-offs at the end of the product life. To help make a decision about the optimal versions of the product to offer, we consult the ancillary data on genre and color preferences. Exhibit 5-7 is the raw data on color and genre preferences. Respondents were asked to identify the colors and genres in which they were most interested. This resulted in multiple votes by several of the respondents, which we rank equally. In retrospect, we would have been better off asking for their ranking of colors and genres. We reorganized the data from Exhibit 5-7 to show unique versus shared preferences for each genre and each color. This reorganization is shown in Exhibit 5-8a for genres, and 5-8b for colors.

To determine the appropriate number of genres and colors to carry, we need to organize the genres and colors in decreasing marginal value. We make the assumption that anyone who voted for a genre (even if that respondent cast multiple votes) would buy it, if it were the only genre available. Exhibit 5-8a indicates that the genre with the greatest value is "literary quotes." As a sole genre, it captures 52% of the market, while "inspirational quotes," the next most popular genre would capture 48% of the market. Thus if we were to choose one genre, it would be "literary quotes."

If we choose to offer two genres, we imagine that "inspirational quotes" would be the second choice. However, it is possible that people who like "inspirational quotes" are merely a subset of those who like "literary quotes." Reading down the literary column and across the inspirational row of Exhibit 5-8a indicates that half

Exhibit 5-7. Raw data on color and genre preferences

Colors							Genres				
Gold	Silver	Hunter	Burgundy	Blue	Black	White	Literary	Humor	Inspire	Sports	Movies
0	0	1	0	0	0	0	1	0	0	0	0
0	0	1	1	0	1	1	1	0	0	1	1
0	0	0	0	0	1	0	0	0	1	1	0
0	0	1	0	0	1	0	1	0	1	0	0
1	0	0	0	0	0	0	1	0	0	0	0
1	0	1	1	1	0	0	0	1	1	1	0
0	0	1	1	0	0	0	1	0	1	0	0
1	0	1	1	1	1	0	1	0	0	1	1
1	1	0	0	0	1	0	0	0	1	0	0
1	0	1	1	0	1	0	1	0	0	0	0
0	0	1	1	1	0	1	1	1	0	0	0
0	1	0	1	1	1	0	0	1	1	1	0
0	0	1	0	0	0	0	0	0	0	0	0
1	1	0	0	0	0	1	1	1	0	0	1
0	0	1	0	0	1	0	1	1	1	0	0
1	0	0	1	1	0	0	0	0	0	0	1
1	1	0	0	0	1	0	0	1	1	0	0
0	0	1	1	0	1	0	1	0	0	0	0
1	0	0	0	1	0	0	1	0	0	0	0
0	1	1	1	0	1	0	0	1	1	0	1
0	0	0	0	0	0	0	0	1	0	1	0
0	0	0	0	0	0	0	0	0	0	0	0
0	1	1	0	0	1	0	1	0	0	0	1
0	1	0	0	1	0	1	0	0	1	0	0
0	0	0	0	0	0	0	1	1	1	0	1
0	0	1	0	1	1	0	0	1	1	0	0
0	0	0	0	0	0	0	0	0	0	0	0
1	1	0	0	0	1	1	1	1	1	0	0
0	0	1	1	1	1	0	1	0	1	0	1
0	0	0	0	0	0	0	0	0	0	0	0
0	0	1	1	0	0	0	1	0	1	0	0
0	0	1	0	0	0	0	0	0	0	1	0
0	0	1	1	0	1	0	1	0	1	0	0
0.30	0.24	0.55	0.39	0.27	0.48	0.15	0.55	0.33	0.48	0.21	0.24
0.47	0.44	0.51	0.50	0.45	0.51	0.36	0.51	0.48	0.51	0.42	0.44

Exhibit 5-8. Paired genre and color preferences

	literary	humor	Inspiration	sports	Movies
literary	0.15				
humor	0.12	0.00			
inspiration	0.24	0.15	0.06		
sports	0.06	0.06	0.03	0.03	
movies	0.15	0.03	0.00	0.00	0.03
Total	**0.52**	**0.30**	**0.48**	**0.21**	**0.21**

Exhibit 5-8a. Paired genre preferences

	gold	silver	hunter	burgundy	blue	black	white
gold	0.03						
silver	0.15	0.00					
hunter	0.09	0.06	0.09				
burgundy	0.12	0.06	0.21	0.00			
blue	0.12	0.06	0.06	0.18	0.00		
black	0.18	0.09	0.18	0.24	0.12	0.03	
white	0.03	0.03	0.06	0.06	0.06	0.06	0.00
Total	**0.30**	**0.24**	**0.55**	**0.39**	**0.27**	**0.48**	**0.12**

Exhibit 5-8b. Paired color preferences

of the respondents choosing "inspirational quotes" also chose "literary quotes" (their intersection). Thus the value added of the inspirational genre is only 24% of the market (.48 total inspirational genre - .24 shared literary/inspirational).

We systematically consider the value-added of each genre by examining its market capture minus the intersection of its capture with that of all prior genres. Exhibit 5-8a indicates that the pair of genres with the highest market capture is indeed "literary quotes" and "inspirational quotes" with 76% of the market. If we look at the market for the remaining genres, and exclude intersections with literary and inspirational quotes, then the next most valuable are humor and sports. Either would add 9%, to increase the capture to 85% of the market. Exhibit 5-9a shows the market capture for the optimal combination of genres as the number of genres is increased. We determine the optimal number of genres by comparing the value-added of each new genre by the marginal cost of offering an additional genre.

Equivalent analysis of colors is given in Exhibits 5-8b and 5-9b. Complete coverage of the market is achieved with three colors: hunter captures 55%, black adds 30%, silver adds 9%. All remaining colors are redundant with the first three, in that anyone who expressed interest in the remaining colors, also expressed interest in one of the first three. Since there is no up-front fixed cost associated with offering each color, the relevant cost in determining optimal number of color choices is the additional inventory and obsolescence cost for each color. Thus it is easier to offer color options than genre options.[9] In the absence of cost data on cutting new genre dies and holding inventory for the entire distribution system, there appears to be little value in offering more than two genres and two colors (four color-genre combinations).

Determining Price and Product Configuration Under Competition

While establishing monopoly price and product configuration uses decision theoretic principles (optimization logic), examining the same decisions under competition requires the use of game theory. There are four steps in assessing price and product configuration under competition (the same steps used in solving any game):

- Defining the actions and reactions of both firms
- Defining payoffs for each firm for each path of the game—characterizing the impact of "strategy pairs" on both firms' market shares and profits
- Assessing each firm's best strategy given the payoff structure—is there an equilibrium strategy?

Actions. While the complete action space is infinite, the likely action space confronting an entrant is comparable to that you considered in the monopoly setting. The set of actions between you and a later entrant is thus the same. What differs is the relative attractiveness of each action. The set of actions for Epigraphs include distribution channels, the product attributes, and their prices. If there are n such options, there are n^2 paths in the game (I can match each of your n actions with any of the n actions). Fortunately, some of these paths are clearly inferior, and we can ignore them. The first step then is to create the list of actions. In the case of Epigraphs the set of actions are distribution channels X genre-color combinations X price. Because this quickly becomes quite complex, we treat each dimension of strategy in sequence.

a. Distribution

We assume that Epigraphs has an exclusive distribution contract. This implies both that the chain carries only Epigraphs product, and that Epigraphs is not available in any other retail outlet. Accordingly the entrant must choose an alternate distribution channel. Assume it chooses the next most attractive channel. What is really nice in constructing this game is that you know from your own research which action is next most attractive. There is symmetry in the actions and their associated

Exhibit 5-9. Value-added of colors and genres

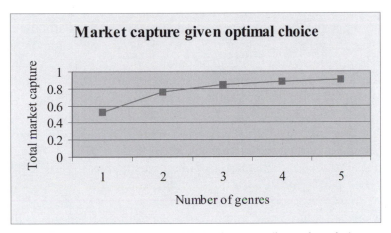

Exhibit 5-9a. Value added of genres (in rank order)
genre 1 is literary, genre 2 is inspirational,
genres 3 and 4 are humor or sports, genre 5 is movies

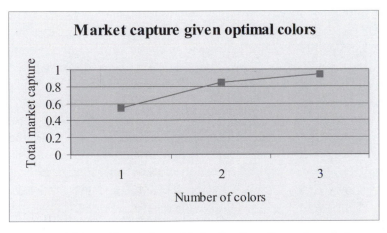

Exhibit 5-9b. Value added of colors (in rank order)
Color 1 is hunter, color 2 is black, color 3 is silver
All other colors are redundant

demand and cost structures. In this case, the next most attractive option is a home superstore.

b. Product configuration

   The next choice facing the entrant is the range of product offerings. Here we frame the choice as a simple one of matching Epigraphs product line, or differentiating. Remember, the available product configurations were five genres times seven colors, with options for custom quotes and colors. Epigraphs chose two genres in rank order of customer preference. The third genre is unlikely to have sufficient demand to justify the fixed cost of new dies. Epigraphs chose two colors, also in rank order, where the third color is unlikely to have sufficient demand to warrant the switching costs between production batches, scale economies in material purchases, and additional obsolescence costs. Thus if the entrant chooses a differentiation strategy, it will be left with less popular genres and colors.

   We examine firms' strategies through a game (normal form rather than a game tree). In the normal form of a game, the columns of the matrix depict your (the first mover) strategies. The rows of the matrix depict the entrant's strategies. Each cell defines the payoff to you and to the entrant for the combination of your strategy (column) and the entrant strategy (row). Note: The matrix characterizes a two-stage game: you create the market with a given strategy, another firm observes your strategy, and then enters the market with their own strategy. We could make the game more complex. We could allow the first mover to respond to the entrant with a revised strategy. The basic methodology is the same, but far more complex. We leave that exercise to the reader. Exhibit 5-10 is the normal form of the genre-color component of the Epigraphs game.

Defining payoffs. To determine the market splitting shown in the cells, we need to assess how each consumer would behave given the choice among both firms' product offerings. The demand curve we generated earlier tells us how much demand will exist for a new product configuration given the existing set of products. It does not tell us the relative demand of one configuration when multiple configurations coexist. We can, however, derive this from the ancillary data summarized in Exhibit 5-8. When a color or genre is unique to one firm, we give it that share of the market, when colors or genres are shared, firms split those colors or genres. The payoff for each firm is thus the sum of all unique and common colors and genres. Note that the shares are of the *potential* market—by not offering the full complement of colors and genres, firms exclude portions of the market.

Exhibit 5-10. Normal Form of Epigraphs Game
(Values are market shares to the respect firm)

		Epigraphs Strategy			
		1 X 1 (one genre X 1 color) Literary Hunter		2 X 2 Literary/Inspiration Hunter/Black	
Monopoly share		**28.1 %**		**64.6 %**	
		Epigraphs	Entrant	Epigraphs	Entrant
Entrant Strategy	1 X 1 Matching Literary Hunter	14.3%	14.3%		
	1 X 1 Complements Inspiration Black	17.8%	13.5%		
	2 X 2 Matching Literary/Inspiration Hunter/Black			32.3%	32.3%
	2 X 2 Partial Complements Literary/Inspiration Gold/Burgundy			49.7%	21.7%
	2 X 2 Complements Humor/Sports Gold/Burgundy			37.7%	7.8%

Assessing equilibrium strategies. Exhibit 5-10 assumes that both firms introduce the product at monopoly price. The logic is that both firms have "local monopolies" in their respective channels.[11] Under this assumption, there is a Nash Equilibrium. Remember that a Nash Equilibrium is a pair of strategies that represents each firm's optimal strategy, given the strategy of the rival. In this game the Nash Equilibrium is for both firms to choose the monopoly product configuration. The optimal strategy for the entrant is to match Epigraphs' product strategy. To illustrate this assume that Epigraphs enters with one color and one genre (column 1). The market share for the entrant if they match Epigraphs' strategy is 14.3%. If instead they offer a different color and genre, their market share is only 13.5%, thus they are better off matching. Similarly, if Epigraphs offers two colors and genres (column 2), the maximum share for the entrant is obtained by matching (32.3%).

This is true because Epigraphs chooses the most popular colors, leaving the less popular colors. While in essence Epigraphs cedes the entrant a monopoly to other colors/genres, these monopolies are less attractive than splitting Epigraph's monopoly. This is true whether Epigraphs enters with only one genre-color combinations (1 X 1) or four genre-color combinations (2 X 2). For example, the second best 2 X 2 strategy for the entrant results in a 15.3% share of the potential market. Matching Epigraphs products and colors yields a 32.3% share of the potential market.

Price. Typically a matching strategy would yield price competition driving industry profits to zero. Here, however, we assume differentiated distribution—Epigraphs, through chains, and the entrant, through superstores. With differentiated distribution, firms' incentives to reduce price are suppressed because it is not possible to directly compare products. In essence, each firm has a local monopoly, and splits monopoly profits (like a cartel).

We may be incorrect in this assumption. To assess how sensitive payoffs are to the assumption, we examine payoffs in each of the duopoly games. These are captured in Exhibit 5-11. The Exhibit essentially replicates Exhibit 5-1, but replaces Epigraphs demand curve for the stylized demand curve of q=120-p.

A final pricing issue is cross-price elasticity—to what extent does a 10% reduction in the competitor's price, reduce my sales? and conversely, to what extent does a 10% reduction in my price reduce competitors sales? We basically skirted the issue in the prior analysis. In drawing the cartel conclusion, we implicitly assume that cross-product demand is inelastic by virtue of the physical separation between the products. In contrast, Exhibit 5-11 assumes that the products are homogeneous, and thus are perfect substitutes.

Opportunities for preemption. Given that the entrant's best strategy is matching the leader, Epigraphs has little opportunity to preempt rivals through its

Exhibit 5-11. Epigraphs outcomes under various structural assumptions

Demand: $q = .000875p^2 - .1616p + 8.612$
Marginal cost = $10.73

	Driving Function	Firm a			Firm b		
		p_A	q_A	Π_A	p_B	q_B	Π_B
Monopoly	$\Pi = 0.0006p^3 - 0.12p^2 + 7.88p - 92.41$	$51.55	2.61	$68.01	--	--	--
Perfect Competition	$p = c$	$10.73	3.54	0	$10.73	3.54	0
Cartel	$\Pi = 0.0006p^3 - 0.12p^2 + 7.88p - 92.41/n$	$51.55	1.30	$34.00	$51.55	1.30	$34.00

choice of colors and genres. Thus, choice of colors and genres should conform to the monopoly configurations.

One other consideration is whether Epigraphs should attempt to deter rivals by choosing an alternative configuration and price.[12] Formal analysis would require details of the upfront costs and inventory costs associated with the range of genre-color options. However, it is doubtful that pricing below monopoly levels is warranted in this case. Wallcovering is a durable good, and 60% of a new product line's sales occur within the first year. Thus the incentive for a follower firm to enter with ANY strategy is decreasing over time. There is little need for Epigraphs to fuel this process by lowering its price. This is particularly true since Epigraphs would be expending near-term profits on a large sales base to preserve future profits on a small and decreasing sales base.

Summary

Ignoring later analysis that will introduce additional considerations to the choice of distribution channel, and may modify the firm cost structure, it appears that the optimal strategy for Epigraphs is as follows:

Introduce a product line consisting of 4 color-genre options (Hunter and Black) X (Literary and Inspirational). These products should be sold through wallcovering chains at a price of $50.00 per set. This strategy should produce average sales of $87.86 per person in the target market (.646 truncation of product line * 2.72 rolls per person * $50.00 per roll). The corresponding profits are $69.00 per person in the target market.

This strategy appears to be the best strategy not only in monopoly, but also in anticipation of later entry. Epigraphs would cede distribution in superstores to entrants, with the anticipation that the entrant would match Epigraphs product line. This will reduce the rate of subsequent sales of Epigraphs products by 50%.

However, since 60% of product line sales occur in the first year, and the entrant will take time to respond, the net impact on lifecycle sales is minimal.

CONCLUSION

This chapter treated the first of the strategic decisions facing the venture. This is the competitive strategy of what product configuration and price to introduce in the market. What makes this decision strategic is the fact that your choice affects the product configuration and price choices of later entrants, and potentially their decision of whether to enter at all.

As we saw in Chapter 2, the number of competitors and the level of product differentiation determine the industry structure. The industry structure in turn determines the level of prices and profitability in the industry. What is distinct here is that Chapter 2 treated the industry structure as given and drew general insights about the relationship between that structure and industry attractiveness (potential profits). Here we focused exclusively on one aspect of industry structure—rivalry. We showed that competitive strategy not only affects how well your venture does within an industry structure, but it also helps to determine that structure.

We began the chapter by reviewing principles of strategic behavior for an industry with a simple stylized demand curve. We used decision theory to find the optimal price and product configuration for the monopoly, and then used game theory to examine the same decisions under competition.

In the Analysis section we applied these tools to the Epigraphs demand curve derived in Chapter 4. We showed how to extend game theory beyond principles to real mechanics. We generated the actual payoff matrix for Epigraphs and a potential entrant, and used that payoff matrix to find the Nash Equilibrium—the Epigraphs strategy that generates the highest profits for it assuming the entrant is maximizing its profits.

While the price, demand and profits from this strategy will be fed into the financials in Chapter 11, the most important conclusions from this chapter are 1) the insight that Epigraphs' choices constrain those of the potential entrant, and 2) the monopoly strategy is also the best preemptive strategy. Thus, there is no cost to behaving strategically in this scenario.

One "configuration" choice we examined for Epigraphs in this chapter was the distribution channel. We derived demand curves for both Internet distribution and chain distribution. Since expected profits for the two channels are comparable, the final distribution decision hinges on other factors. In the next chapter we discuss these other factors, and present alternative methods for making the distribution decision.

notes

1 For examples, see Teece, David J. 1987., "Profiting from Technological Innovation: Implications for Integration, Collaboration, Licensing and Public Policy," in Teece, D.J. (Ed), "The Competitive Challenge: Stratgies for Industrial Innovation and Renewal," New York: Harper and Row.

2 Nash, John. F., 1950. "Equilibrium Points in n-person Games. Proceedings of the National Academy of Sciences," 36, pp. 48-49.

3 Bertrand, J., 1883. "Theorie Mathematique de la Richess Sociale," Journal des Savants, pp. 499-511.

4 Cournot, A., 1838. "Recherches sur les Principes mathematiques de la Theorie des Richesses," English edition: Bacon, N. (Ed), "Researches into the Mathematical Principles of the Theory of Wealth," New York: Macmillan, 1897.

5 Von Stackelberg, Heinrich., 1934. "Marktform und Gleichgewicht," Vienna: Julius Springer.

6 Hotelling, H., 1929. "Stability in Competition," Economic Journal, 39:41-57.

7 Many calculators will do this regression for you. You merely enter the three data points (where each data point is the set of demand and price), and the calculator will come back with the equation that best fits those points, along with the r-squared that assesses the fit. Unfortunately, Excel only does linear regression, so you need to manually create exponential variables in the case of the quadratic. In the quadratic regression, your dependent variable is the demand, one of your independent variable is price, and the other is a new variable that you create by squaring price. For the power curve, you take logs of both the dependent variable (demand) and the independent variable (price): $Ln(q) = ln(intercept) + ln(p)$.

8 Remember to check second order conditions.

9 Each new genre requires a new set of dies/templates used to cut the quotes from the material.

10 This structure of play is similar to Stackelberg except that Stackelberg assumes homogeneous products across firms.

11 In order for the firms to have local monopolies, then price minus consumer surplus must be greater than 1/2 the transportation cost between the chain and the superstore.

12 See Chapter 8 in Tirole, Jean 1988. "The Theory of Industrial Organization," Cambridge, MA: MIT Press, for a nice tutorial on entry models.

marketing channel decisions

INTRODUCTION AND GOALS

The marketing channel is the second strategic decision in the venture design. The marketing channel is the means by which your product or service is made available to the end customer. The marketing channel decision has implications for both reach (the number of customers who have access to your product) and effectiveness (the likelihood that customers will purchase your product, given it is accessible to them). The goal in the marketing channel (as with all the strategic decisions) is maximizing firm profits. The maximization problem trades reach and effectiveness against the cost of distribution through the channel.

The decision is important because it is one of the two means available to the firm to control realized demand (the other being advertising). Chapters 4 and 5 defined the potential demand for the product. This potential demand assumes that all customers in the market are aware of the product and have access to it. While it is reasonable to assume that we want all customers to be immediately aware of the product and have unlimited access to it, this is probably unwise. We may want demand to unfold slowly over time to minimize the repercussions of early mistakes.

This chapter begins by reviewing the principles underlying the distribution channel decision, both the vertical contracting literature in economics and the marketing literature. Next we introduce tools to assess distribution channels: demand curves, breakeven analysis, and channel contribution. Finally, we apply these analyses to Epigraphs and draw conclusions about the appropriate distribution channel.

PRINCIPLES

Vertical contracting

The vertical contracting literature[1] treats the marketing channel decision as a principal–agent problem, where the manufacturer (or other upstream party) is the principal, and the dealer (downstream party) is the agent. While the literature is primarily concerned with designing the optimal contract between the principal and the agent, rather than choice of agent or channel (which we consider here) the theory is useful for framing the channel decision.

The basic structure of the theory has the manufacturer attempting to design a contract that jointly increases manufacturer revenues and minimizes payments to the dealer. The goal in designing the contract is providing incentives to the dealers that cause them to simultaneously maximize manufacturer revenues while maximizing their own profits. By creating a contract where the dealers' incentives are aligned with the manufacturer's, the manufacturer can minimize monitoring costs.

Since the dealer network likely exists, and likely follows fairly standard contracts, the vertical contracting literature is less useful in contract design than it is in merely illuminating the issues that confront you in making the channel decision. These issues are dealer attributes and behaviors that increase demand, and dealer attributes that minimize cost.

Dealer attributes affecting demand. To the extent that the dealer has reputational advantages that imbue your product with higher quality, the dealer may be able to "shift up" the demand curve for your product. This would (or may be) the case, for example, if Hammacher-Schlemmer carries your product. Since Hammacher-Schlemmer claims to test several manufacturers' versions of each product it sells, carrying your product is an endorsement of its quality. To the extent that customers ordinarily would be uncertain about the quality of your product, Hammacher-Schlemmer may be able to increase the number of people willing to buy your product at any given price.

We already saw evidence of the potential for the distribution channel to shift demand for Epigraphs. The demand curve for chains was above that for the Internet. While we didn't probe why the demand curve for chains is higher, there are likely reputation effects as well as experience effects. The reputation of the chain provides confidence to the buyer that if they are unhappy with the product they will have recourse. The experience effect is that customers can view samples of the product firsthand to get a sense of the product's size and texture.

This leads nicely to the second dealer attribute affecting demand, reach. While Hammacher-Schlemmer may shift the demand curve up, you may not realize any greater demand through it than through other more conventional dealers because of the limited reach of its catalog. If Hammacher-Schlemmer mails its catalog to one million households, you can never sell your product to more than one million households if you choose the catalog as your exclusive outlet. In essence, while the catalog may shift the demand curve, generating greater demand at any given price for customers within its reach, it truncates total demand by not providing access to all those with a willingness to buy the product at the higher price.

Dealer attributes affecting cost. In addition to the demand implications of channel choice are the cost implications. The wholesale price to Hammacher-Schlemmer may be lower than that to other channels. Since Hammacher-Schlemmer knows it has the ability to increase demand relative to other dealers, it may require a contact that allows it to capture much of the benefit of the demand increase. It may "charge higher cost" to sell each unit by requiring a lower wholesale price.

The example so far has been primarily a passive channel. Hammacher-Schlemmer "sells" by distributing its catalog. The issues addressed above become more pronounced with industrial products requiring personal selling. There, the opportunity to increase demand is active selling by an agent. Here, incentives become tremendously important not only through increasing overall selling activity by the agent, but relative emphasis on your product versus the other products the dealer represents. (In the case of a direct sales force, the emphasis is on the former rather than the latter.)

Marketing Literature

The vertical contracting literature does a nice job of laying out the theory underpinning the marketing channel decision. However, as a start-up venture, the challenge will be choice among a set of existing channels and associated contracts rather than design of entirely new contracts. The marketing literature helps us translate the profit maximization structure of the vertical contracting literature into a set of guidelines that help inform the channel decision. While the cost implications and reach implications translate directly, the demand implications are treated through the lens of "channel length."

Channel length refers to the number of intermediaries between the manufacturer and the final customer. In the case of a direct sales force to the end customer, the length is zero; in the case of the GAP, which manufactures its own goods, and sells them through its own stores, the length is also zero. In the case of toys, a small manufacturer works through independent sales representatives, who market to retailers, who in turn sell to consumers. There the channel length is two.

In general, the trade-off between channels of different lengths is one of high fixed cost, high effectiveness, and limited reach (short channel length) versus low fixed cost, reduced effectiveness, and greater reach (long channel length). One of the exciting promises of Internet commerce is the prospect of combining the advantages of short and long channels at relatively low cost. To the extent that your product does not require personal selling, the Internet provides unlimited reach, with in-depth product information at close to zero unit transaction cost, in an environment where your product may not be competing with others.

Currently the reach is only limited by the number of people willing to engage in e-commerce transactions.

A number of factors influence the feasibility of short versus long channels: a) *customer characteristics* such as geographic dispersion, frequency of purchase, need for information, b) *product characteristics* such as product weight, perishability, unit value, degree of standardization, and need for maintenance/service, and c) *company strategy* such as delivery policies, financial resources, scope of product mix. Exhibit 6-1 summarizes the factors that tend to move distribution toward short or long length channels.

Relating the marketing principles to the vertical contracting principles: short channels tend to shift the demand curve—they enhance the product through superior delivery, service, and information. On the flip side, they tend to truncate demand due to their limited reach. In contrast, long channels provide more complete reach (movement along demand curve). We tend to see short channels in small markets and ones for which the product's value is high relative to customer income. We tend to see long channels for mass markets of lower priced goods.

Exhibit 6-1. Characteristics driving distribution toward long or short channels.

	CHANNEL LENGTH	
	Short	Long
Customer Characteristics	Concentrated Market	*Dispersed market* Well–informed Frequent purchaser
Product Characteristics	*Perishable* *Custom product* High unit value *Requires maintenance/service*	Standard product *Low unit value*
Company Characteristics	*Rapid delivery policy* *Single product*	*Financial constraints* Wide product mix

Enables use of channel
Precludes use of alternative channel

Two distribution innovations attempt to combine the advantages of long and short channels. Franchising creates a network of short channels, thereby combining increased demand with greater reach. While this is typically a high-fixed cost strategy, franchising overcomes the financial constraints, by having the local owner/managers finance their own outlets. Similarly, as mentioned previously, e-commerce provides unlimited reach, with in-depth product information at low cost, in an environment where your product is not competing with others.

All the above considerations flow nicely into an economic analysis that allows us to choose the channel that maximizes firm profits. We will illustrate that in a moment, but before doing so, we need to mention three other characteristics of channels that are probably best treated outside the analysis. (Note, that with adequate information, these too could probably be folded into economic analysis.)

The first issue is flexibility. In general, it is quite costly to change distribution channels. Distributors or representatives often require long-term contracts with high degrees of exclusivity. Thus if you begin with long channels, and then realize that your product requires shorter channels, you may not be able to implement them for a considerable period. Additionally, there may be switching costs—some retailers may not be willing to deal with you if you have already established other channels. Neiman Marcus, for example, is unlikely to carry your product if it was first introduced at WalMart. Beyond the issue of switching, some channels provide greater flexibility in that they tolerate parallel channels. This is probably the exception. Many outlets require not only exclusivity in the channel, but also restrict selling in other channels. Retailers, for example, are generally intolerant of direct sales by the manufacturer.

To the extent you believe you may ultimately want direct channels (zero level), you should take that into account when choosing current channels, and when structuring their contracts.

A final consideration is reverse information flow. We have seen that shorter channels facilitate greater information flow to the customer. Even if your product allows you to utilize longer channels, you may want to consider short channels if customer information is important. Short channels permit you to learn what customers think about your product, and how they use the product. Timely receipt of such information may lead to superior innovation capability. Similarly, short channels allow you to track changes in demand more quickly and more accurately. Such tracking helps preclude the possibility that customers will shift to competitor's products during stock-outs, or that you will be left with obsolete inventory. Yellow Cab shoes moved to direct sales for precisely that reason.

Analytical Process

While the task of designing a distribution channel from scratch would be overwhelming, the task is made considerably more tractable by the prevalence of existing channels. The starting point for the channel analysis is the industry analysis conducted in Chapter 2. To complete that analysis, you needed to identify all the industry players, including the buyer channels. For each channel, and possibly for each firm in that channel (if firms are not perfect substitutes), you need to gather the information called for in Appendix 6-1.

For channels with multiple levels (through dealers to retailers, for example), you can treat each level separately, and then sum the levels for the channel. Thus, for a two level channel, the distributor may charge a 30% markup over manufacturer price, and the retailer may charge a retail price that represents a 40% markup over wholesale price. You would combine these to determine manufacturer's revenues as a function of retail price. With the markups just mentioned, the manufacturer's revenues would be 55% of retail price [= retail price/(1.3*1.4)].

There are two approaches to analyzing these data once they have been compiled. One approach is merely to compute a single profit number for each channel, then compare channels. The second is to do a break-even analysis of each channel, then assess the likelihood of achieving breaking-even volume. We advocate doing both. We begin with break-even analysis.

Break-even

Break-even analysis compares fixed costs to unit margin, to determine the number of units that must be sold to "break-even" or cover fixed costs. While this results in a single number, generally, break-even analysis is depicted as a plot of net income versus number of units sold (as shown in Exhibit 6-2). To do the analysis then, you merely sum the fixed costs, compute the unit margins, and divide fixed costs by unit margins to determine break-even volume.

$$\text{Break-even Volume} \ = \ \frac{\Sigma \text{ fixed costs per channel}}{\text{unit margins per channel}}$$

Below break-even volume, the channel is a net cost to the firm. Above that volume, the channel contributes to firm profits. As a simple example, assume the firm has a product with two channel options: selling direct, and selling through a wholesaler, then retailer. Assume that a direct sales force with comparable reach to the retail channel incurs fixed costs of $100,000 per year and that the commission is 10% on a unit price of $500. Thus, each sale generates $450 in unit margin. Further, goods are paid for via credit card, so the cash cycle and attendant carrying costs are zero (possibly even negative—suggesting the poten-

Exhibit 6-2. Sample comparison of channels showing break-even volumes as well as cross-over volume

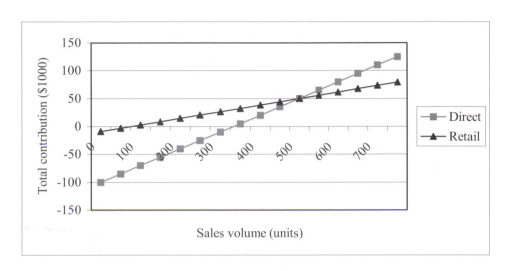

tial to earn interest on the float). Assume that the retail channel consists of 100 outlets and that each outlet requires one display unit and two units in inventory (shared between wholesaler and retailer). Thus, 300 units are required to fill the channel. Assume further that the wholesaler markup is 30% and the retailer markup is 40%. This yields unit revenues to the manufacturer equal to 55% of retail price ($500 * 0.55 = $275).

There are two approaches to the break-even here: one is the lifetime break-even approach, in which we consider the actual manufacturing cost of the 300 units in inventory; the other is the annual break-even approach, in which we consider only the carrying cost of the 300 units. Since the 300 units will ultimately be sold, the annual approach is more appropriate (though the lifetime approach is important for start-up cash flow analysis). Assume also that the manufacturing cost is $150/unit. Finally, assume that the cost of capital is 20%, and that the cash cycle for units sold through the wholesale channel is 90 days (meaning, on average, you finance inventory for 90 days before you receive payment, whereas for direct sales, the cash cycle is 2 days).

Sales force break-even $= \dfrac{\$100{,}000 \text{ fixed cost}}{\$450 \text{ revenue} - \$150 \text{ mfr cost} - .20(2/365)*\$150 \text{ carrying cost}} = 333.5$ units

Retail break-even $= \dfrac{(300 \text{ units}) (.20*\$150 \text{ carrying})}{(\$500 \text{ retail price}/(1.3*1.4)) - (150 + (.20(90/365)*\$150 \text{ carrying}))} = 76.7$ units

We depict this graphically in Exhibit 6-2. The exhibit plots the net contribution for each distribution channel as a function of sales volume. Note that while retail breaks even more quickly, its slope is shallower. Thus at some volume, sales through the direct channel are more lucrative. We can solve for this "channel indifference" volume:

$$\text{(Unit Margin)}_a x - \text{Fixed Cost}_a = \text{(Unit Margin)}_b x - \text{Fixed Cost}_b$$
$$\$299.83x - \$100,000 = \$117.63x - \$9,000$$

$$x = 499.5 \text{ units}$$

Thus, if the firm anticipates selling more than 500 units per year, it prefers to sell through direct channels. The issue then, is how likely are sales of 500 units.

Total Contribution Per Channel

A second approach to assess the optimal channel is to combine demand considerations with cost considerations. Since direct sales is a shorter channel, we would expect it to produce greater sales, holding reach and price constant. Thus, not only is direct sales a more lucrative channel above 500 units, but because it is an information-intensive channel, it is more likely to reach sales of 500 units than is a retail channel with the same reach.

The total contribution approach to the channel decision requires the demand data derived from conjoint analysis. Assume that conjoint analysis indicates sales through direct channels produces 10% probability of purchase, while sales at retail produces 7% probability of purchase. Assume further that the reach of each channel is 50,000 consumers, then the expected contribution for direct sales is:

$$(.10)(50,000)(\$299.83) - \$100,000 = \$1,399,150$$

For retail, the expected contribution is:

$$(.07)(50,000)(\$117.33) - \$9,000 = \$410,655$$

Thus, both analyses indicate that the firm should sell directly to end users rather than through the retail channel.

Other considerations

One final consideration for marketing channel pertains to life cycle issues. Remember from studies of diffusion, that different types of customers buy products at different points in the life cycle, and accordingly, different selling methods/media are used throughout the product life cycle. Early users tend to make independent decisions based on mass media. Later users tend to imitate early users. Relatedly, it is easier to degrade reputation, than to enhance it. These life cycle considerations suggest two things for marketing channel decisions:

1) There may be a natural flow from short, information-intensive channels with truncated reach to lead users in early stages. Once lead users have adopted the product, and have begun to fuel imitation, then the firm can move distribution to longer channels with greater reach. We saw this with personal computers. Early personal computers were sold as kits through the mail to technologists. Now that people understand their function, they can be sold through office supply stores.

2) There may be a natural flow from high margin, high reputation channels with truncated reach in early stages to mass market discount retailers in later stages. We saw this for the TV Guide game.[2] Early sales were to exclusive retailers like Neiman-Marcus. In the next stage, sales were through department stores, like Sears. In the final stage, sales were through discounters like Toys-R-Us and Walmart.

Accordingly, marketing channels play a secondary role promotion /advertising—stimulating demand. This is in addition to their primary role of providing access to the product.

We now apply these tools to the Epigraphs case.

EPIGRAPHS

Data on markups and inventory requirements for the wallcovering retail channels are shown in Exhibit 6-3. These data were obtained from one of the manufacturers. The three main channels are independent retailers, chains, and superstores.

Industry analysis had indicated that there were approximately 15,000 independent retailers served by 100 distributors with an estimated reach of 15 million consumers. Because there are 40% markups both at the distributor and at the retailer, the unit revenue is $0.51*$retail price ($=price/(1.4)^2$).

There are fewer chains—Sherwin-Williams, the largest chain, has 2200 outlets. There are even fewer superstores—Home Depot, the largest superstore has approximately 750 outlets. Despite the fewer numbers of chains and superstores, their reach is equivalent to the independents. Sherwin-Williams has approximately 2200 stores, with 1500 transactions per quarter. This number exceeds the number of wallcovering transactions per month, thus it appears that distribution through Sherwin-Williams provides 100% availability to the target market.

Because manufacturers sell directly to the chains and superstores, without distributors, there is only a single markup of 40%. The unit revenues through this channel are therefore $0.71*$retail price. At this point we add the new Internet channel, which has no intermediaries, and therefore no markup. The Internet

Exhibit 6-3. Wallcovering flows through the distribution channels

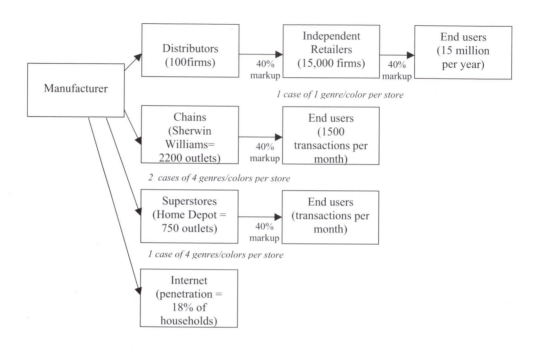

reach is lower than that for the bricks and mortar retailers because not all customers have adopted Internet purchasing. The current estimate for Internet purchase penetration is 18% of households.[3]

We combined these contribution numbers with considerations for inventory and other fixed costs to derive the break-even volume for each channel. These are given in Exhibit 6-4. Break-even analysis indicates that the most lucrative channel is direct sales through the Internet. The three channels have breakeven volumes that differ by an order of magnitude: break-even volume for the Internet is 626 units; for sales through chains or superstores, break-even volume is 6556 units; for sales through distributors to independents, break-even volume is 50,038 units.

While the Internet appears at this point to be the most attractive channel, there are two other issues: the demand issue—will the Internet attract sales, since the customer can't "feel" the product, and if so, at what volume? The other issue is the life cycle issue: is there value in initiating sales through a channel that packages design consulting with the wallcovering sales? This is the advantage of independent retailers over the other channels.

Exhibit 6-4. Epigraphs break-even analysis

	Internet	Independents	Chains	Superstores
DEMAND				
Units per person at optimal price/config (Chap 5)	2.63	not done	2.61	2.61
Market size (Chap 2)	15,000,000	15,000,000	15,000,000	15,000,000
Reach--percent people reached by channel (Chap 2)	0.18	1.00	1.00	1.00
TOTAL EXPECTED DEMAND: (units*mkt*reach)	7,101,000	--	39,150,000	39,150,000
FIXED COST				
Outlets in channel (Chap 2)*	1	15,000	2,200	750
Inventory required to fill outlet (Chap 2) (Exhibit 6-3)	--	12	48	96
Inventory required to fill channel: outlets*inventory	--	180,000	105,600	72,000
Unit cost	10.73	10.73	10.73	10.73
Cost of capital	0.20	0.20	0.20	0.20
Inventory carry cost: inventory*unit cost*capital	--	386,280	226,618	154,512
Training cost per outlet		100	100	100
Training cost: outlets*training		1,500,000	220,000	75,000
Other fixed costs (website plus phone sales)	100,000	100,000	100,000	100,000
TOTAL FIXED COST: Inventory+training+other	100,000	1,986,280	546,618	329,512
UNIT MARGIN				
Optimal price given channel (Chap 5)	38.06	51.55	51.55	51.55
Total channel markup (multiplier of wholesale price)(Chap 2)	1.00	1.96	1.40	1.40
Revenue per unit sold=price/markup	38.06	26.30	36.82	36.82
Marginal cost (MC)	10.73	10.73	10.73	10.73
Unit selling cost (commission, if any) (SC)	0	0	0	0
Accounts payable cycle (time from shipment to payment)	0	45	45	45
AP carry cost (AP): AP cycle/365*cost of capital*unit cost	0.00	0.26	0.26	0.26
NET UNIT MARGIN = Revenue-MC-SC-AP	27.33	15.31	25.83	25.83
BREAKEVEN VOLUME=Total fixed cost/unit margin	3659	129768	21165	12759
CONTRIBUTION=Expected demand*unit margin ($million)	194	--	1011	1011

*Assumes use of only one firm (the largest) in each channel: chains=Sherwin Williams, superstore=Home Depot

To answer these questions we turn to the results from conjoint analysis. Exhibit 5-4 indicated that the optimal price for distribution through chains was $50. This yields demand of 2.72 rolls and contribution of $67.94 per person in the target market. The Internet has a lower sales forecast—2.45 rolls, at its optimal price of $40, but this is still very healthy demand. The chain/superstore demand advantage is not sufficient to compensate for the order of magnitude difference in break-even sales between chains and the Internet.

The final issue in comparing the distribution channels is the reach. So far we know the break-even volume for each channel, and the average demand for each person through each channel. The total demand for each channel applies the average demand per person with the total people reached by the channel.

Epigraphs Summary

We combine all the above information in Exhibit 6-4 and show the breakeven plot in Exhibit 6-5. The table indicates that the break-even approach yields a different conclusion than the contribution approach. The preferred channel from the break-even analysis is the Internet. The Internet channel breaks even at 3659 rolls, while chains break-even at 29,935 rolls. This is true because the fixed costs of the Internet channel are quite low. In contrast, the preferred channel from the contribution analysis is chains. The expected contribution from chains is $1 billion, while that from the Internet is $0.2 billion. This is because chains have greater reach.

Break-even analysis is the preferred approach if you want to minimize financial risk. Total contribution is the preferred approach if you want to maximize profits. Accordingly our quantitative analysis indicates we should distribute Epigraphs through chains. Qualitative analysis also tends to support that conclusion. Chains have the potential to shift the demand curve, because they cre-

Exhibit 6-5. Break-even and Indifference Volumes for Epigraphs Channels

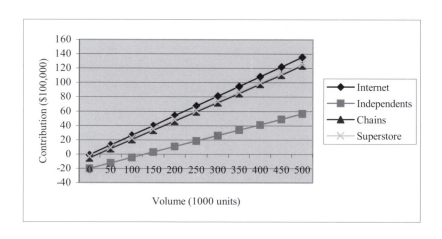

ate awareness (people who hadn't seen Epigraphs advertising, may see the product when they look for wallpaper), and chains also provide experience with the product. Customers can see the real size and texture in context. Thus, we retain the tentative conclusion reached in Chapter 5 regarding chain distribution.

CONCLUSION

This chapter examined the second strategic decision of the new venture—the choice of distribution channel. The distribution channel has a major impact on the venture's ability to realize the potential demand forecasted by conjoint analysis. The distribution channel determines reach—the number of customers who actually have access to the product.

To analyze the decision we took data from Chapter 2 regarding the structure of existing distribution channels and data from Chapter 5 estimating demand within each channel. We introduced two quantitative techniques to compare channels: break-even analysis and total channel contribution. We augmented quantitative analysis with qualitative considerations of channel attractiveness. In particular we evaluated the channels' ability to shift demand, their reversibility, and their potential for customer feedback. We applied these tools to Epigraphs.

The distribution channel decision is one of two decisions affecting the venture's ability to realize potential demand. The second decision affecting realized demand is advertising. We treat that decision in the next chapter.

Appendix 6-1. Channel comparison worksheet

	Channel 1	Channel 2	Channel 3	Channel 4
DEMAND Units per person at optimal price/config (Chap 5) Market size (Chap 2) Reach--total people reached by channel (Chap 2) TOTAL EXPECTED DEMAND: (units*mkt*reach)				
FIXED COST Outlets in channel (Chap 2) Inventory required to fill outlet (Chap 2) Inventory required to fill channel: outlets*inventory Unit cost Cost of capital Inventory carry cost: inventory*unit cost*capital Training cost per outlet Training cost: outlets*training Other fixed costs TOTAL FIXED COST: Inventory+training+other				
UNIT MARGIN Optimal price given channel (Chap 5) Total channel markup (Chap 2) Revenue per unit sold=price/markup Marginal cost (MC) Unit selling cost (commission, if any) (SC) Accounts payable cycle (time from shipment to payment) AP carry cost (AP): cash cycle/365*cost of capital*unit cost NET UNIT MARGIN = Revenue-MC-SC-AP				
BREAKEVEN VOLUME=Total fixed cost/unit margin				
CONTRIBUTION=Expected demand*unit margin				

Plot Channel Indifference

Using an Excel spreadsheet, create sample volume levels in column 1. Choose a channel for column 2. In column 2 insert function: = TOTAL UNIT MARGIN*volume in column 1 – TOTAL FIXED COST. Assign a column for each of the remaining channels. In each of the remaining columns insert the same function, but apply the new UNIT MARGIN and new FIXED COST.

Set column 1 (volume) as the x axis and plot the remaining columns (channels) against it.

notes

[1] For a summary, see: Katz, Michael, L., 1989. "Vertical Contractual Relations" in Richard Schmalensee and Robert Willig (Eds), Handbook of Industrial Organization, Volume 1.

[2] Mossi, J. and H. Stevenson, 1985. "R&R," Harvard Business School Case 9-386-019.

[3] Forrester Research, March 2000

chapter 7

advertising decisions

INTRODUCTION AND GOALS

The advertising program is the third strategic decision in the venture design. The advertising program is the means by which potential customers are made aware of your product. The ultimate goal of the advertising program is to stimulate purchase through a paid program of communication to the target market. The advertising program is designed to make the target market aware and fully informed about the product. The advertising program is the second means (distribution channel being the first) by which firms transform potential demand into realized demand. To realize demand, customers must be aware of the product and its benefits, and must have access to it. Advertising controls awareness, while distribution channel controls availability.

The advertising program is important because it solves a common misperception among entrepreneurs—particularly those with a new innovation, that, "If you build a better mousetrap, the world will beat a path to your door." In essence, these entrepreneurs believe the product will sell itself. This just isn't plausible—customers need to know there is a new mousetrap, and they need to know what makes it more effective than their existing mousetrap.

We are unable to provide enough guidance in a single chapter to develop a complete advertising campaign. In fact, we advocate use of an agency. Our goal rather is to define the principles underlying adoption of new products. We then translate these principles into tools to specify campaign goals, link them to demand implications, specify a budget likely to accomplish those goals, and provide you with enough information to make you a sophisticated buyer of advertising. We end the chapter by specifying the advertising budget and vehicles for Epigraphs.

PRINCIPLES

There are two levels of analysis in research on advertising design and effectiveness. At the micro-level, we are interested in the effort necessary to induce a single customer to purchase the product or service. The theoretical underpinnings at this level are from behavioral psychology. At the macro-level of analysis, we are interested in the impact social structure will have (and how we can take advantage of it) on the rate at which product adoption will move through the population. Here the theoretical underpinnings come from many fields, but are subsumed under the heading "Diffusion of Innovation."[1]

Micro-Level

There are two basic frameworks of interest to advertising from behavioral psychology: response hierarchy models[2] and studies of communication format effectiveness.[3]

Response Hierarchy Models. Response hierarchy models propose that buyers pass through cognitive, affective, and behavioral stages toward purchasing a product. In the AIDA model for example, buyers pass through **A**wareness, **I**nterest, **D**esire, and **A**ction.

In the *awareness* stage, the goal is merely to gain attention for your product amidst the 1500 commercial messages people are exposed to each day. Repeating simple messages is probably the most effective means to accomplishing this. In the *interest* stage, customers move from knowing the product exists, to wanting to know more about how the product meets their needs (holding interest). In the *desire* stage, customers know enough about the product to recognize it to be superior to alternatives—the goal is to arouse desire. In the *action* stage, advertising moves customers with desire toward actual purchase (obtain action). Other versions of the basic model propose that there are sub-stages within these stages. We are less interested in determining exactly how many stages, than we are in surfacing the idea that there is a progression through stages.

The joint contribution of these models is:
1) The insight that even an effective campaign will have delayed impact, since customers are not immediately moved to action.
2) The implication that it may be necessary to create different ads for each of the stages.
3) Accordingly, products in different parts of their life cycle may require different types of campaigns. For entirely new products, a good portion of advertising is devoted merely to generating awareness. In the mature stage, customers are likely aware, and may only need to be reminded of the product.

Knowledge of these models forces firms to be specific about the response sought from the buyers.

Format Effectiveness. Once you have established a response goal, the next issue is how to accomplish it. Here behavioral psychology contributes frameworks that define types of appeals and their effectiveness in achieving desired responses. *Rational appeals* are ones that attempt to educate the customer about the specific benefits of the product: its quality, features, value, and performance. These types of appeals are essential for industrial customers, and for big-ticket consumer purchases. The presumption here is that customers are gathering information and carefully comparing alternatives—thus they want advertising to support their data gathering and analysis. The recent raff of pharmaceuticals ads in the mass media are rational appeals that attempt to educate consumers about the benefits and side effects of ethical drugs—thus making consumers, rather than doctors, the source of primary demand. *Emotional appeals* attempt to stir up negative or positive emotion to stimulate purchase. Automobile ads are typically emotional appeals that try to capture how you will feel driving the car. Similarly DeBeers ads for diamonds are emotional appeals that try to capture wives' reactions to a gift of diamonds. *Moral appeals*, used primarily for social causes and non-profit contribution campaigns, attempt to stimulate the audience's sense of right and wrong to induce action. One example of moral appeals are "The More You Know" ads on NBC featuring stars who convey messages such as "spend more time with your children."

Structure considers issues of conclusion drawing, argument dimensionality, and order of argument presentation. *Conclusion drawing* pertains to whether the message should explicitly draw a conclusion or whether it is better to let the audience do so. Generally, letting the audience do so is more effective,[4] but if there is a chance that they will draw the wrong conclusion, you may want the ad to do so for them. *Argument dimensionality* is the issue of whether to present one-sided or two-sided arguments. Two-sided arguments project greater credibility, and provide an opportunity for you to preempt any arguments that the customer might naturally raise. Accordingly, two-sided arguments may be more compelling. The risk in presenting opposing arguments is that you may introduce shortcomings that the customer would not have considered otherwise. Some of the pharmaceutical ads, for example, seem to raise more concerns over the side effects than interest in the product. The final structure issue, *order of presentation,* considers whether to present the strongest arguments first (to gain attention), or last (to reach a climax toward action).

Macro-level

While the micro-level studies (behavioral psychology) help us understand the behavioral mechanisms involved in stimulating purchase at the individual level, macro-studies (diffusion of innovation) help us understand how individual behavior will aggregate to the population level and unfold over time. The contribution of greatest interest here is the notion that different portions of the population are moved to action by different mechanisms.[5]

In particular, if individuals are arranged in the order in which they adopt an innovation, relative to the time it was introduced, they form a normal distribution as shown in Exhibit 7-1. "Adopter categories" correspond to the deviations from mean adoption time. Individuals who adopt innovations earlier then two standard deviations before mean adoption (μ -2σ) are termed "innovators" (2.5% of the population); those who adopt earlier than one standard deviation are termed "early adopters (13.5%); those who adopt before the mean are "early majority" (34%); those who adopt up to one standard deviation after the mean are "late majority" (34%); and the remaining population is termed, "laggards."

There are a number of characteristics that tend to discriminate between these groups. Innovators tend to have six times the mass media exposure of laggards; they tend to have more education; they tend to communicate with non-local sources to a much higher degree; and tend to have greater wealth (necessary to afford both the volume and higher price of new innovations). While innovators are the earliest adopters, the real opinion leaders fueling the critical mass—the point at which the diffusion process is self-sustaining—are the early adopters. Innovators are often considered to be outliers—both behaviorally and socially. Their willingness to try anything leads others to discount their opinions, and their limited connections with local social networks minimize the interpersonal inter-action fueling diffusion.

Exhibit 7-1. Adopter categories

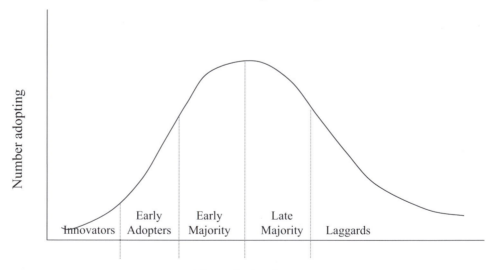

Reprinted with permission of The Free Press, a division of Simon and Schuster, Inc. from "Diffusion of Innovations," Fourth Edition by Everett M. Rogers. Copyright © 1995 by Everett M. Rogers. Copyright © 1962, 1971, 1983 by The Free Press.

In contrast, early adopters are perceived to use greater discretion in adopting new products, and are more integrated in the local social system. Thus their opinions are both valued and accessible. Early adopters are the role models for the remainder of the population. Their example and word-of-mouth stimulates action by others.

These early use and personal influence mechanisms carry the greatest weight when the product is expensive and purchased infrequently. Here, buyers will consult with trusted sources that they know to have superior information. Personal influence is also critical in products with substantial social character—those that convey status or taste. Here, customers will tend to imitate those whose tastes they admire. The implication, then, is that early appeals in mass media should target opinion leaders rather than the population at large. Note that publicity (unpaid ads incorporated in news and magazine articles) is particularly effective here. Publicity follows similar principles to advertising, but conveys greater credibility, because information about the product is implicitly endorsed by the given vehicle (publisher or station). While we don't treat publicity in this book, we highly recommend a public relations campaign as a companion to the advertising campaign. A good ad agency ought to provide these services as part of the total communications package. Once early campaigns have stimulated purchase by innovators and early adoptors, later campaigns can take advantage of these opinion leaders to stimulate imitative adoption in the remaining population.

The second contribution of diffusion literature is quantitative tools to forecast the rate and extent of diffusion of product adoption. We will discuss these models in greater detail in Chapter 8, Demand Forecasting, however, we discuss the Bass Diffusion Model here because of its specific link to advertising. The Bass Diffusion Model[6] marked the beginning of marketing contributions to the diffusion literature. The intent of the model was to forecast the diffusion of new consumer products as a function of advertising policy.

The model is particularly interesting because of its comprehensive consideration of diffusion phenomena. In particular, the model decomposes diffusion into mass media influence (p), as well as interpersonal influence (q). Studies that have empirically examined diffusion using the Bass Model have found that the coefficient for interpersonal influence is 12 times that for mass media influence.[7] While this would tend to suggest the futility of advertising, mass media influence precedes and initiates interpersonal influence (as shown in Exhibit 7-2). Thus advertising is crucial.

A variant of the Bass model tailored to sales and advertising expenditure[8] models sales, S, as a function of advertising expenditure, A, an advertising response constant, R, saturation level of sales, M, and a decay constant, λ.

$$dS/dt = rA\,[(M-S)/M] - \lambda S$$

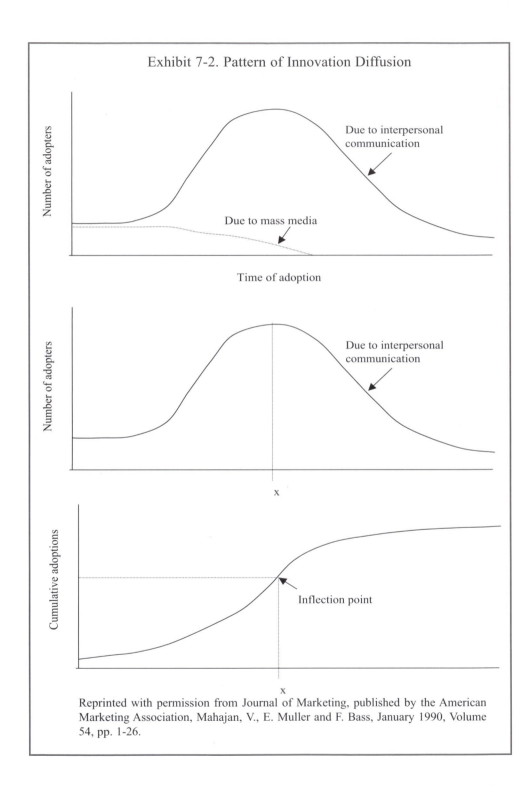

Exhibit 7-2. Pattern of Innovation Diffusion

Number of adopters

Due to interpersonal communication

Due to mass media

Time of adoption

Number of adopters

Due to interpersonal communication

x

Cumulative adoptions

Inflection point

x

Reprinted with permission from Journal of Marketing, published by the American Marketing Association, Mahajan, V., E. Muller and F. Bass, January 1990, Volume 54, pp. 1-26.

where:

	S	is sales in period t
	A	is advertising expenditure in period t
	r	is sales response consant (dS/dt at time 0)
	M	is saturation level of sales
	λ	is sales decay constant (fraction sales lost when A=0)

The basic intuition of the model is that advertising costs grow exponentially with sales: this obtains quantitatively because as the sales base grows, so too does the cost to maintain those sales (λ). This occurs in practice for the same reason, but also because the laggards are intrinsically those individuals who are either hard to reach, or for whom the product holds little utility.

We demonstrate use of the model via example. Assume conjoint analysis indicates that potential sales are $10 million sales. Assume also that sales response in year 0 was 5 (each dollar of advertising produced $5 of sales), sales in year 3 are $4 million, and sales decay by 10% in the absence of advertising. Given this information, we can forecast year 4 sales as a function of advertising expenditures:

$$dS = 5\ A * [(10,000,000 - 4,000,000)/10,000,000] - .10 * 4,000,000$$
$$dS = 3A - 400,000$$

Thus, I need to spend $133,000 in advertising merely to maintain current sales (400,000/3). Further, each additional sale costs 65% more than the first sale (5A/3A). This is pretty dismal. However, the most frustrating problem as a new venture, is that while we know M ($10 million) from conjoint, we don't know r or λ.

This leads nicely to the applied discussion. Before doing so, we would like to reiterate the conclusions we draw from the foundation literature:
1) A single advertising message does not fit all individuals
2) A single message does not fit all stages of the AIDA process even for a single individual.

Thus at any given time, you may need to send separate messages to separate audiences. Exhibit 7-3 is an effort to convey the idea that during most periods you will be appealing simultaneously to different groups with different messages. While the exhibit is discrete for purposes of clarity, the distribution of adopters is actually continuous. Thus, so is the distribution of needed messages.

The implications from the exhibit are that messages and media will vary over the product life cycle. The introduction stage calls for rational, information intensive advertising in fairly exclusive vehicles (high income/education demo-

Exhibit 7-3. Message cascading

	Time ->											
Innovators	Aware	Interest	Desire	Action								
Early Adopters					Aware	Interest	Desire	Action				
Early Majority									Aware	Interest	Desire	Action
Late Majority										Aware	Interest	Desire	Action
Laggards											Aware	Interest	Desire	Action

graphics) matched to the product characteristics. Such advertising stimulates awareness, interest, desire, and action for innovators in the product category. As innovators begin purchasing the product, campaigns expand into broader media with messages that may relax information intensity. These campaigns may feature testimonials by early adopters.

Fortunately, technology and deregulation trends have fostered the growth of highly targeted advertising vehicles in magazines, radio, and cable television. These media are not only more efficient than mass media (in that you can send separate messages to separate audiences), but they are also less expensive on an absolute basis, because the audiences of each vehicle are smaller than those for mass media. Thus you aren't wasting money advertising to customers who aren't in the target market.

DEVELOPING THE ADVERTISING PLAN

The key elements of the advertising plan are identifying the target audience, determining the communication objectives, designing the message, selecting the advertising channels, and establishing the budget. We discuss each of these in turn.

Identifying the target audience.

The broadest definition of the target audience is the set of customers who are potentially interested in your product/service at some price. This is the audience that you sampled to develop the perceptual map (focus group) as well as the demand curve (conjoint analysis).

This broad specification is refined passively by information obtained via from the survey (segments of the target who have no interest in your product). The target is also refined actively, when you make pricing, product configuration, and distribution decisions that exclude further segments of the target.

It may help to clarify the distinctions by way of example. Imagine I have developed a noise cancellation system that replaces an automobile muffler. The advantages of this product are 1) that it is more effective than the muffler in reducing engine noise, 2) it reduces the cost to operate the automobile, because the muffler consumes fuel, and 3) it reduces pollution (again because it does not consume fuel). Assume I am only interested in the aftermarket for the system (since I have struck separate arrangements with each of the automobile manufacturers for new automobiles). The broadest definition of the target market is all U.S. registered automobiles: roughly, 130 million vehicles.

Conjoint analysis reveals that people are not interested in purchasing the system for automobiles older than 5 years. Even though consumer breakeven for the system (dollars saved in fuel consumption versus nominal cost of the system and installation) is estimated at 12,000 miles, consumers appear unwilling to make sunk investments in cars that they don't plan on driving much longer. Thus, the passive refinement of the target market yields an estimate of 45 million vehicles (shrinking over time, as existing cars age further, and new cars come factory-equipped with the system). Finally, active refinement of the target market, based on choice of optimal price, excludes 50% of the prior market— leaving a potential market of 22 million vehicles. Fortunately the conjoint analysis provides demographic characterization of a) people likely to have cars 0-5 years old (versus older or newer cars), and b) people willing to pay at least the optimal price. Thus we know not only *how* large the target market is, but more importantly, we have insight on *who* it is.

Determining communication objectives

The communication objectives pertain to the desired advertising outcome. While ultimately the objective is to move the entire potential market to purchase, this objective is not reached immediately. The communication objectives specifically address the cascading in Exhibit 7-3, where separate messages are sent to distinct adopter categories, and where each adopter category is moved at different points in time through the response hierarchy. For example, in the first time period in Exhibit 7-3, the communication objective is merely to make innovators aware of the product. In the second period, there are two objectives: generating product interest among innovators, and creating awareness among early adopters. Within these qualitative objectives are quantitative objectives regarding how many innovators and early adopters to reach.

Designing the message

As mentioned previously, the actual message design is outside the scope of the book. We strongly recommend the use of an advertising agency for message design and copy execution. In general (at least in the past), the services of advertising agencies were included in the cost of the advertising through the commission paid to them by the advertising vehicles. Thus, these services are "free" to the advertiser, and are certain to be of higher quality than ads you can produce yourself. Having said that, there will be differences across agencies, and therefore you will want to be an educated customer of their services.[9] Thus we will touch on message basics. We also recommend the book, "Guerilla Marketing",[10] for a good hands-on guide to some of these design issues.

The message itself has four elements: content (what to say), structure (how to say it logically), format (how to say it symbolically—the actual copy), and source (who should say it). We will discuss content and structure briefly, but ignore format and source, since they are in the details of the message design.

The most important component of the message *content* is the core benefit proposition that emerges from the focus group, and is refined by conjoint analysis. In addition, content pertains to the type of appeal: rational, emotional, or moral. We discussed these types of appeals previously. Rational appeals convey the message that the product will produce the claimed benefits; emotional appeals attempt to stir up emotion to motivate purchase; and moral appeals (a variant of emotional appeals) stir up a sense of civic responsibility to induce a desired action. Knowledge of your product, and the response it engenders in the audience (obtained from focus group and qualitative comments in the survey) will help you determine which of these appeals is best suited to your product for each of the audience segments.

Selecting Advertising Media and Vehicles

In our discussion of diffusion models we drew the distinction between mass media channels and personal channels of communication. Personal communication refers to advocates (sales people), experts (independent persons with expertise), and social channels (word-of-mouth). Personal communication as an "advertising" medium is most effective for the population at large, when the product is expensive, risky or purchased infrequently (where there is high information seeking), or when the product has significant social character—when it implies status or taste.

Mass media channels are those typically associated with advertising. These include print (newspapers, magazines), broadcast (radio, TV), display (billboards, signs) and now Internet. There is no "best medium." Each medium has characteristics that make it attractive for some product advertising, and less attractive for other products. Exhibit 7-4 is an effort to summarize these qualitative differences, as well as cost and reach differences.

Mass media are critical in reaching innovators and early adopters, since this is their main source of information on new products. These opinion leaders can then stimulate communication to the later adopters. While it is easiest for advertisers to control mass media channels to reach early adopters, there are things a firm can do to stimulate personal channels to reach later adopters. They can create opinion leaders by supplying certain people with the product on attractive

Exhibit 7-4. Comparison of media characteristics

Medium	Pene-tration	Segment	Ad cost	Audience 1000	CPM $	Total $billion	Advantages	Limitations
TV	1.0		30 sec			29.4	High attention	High cost
		ABC Daytime (10:00-16:30)	12724	4341	2.93		High reach	High clutter
		ABC Primetime (20:00-23:00)	102428	11095	9.23		Most capable of	Fleeting exposure
		CBS Daytime	6984	2910	2.41		capturing full	New technology
		CBS Primetime	105648	11844	8.92		product experience:	blocking commer-
		NBC Daytime	11857	2731	4.34		3D color, plus time	cials
		NBC Primetime	64931	8739	7.43			
Radio	95.1		60 sec			8.7	High geographic	Audio only
		AM Drive (6:00-10:00)	510	175	2.91		targeting	Lower attention
		Daytime (10:00-15:00)	405	155	2.61		Timeliness (suitable	than TV
		PM Drive (15:00-19:00)	470	135	3.48		for one day events)	Fleeting exposure
Cable TV	61.5		30 sec	Subscribers		3.9	All benefits of TV	High clutter
		CNN	1300	61738			but at lower cost	Fleeting exposure
		ESPN	2400	61600			High demographic	New technology
		USA	1700	60046			targeting	blocking commer-cials
Newspaper	64.5		1pg B&W	Circulation		30.7	High geographic	Short life
		Wall Street Journal	114605	1795			targeting	Poor reproduction
		USA Today	57505	1506			Timeliness (suitable	Black and white
		NY Times	53298	1146			for one day events)	
		Philadelphia Inquirer	18525	695			Air of credibility	
							Dwell time	
Magazines	3335 consumer		1 pg 4color			7.0	High geographic	Long lead purchase
	7015 trade	TV Guide	119500	14919			and demographic	No position
		Time	142500	4160			targeting	guarantee
		Better Homes and Gardens	143000	8002			Good reproduction	
		Sports Illustrated	134620	3432			Long life	
							Pass-along audience	
							Credibility/prestige	
Cinema	6500 theatres		4 week run				High geographic	High cost per CPM
			800,000	47000	20		and demographic	
							targeting	
							High attention	
Outdoor	84% exposure		month			29.1	High repeat exposure	No demographic
		12 X 25	567				Low cost	targeting
		14 X 48	2315				Geographic targeting	
Direct Mail					1000	23.4	High targeting	High cost
Internet								
TOTAL						129.3		

All cost, audience data from Leo Burnett, Worldwide Advertising and Media Factbook 1993
qualitative comparisons from Kotler, Marketing Management

189

terms. It is quite common for manufacturers of sporting goods to sponsor athletes so that they will endorse the product. In fact, many athletes make more money from endorsements than they do from actual play. Tiger Woods, in 1999, for example, made $6.9 million from golf purses, but earned approximately $20 million per year from endorsements.

Within each mass medium there are thousands of specific advertising vehicles. For example, there are over 3000 consumer magazines, and 7000 trade magazines. The goal in choosing a specific vehicle is to find the most cost effective way to deliver the desired exposures to the target audience. Cost effectiveness is a function of the reach of a given vehicle (number of persons exposed to the medium during a given period), the frequency (the number of times a given person is exposed to the medium during the same period), and the impact (the value of an exposure for that product in that medium). While reach and frequency are characteristics of the vehicle itself, impact is a function of the match between the product and the vehicle. Exhibit 7-4 includes a comparison of several representative publications to provide a sense of how cost varies with vehicle characteristics.

Media choice to achieve the highest impact is based on audience quality, characteristics of the advertising vehicle, product characteristics, the message, and cost.

With respect to the *audience quality*, the issue is exposure value (the portion of the audience that is in the target market). Since advertising pricing is based on audience size (cost per thousand—CPM), the amount you pay per person in the target audience is a function of the alignment between your target and the vehicles audience. Modern Maturity, for example, is a cost effective means to reach a large portion of the US population. It has paid circulation of 22 million readers and a 1/3 page ad has a CPM of $9.50 (versus a range of $7.00 to $400). If you are selling health insurance this is probably a great place to advertise, but if you are selling birth control, you have wasted $90,000. There are a number of good means to identify vehicles that are aligned with the target market. From secondary research, Simmons Marketing Research Bureau[11] and MediaMark[12] cross-match product categories and media habits. In your primary research, we recommend asking focus group interviewees as well as survey respondents their media habits, as well as their sources for information on new products.

The main characteristics of the *advertising vehicle* that affect advertising impact are attention probability and editorial quality. Attention probability is the likelihood that the audience will pay attention to your ad versus the 1500 other communications they see each day. Editorial quality affects how they will interpret the ad, given that they have paid attention to it. Radio spots during rush hour have high attention probability because the drivers are captive. While drivers could channel surf to avoid ads, doing so increases the stress of rush hour driving. If the radio spot airs on the Kevin and Bean show on KROQ in Los Angeles, and better yet, Kevin and Bean produce the ad, and it pertains to new music, then the ad not only is attended to, but is interpreted as being credible by the show's audience.

With respect to *product* characteristics, the issues are how to best convey information about the product. If the product requires demonstration, you will need to utilize visual media—most likely television. If the product requires explanation, you may need print media, so that audience can take time to read through all the details.

Characteristics of the *message* also constrain choice of vehicle, most notably through timing. If, for example, you are advertising a one-day sale, the most effective vehicles are dailies (ones with daily frequency), such as newspaper or television.

Establishing the advertising budget.

There are two basic approaches to establishing an advertising budget: rules of thumb and goal-oriented. Until the days of e-tailing, rules of thumb methods were probably most common.

Generally, rules of thumb establish advertising budgets on a percentage of sales (advertising intensity) basis. While such an approach seems backward in that it ignores opportunity, and nonsensical for startups with zero sales, rules of thumb approaches are supported by reasonable logic. Generally, industries are characterized by fairly consistent advertising intensities across firms. These intensities reflect collective wisdom on the amount of advertising required to generate a given level of sales. Accordingly, advertising intensities provide focal points that lead to stable advertising equilibria in an industry. Many industries are best characterized as zero-sum games, in which any sales increase I achieve comes at a competitor's expense. In such settings, increases in advertising, aimed at increasing market share, can lead to advertising wars that are harmful to the industry in that they increase total spending without increasing sales.[13] Even in cases where the increased spending results in higher share, generally the cost to increase market share equals the net present value of the increased profits associated with the increased share.[14] Thus, rules of thumb are not a bad way to go. Even if you use a goal-oriented approach, you should compare your resultant advertising intensity with those in the industry (available in industry ratio studies).[15] The approach we advocate here, and the approach that characterizes advertising by e-tailers, is a goal-oriented approach. Here we take the objectives defined in step 2, determine the advertising needed to accomplish those goals, and estimate the costs to conduct that advertising.

Remember that our goal for the noise cancellation system was 22 million units from the target audience of 45 million car owners with automobiles that are 0 to 5 years old. The first issue is choosing a cost-effective advertising vehicle that reaches these 22 million people. *Car and Driver*, while offering a good editorial match with the product only reaches 1 million people. For the moment however, assume that there is such a magazine and that the CPM for a 1/3 page ad is $45.00 (about average).

Trial, for those likely to respond, is induced by three "attention episodes."[16] The first episode creates awareness, the second stimulates response, and the third either causes the audience to engage or withdraw. Not all exposures produce attention episodes. In order to compensate for failure to gain attention and/or forgetting between episodes, you may need three or more exposures to gain one attention episode. Accordingly, a good budgeting estimate is that you will need 9 exposures per member of the target audience to induce purchase.

Thus the total budget would be:

audience size/1000 * (CPM)* 9 exposures

In our noise cancellation system example, this would be:

22,000,000/1000* $45.00* 9 = $8.9 million

It is likely that the true cost would be much higher, because it is unlikely that there is an advertising vehicle perfectly matched to the target audience (or a set of vehicles combined that perfectly matches the target audience without overlap). In practice, you would need to identify the specific vehicles before establishing the budget.

EPIGRAPHS ADVERTISING PLAN

Identifying the target audience

We identified the broadest target market for wallcovering as the 67 million owner-occupied households. American Marketplace reports peak household textile use among households as married couples, age 45-54, with annual incomes in excess of $70,000. Our market survey confirms these basic trends for Epigraphs' demand. However, we find that demand peaks at incomes of $100,000-$150,000.

Determining communication objectives

Ultimately our objective is to induce purchase in the entire market. Before discussing more specific objectives, it is worth commenting on some idiosyncrasies of the wallcovering market. First, sales are "skewed left." An average wallpaper pattern sells 7 million single rolls over a 3 year life. Sixty percent of the rolls are sold within the first year, as shown in Exhibit 7-5 (same as Exhibit

2-7). Second, ratio studies of the industry indicate that advertising intensity is less than 1%. Thus, a wallpaper manufacturer with first year sales forecast of $75 million at wholesale ($105 million retail) only spends $750,000 on advertising. The low level of advertising, as well as the fact that sales peak early (antithetical to the slow diffusion associated with the AIDA process), tend to suggest that advertising is a relatively unimportant component in the communication process. It appears, rather, that 20-25% of homeowners decide to purchase wallcovering each year irrespective of advertising, and *then* shop among patterns. In fact, our survey data (Exhibit 4-9) indicate that store displays are the second most prominent source of ideas (magazines being first).

An additional issue, raised in the focus groups is that consumers seek uniqueness in their décor. To the extent that customers repeatedly see a wallcovering in advertisements, they may reject it as something that is no longer unique. The skewed three year life cycle corroborates the importance of uniqueness—a wallcovering's greatest sales occur when it is new and unique, and then diminish as it becomes more common.

The implications for advertising in this context are first, that ads at most play an attention/interest role. The final stages of the AIDA process occur at the retailer, where the consumer makes on-site comparisons of wallcovering alter-

Exhibit 7-5. Profile of wallcovering sales over time

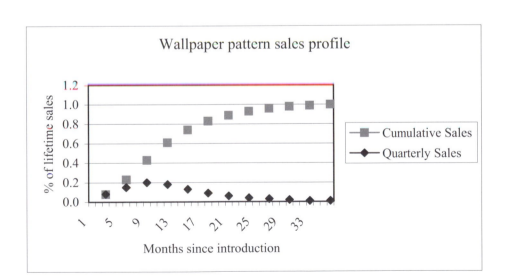

natives. Second, and more importantly, any advertising beyond that point may truncate sales by overexposing the product and eliminating its novelty. Thus wallcovering by nature, rather than strategic choice, is a low advertising-intensive industry.

If we examine the wallcovering life-cycle (Exhibit 7-5) once again, we see that demand peaks in Quarter 3. We recommend advertising to create awareness only until the product reaches critical mass in that quarter, and rely on interpersonal influence (including the retailer) thereafter. We can revisit this tentative decision at the critical mass point.

Designing the message

While we will leave the structure, format, and source decisions of message design to an ad agency, we need to supply the content. The content of the message is the core benefit proposition that emerged in the focus group and was confirmed by conjoint results. The proposition is a whimsical wallcovering with the versatility and uniqueness of custom finishes (faux, stenciling), with greater durability, and easier installation than wallpaper.

One interesting observation with respect to the message is that we have already pre-tested a preliminary message in the product literature sheet that we distributed with the conjoint survey. The relatively high potential demand suggests that in general we have compelling ad copy. However, a review of the qualitative comments about the product suggests that we created a misperception regarding the quotes. People seemed to believe that they would be reading a single quote over and over rather that 50 feet of different quotes. Thus the product literature sheet is a valuable opportunity to examine both the core benefit proposition and the effectiveness of the ad copy in communicating that proposition.

Selecting the advertising media and vehicles

MediaMark[17] identified the main demographics and media habits tied to remodeling. These are listed in Exhibit 7-6. While the Audit Bureau of Circulations (www.accessabc.com) maintains data on circulations and audience demographics for these vehicles, the data are only available to ABC members. The next best reference is SRDS.[18] SRDS provides rate information for every advertising vehicle (organized in volumes by medium, and then within medium by genre). Thus, we can compare rates but not audience demographics. To get demographics we requested media kits from the vehicles we felt (from personal experience) would be most attractive. Exhibit 7-7 is a brief overview of the major "home service and home" vehicles identified by SRDS.

Media kits provide information on circulation, detailed audience demographics, audience media habits and spending habits, editorial content, advertising rates, and any advertising format requirements. Media kits for print media usu-

Exhibit 7-6. Demographics and media habits of remodelers

Education			Radio formats	Adult contemporary	118
Education	BS	124	Radio formats	Adult contemporary	118
	Some college	125		All news	68
	HS diploma	89		Prog rock	123
	< HS diploma	62		Classic rock	143
				Easy listening	171
Age	18-24	74		Golden oldies	124
	25-34	118		Soft contemporary	152
	35-44	151			
	45-54	111	Internet	AOL	185
	55-64	74		Compuserv	161
	>64	36		Prodigy	150
Income	>75000	132	Cable TV	CNN	113
	60-75000	144		Discovery	119
	50-59999	136		ESPN2	109
	40-49999	147		Nickolodeon	121
	30-39999	113		TBS	109
	20-29999	70		TLC	119
	10-19999	53		VH1	145
	<10000	27		Weather	114
				AMC	51
Region	Northeast	118		Court TV	60
	North Central	119			
	South	78	Correlated hobbies	Fashion clothing	241
	West	98		Fine art/antiques	236
				Real Estate	185
Marital Status	Single	65		Fine Arts	180
	Married	126		Gourmet food	177
	Other	60		Collectibles	174
	Parent	139		Self-improvement	173
	Working parent	150		Moneymaking	172
				National Heritage	170
				Health Foods	168
				Community/civic activities	167

Mediamark Research: Household and Personal, Appliances, Etc, Spring 1995

Base: All Households	98529000
Remodel other rooms	3997000

Interpretation of index: Household rate of participation relative to average US household rate (100)

Exhibit 7-7. Comparison of wallcovering vehicle characteristics

Magazine	Circulation	1 pg B&W	1/3 pg color	1 pg color	CPM 1pg color
Architectural Digest	818,185	43510	30130	60270	7.37
Better Homes & Gardens	7616114	190900	111600	231100	3.03
Elle Décor	436634	26500	19400	35400	8.11
Home	1024238	42800	27100	56400	5.51
House & Garden	580864	31200	22060	45640	7.86
House Beautiful	864585	38260	24730	56170	6.50
Martha Stewart Living	2235723	71957	46258	102795	4.60
Metropolitan Home	602505	38600	23800	51700	8.58
Sunset	1464559	44100	26800	61200	4.18
Traditional Home	812823	39190	30827	53070	6.53

SRDS Consumer Magazine Advertising Source, January 1999

Home service and home (selected magazines)

ally include copies of the publication, so that you can get a first hand sense of the editorial content and tone.

Exhibit 7-8 summarizes circulation, demographic, and rate information for the media kits we received. In general, the demographics are comparable across the vehicles: the audience is predominately female, 40-45 years old, median household income of $50,00-$60,000, and 80% home ownership. Aside from advertising reach and cost, which we discuss in a moment, the main feature discriminating these vehicles is "% medium devoted to home furnishings." Here HGTV (broadcast media), and *House Beautiful* (print media) dominate *Living* and *Better Homes & Gardens*. This distinction is evident in comparing samples of the print media— *Living* primarily focuses on crafts/entertaining, and *Better Homes & Gardens* deals broadly with house, family life, and gardening in addition to home furnishings. Thus, *House Beautiful* and HGTV are a better match to the product—the audience is more conditioned to respond to home furnishings advertisements.

One of the interesting features of media kits is that they are "advertising to advertisers". Thus the vehicles conduct their own audience studies in an effort to distinguish themselves from other similar vehicles. *House Beautiful*, for example, did a set of interesting studies that compared spending generated by their magazine with that of competing magazines. In addition, they created a perceptual map (Exhibit 7-9) of the competitors (which we applaud). The per-

Exhibit 7-8. Demographics and rates from selected media kits
of wallcovering vehicles

	Living	BH&G	HB	HGTV
Audience size	9,634,000	7,600,000	6,555,000	1,140,000
Female	87%	78%	84.10%	66%
Age (Median)	40.8	44.1	46.1	45
HHI (Median)	$60,146	$48,688	$53,524	$55,000
Married	65%	66.00%	64.50%	
Children (% of households)		45.60%	39.50%	
Own Residence	76%	79.00%	80.80%	
1/3 page color ad*	$48,571	$120,600	$81,260	$1,500
Focus (% medium on home furnishings)	25%	25.90%	100%	100%
Cost/million	$5,041.62	$15,868.42	$12,396.64	$1,315.79

ceptual map brought clarity to intuitions we had about the distinctions between the editorial focus of the various "shelter" magazines. The map confirmed that the magazine offering the best match for Epigraphs was *Home*, which is unfortunate since its audience is only one million households. We next consider reach and advertising cost as part of the advertising budget.

Establishing the advertising budget

Our goal is to reach the 15 million homeowners who purchase wallcovering in a given year. Because we don't want to destroy product uniqueness through over-exposure, we only want to achieve awareness/interest through advertising—thus only one or two attention episodes per target member. Assuming failure to gain attention in some episodes, but no forgetting between episodes, we estimate two exposures per attention episode. Thus total, exposures per target is (1 to 2) * 2 = 2 to 4.

A third page color ad in *House Beautiful* costs $37,405 and reaches an audience of 880,206. This yields a CPM (cost per thousand) of $42.69. This is the highest CPM of all the vehicles. It is three times the CPM of *Better Homes and Gardens*, and twice that of *Living*. In contrast, a 30 second spot on HGTV is only $1500 and reaches an audience of 1,140,000. Thus, you could purchase 24 spots on HGTV, and reach a larger audience with more exposures. Additionally, HGTV offers the opportunity for more focused targeting than *House Beautiful*—each show has a particular topic. Thus Epigraphs, ads could be aired during shows having to do with wallcoverings, or do-it-yourself projects, rather than gardening.

HGTV appears to be the most cost-effective means to reach the target. While each show has only 1.1 million viewers, the total subscribers to the channel is 55

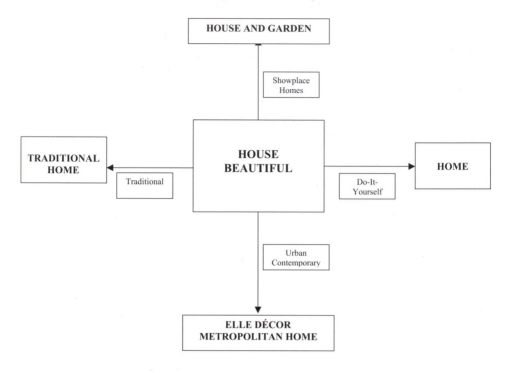

Exhibit 7-9. Perceptual map of home decorating magazines done by *House Beautiful*

million. Thus, there is the possibility of reaching the entire target. If so, the total advertising budget would be:

10 million target market/1.1 million viewers per show = 9 shows

9 shows * $1500 per show * 3 exposures on each show = $40,500

One caveat is that our primary research indicates that magazines outrank television by a factor of 2:1 as a source of decorating ideas. Thus, we plan to augment HGTV advertising with print advertising in three issues of *Home*:

3 issues * $27,000 per 1/3 page color ad = $81,000.

Summary

Thus, the tentative advertising program for Epigraphs is to place 27 spots on HGTV. This comprises 3 spots each across 9 different weekly shows in an effort to reach all 10-million people in the target market. In addition, we will place 3 1/3 page color advertisements in *Home*.

The timing of this advertising is shown in Exhibit 7-10. The advertising will be concentrated in the first three months following introduction. The televisions spots will occur at a rate of roughly three per week. The print ads will be placed in each of the first three months. This is a tentative program. Response to first month advertising will provide an indication how best to manage the remaining two months.

The cost of the program is $40,500 for HGTV and $81,000 for *Home Magazine*, for a total of $121,500. As a test of reasonableness of this budget, we examine advertising intensity. Combining advertising expenditures of $121,500 with forecasted first year sales of $29.9 million at wholesale yields an advertising intensity of 0.4%. This is comparable with an industry average of less than 1%.

CONCLUSION

This chapter examined the third strategic decision of the new venture—the advertising program. The product configuration, advertising, and distribution decisions jointly determine how much of the potential demand from conjoint analysis is actually realized. All three strategic decisions assess the marginal value of appealing to less attractive portions of the target market.

In the case of the price and product configuration decisions, "less attractive" was defined as portions of the market with lower values for the product; in the distribution decision "less attractive" meant harder to access physically; and in the advertising decision "less attractive" meant harder to access through media. Thus, the product and pricing decisions exclude customers with low reservation prices and obscure preferences; the distribution decision excludes customers that are hard to reach; and the advertising decision excludes customers with obscure media habits.

Exhibit 7-10.   Epigraphs Advertising Program

	Week 1	Week 2	Week 3	Week 4	Week 5	Week 6	Week 7	Week 8	Week 9	Week 10	Week 11
HGTV											
Show 1	x	x	x								
Show 2		x	x	x							
Show 3			x	x	x						
Show 4				x	x	x					
Show 5					x	x	x				
Show 6						x	x	x			
Show 7							x	x	x		
Show 8								x	x	x	
Show 9									x	x	x
Home Magazine	x				x				x		
Total Cost	$28,500	$ 3,000	$ 4,500	$ 4,500	$31,500	$ 4,500	$ 4,500	$ 4,500	$31,500	$ 3,000	$ 1,500

To analyze the advertising decision, we combined audience data from various vehicles with ancillary data from the conjoint survey. We chose vehicles that cover the target market cost-effectively. While we didn't provide details sufficient to design an advertising campaign, we did provide enough background to make the entrepreneur a sophisticated advertising customer.

In the next chapter, we combine all the strategic decisions to develop a dynamic forecast for venture sales.

Appendix 7-1
Advertising Decision Worksheet

1. Identifying the target audience

Since chapter 2 you have been working with a definition of who the target audience is. In Chapter 2, the definition is broad--all possible individuals /households /firms with potential need for your product/service. As we progressed through focus groups and conjoint analysis, we found that some portions of the market are not worth pursuing (less heavy use, too costly too reach, willingness to pay is below optimal price).

    Who is your target audience?

    How large is it?

2. Determining communication objectives

a) What is the average advertising/promotion intensity in your industry ($ad/$sales)?

A good source for this is LNA/Media Watch (Lippincott reference desk). They have advertising expenditures for each firm, by product line.

b) What is the relative emphasis you need to place on awareness, interest, desire, and action? Take into account the maturity of the industry.

3. Designing the message

What is your core benefit proposition—What is the unmet need that surfaced in focus groups that you will be able to satisfy?

4. Selecting the advertising media and vehicles

If you have not already done so, and your product/service is consumer-based, you should consult Mediamark Research(a hard copy is at the reference desk in Lippincott). Mediamark Research characterizes consumers by a seemingly infinite number of buying behaviors, and matches that to demographics, psychographics, and media habits. Summarize this for your product/service using Exhibit 7-7 as a guide.

    If your product/service serves a commercial market, then psychographics are not useful, but you will want to characterize firms by their size, and will want to identify the major journals, trade shows, and associations in the industry. You will also want to know what % of firms in the industry participate in each of these.

Attribute	Category	Index	Medium	Formats	Index
Education	BS		Radio formats		
	Some college				
	HS diploma				
	< HS diploma				
Age	18-24				
	25-34				
	35-44				
	45-54		Internet	AOL	
	55-64			Compuserv	
	>64			Prodigy	
Income	>75000		Cable TV		
	60-75000				
	50-59999				
	40-49999				
	30-39999				
	20-29999				
	10-19999				
	<10000				
Region	Northeast				
	North Central				
	South		Correlated hobbies		
	West				
Marital Status	Single				
	Married				
	Other				
	Parent				
	Working parent				

b) Once you have identified candidate advertising vehicles, you need to characterize them by demographics, reach, and cost (see Exhibit 7-8). This cost and reach data is available from SRDS for both consumer and trade magazines (Lippincott reference desk).

Magazine	Circulation 1 pg B&W	1/3 pg color	1 pg color	CPM 1pg color

Do an equivalent characterization for any non-media promotion you are considering, e.g.,
Trade shows (identify each, and define cost and attendance)
Direct mail (identify mailing list, and cost to obtain)

5. Establishing the advertising budget
The advertising budget is merely the sum of the number of exposures times the cost per exposure for all advertising/promotion that you are implementing. As a rule of thumb, three attention episodes are generally required to achieve purchase. Note that in crowded media, it may take 3 exposures to achieve an attention episode

Ad/ promo vehicle	Audience size	Number of exposures	Cost per exposure	Total cost

When planning your media, take into account redundancies between vehicles. For example the audience of a CBS show at 10 on Wednesday, has no overlap with an ABC show at 10 Wednesday. Thus if you advertise on both shows, you have doubled the audience, but not the exposures. In contrast, if you advertise on *Law and Order* and in *Time*, and if 60% of people who watch *Law and Order* read *Time*, then your total audience is less than their sum, but you gain more exposures per person in the audience.

As a check, compare your total advertising expenditures with your sales forecast, to determine your advertising intensity.

First year advertising intensity = $\dfrac{\text{planned ad \$}}{\text{Sales forecast}}$ =

How does this compare to the industry?

notes

1   Rogers, Everett M. 1995. "Diffusion of Innovations," New York: The Free Press

2   Strong, E. K., 1925. "The Psychology of Selling," New York: McGraw-Hill.

3   Hovland, Carl I., A.A. Lumsdaine and F. D. Sheffield, 1948. "Experiments on Mass Communication," Princeton, N.J.: Princeton University Press.

4   Hovlad, Carl I. and Wallace Mandell, 1952. "An Experimental Comparison of Conclusion-Drawing by the Communication and by the Audience," Journal of Abnormal and Social Psychology, July, pp. 581-588.

5   Rogers (op cit), Durstmann & Borda, 1962.

6   Bass, Frank, 1969. "A New Product Growth Model for Consumer Durables," Management Science, 15 (5), pp. 215-227.

7   Sultan, F., J. Farley and D. Lehmann, 1990. A Meta-Analysis of Applications of Diffusion Models, Journal of Marketing Research, 2, pp. 70-77.

8   Vidale, M.L. and H.B. Wolfe, 1957. "An Operations-Research Study of Sales Response to Advertising," Operations Research, June, pp. 370-381.

9   The best means to select an agency is to collect ads that appeal to you, and contact the advertiser to see what agency they use. The agencies used by major advertisers are identified in AdWeek and Advertising Age.

10 Levinson, Jay and Seth Godin, 1994. "The Guerilla Marketing Handbook," New York: Houghton-Mifflin Company.

11 Simmons Marketing Research Bureau.

12 MediaMark.

13 Schmalensee, Richard, 1972. "The Economics of Advertising," Amsterdam: North-Holland.

14 Rumelt, Richard P. and Robin Wensley, 1981. "In Search of the Market Share Effect," Academy of Management Proceedings.

15 See for example: Robert Morris Associates (1923-present) "RMA Annual Statement Studies," Philadelphia: Robert Morris Associates; Dun & Bradstreet, Inc. (several years) "Dun & Bradstreet's Key Business Ratios", New York: Dun & Bradstreet.

16 Krugman, Herbert, 1972. "Why Three Exposures May Be Enough," Journal of Advertising Research, 12, pp. 11-14.

17 op cit

18 Standard Rate and Data Service (SRDS).

chapter 8

dynamic demand forecast

INTRODUCTION AND GOALS

Demand forecasting is the linchpin of the entire business plan, yet rarely are forecasts accurate. Venture capitalists indicate that 60% of plans overstate demand by 60%, while 40% of plans overstate demand by 90%. All decisions in the design of the venture are contingent upon the demand forecast—even those that ultimately affect demand. The channel decision, for example, is based on the likelihood of exceeding breakeven demand, yet the channel itself determines product/service availability, which in turn affects realized demand. The goal of demand forecasting is to generate reliable estimates of future revenues, and to support well-informed decisions about the levels of physical, human, and financial resources.

Reliable forecasting techniques are important because erroneous demand forecasts in and of themselves could lead to failure. Optimistic forecasts generate requirements for high levels of physical, human, and financial resources. The associated carrying costs for excess resources could strangle an otherwise viable venture. Similarly, pessimistic forecasts may result in insufficient capacity to meet demand. Inability to meet demand will cause customers to go elsewhere, and may permanently suppress market share.

Because the demand forecast is so critical, we tackle it from two different analytical approaches. The first technique is a bottoms-up approach that combines the potential demand from conjoint analysis with sales formation decisions: the distribution channel decision in Chapter 6 and advertising decision in Chapter 7. The second technique is a top-down approach that utilizes adoption data for comparable prior products (historical analogy). After reviewing these two approaches, the chapter applies the techniques to Epigraphs to generate a 3-year demand forecast.

PRINCIPLES

The first approach we use for demand forecasting is conjoint analysis combined with models of sales formation. This approach utilizes primary data specific to the venture to derive the forecast. The second approach is historical analogy. Here, we examine the diffusion of similar past products to estimate the likely diffusion of our own product. The conjoint approach is "bottoms-up"—building an aggregate forecast using behavioral data at the individual level. In contrast, historical analogy is a "top-down" approach beginning with a set of forecasts of diffusion at the population level. From the set of forecasts, we assess which innovation and associated diffusion path is most similar to our own, and use that path as the basis for estimating our own sales diffusion.

Unless the product is completely new to the world, we recommend using conjoint analysis as the primary forecast and using historical analogy as a validation tool. If the product is new to the world, such that individuals have no sense of why they would want the product, and how they would use it, then stated purchase intentions are highly speculative. Examples of "new to the world" produces are Xerox copiers and personal computers. Until people "experience" these products, they may not believe they have any use for them. For example, the initial forecasted demand for copiers was four units worldwide. In such instances, we recommend historical analogy as the primary forecasting tool.

Conjoint Analysis / Sales Formation Models

Conjoint analysis produces a point estimate of the "potential demand" for the product. By point estimate we mean a single number rather than a growth path. The demand forecasting process uses sales formation models to convert the conjoint point estimate into a dynamic sales pattern (how those sales unfold over time).

Responses to conjoint surveys assume full awareness and availability of the product. This is true because the survey itself makes the customer aware of the product, and has the customer assume it is widely available. Sales formation models convert the point estimate of demand to a dynamic sales forecast, by simply applying firm advertising and channel decisions.

In other words, while *potential demand*, the inherent attractiveness of the new product/service relative to the alternatives, is something outside the control of the firm, *sales formation*, the actual capture of the potential demand over time, *is* controlled by the firm.[1] Strategic decisions by the firm determine the product availability and awareness. Availability is set through the firm's channel decision; awareness is set through the firm's advertising decision. Realized sales (S)[2] in any period (t) is merely the sum over all individuals (i) in the target market (n) of their respective awareness (a_w), availability (a_v) and purchase intention (b_c), where a_w, a_v are expressed as percentages of the target population:

$$S_t = \Sigma_i \ a_{wit} \ a_{vit} \ b_{cit}$$

While in principle we could do this analysis for each individual in the target market, in practice, we will assume that the mean responses in the survey reflect a representative individual. We therefore focus attention on the "reach" of our advertising and distribution across all individuals. (Note: to the *extent* there are market segments that we target differently, the aggregation should be done within segments.)

This is illustrated nicely with the R & R case[3] on the introduction of the *TV Guide* game. With regard to availability, a_{vt}, R & R planned to introduce the *TV Guide* game through exclusive retailers for the first three weeks, expanding to department stores in week four, and finally to discounters in week eight. Assume that exclusive retailers have a total base of 21 million customers, with weekly traffic of 15% of the base (3.2 million), that department stores have a base of 32 million customers (weekly traffic of 4.8 million), and that discounters also have a base of 32 million customers (weekly traffic of 4.8 million). We add the traffic of all outlets in which the product was available, to establish the product availability, a_v, in the first row of Exhibit 8-1.

We follow similar analysis for advertising reach, a_{wt}. We begin by looking at the reach of the planned advertising vehicles. R&R planned to place five ads in *TV Guide*. At the time of the case, *TV Guide* had an audience of 17 million out of 87 million total U.S. households (19.5%). Assume that the first ad only achieves attention in one-third of the *TV Guide* audience, and that each of the next two exposures adds another third. The resulting advertising reach, A_W, is given in the second line of Exhibit 8-1. Remember that customers need repeated exposures to advertising to create awareness (the rule of thumb is three attention events).[4]

Finally, we treat stated purchase intentions. Ordinarily, this is a single number for a homogenous target market—conjoint analysis leads to an optimal product configuration and corresponding price. However, in the case of R&R, the company decreased the price of the *TV Guide* game over time. This is a form of price discrimination—early adopters at exclusive retailers pay one price, majority adopters at department stores pay a lower price, and laggards at discount stores pay the lowest price. Since R&R did not conduct conjoint analysis, we do not know the explicit demand curve for the *TV Guide* game. Let us assume that at $25, customers are 2% likely to buy the game, at $20, they are 3% likely to buy the game, and at $15, they are 4% likely to buy the game. The respective purchase intentions, b_c, for the prevailing price in each period are given in row 3.

To find weekly sales in each period, we merely multiply $a_{vt} * a_{wt} * b_{ct}$. These sales estimates are given in row 5. To find cumulative sales, we merely add sales for the current week and all prior weeks (row 6). This is our demand forecast. Optimistic and pessimistic versions would require demand variance from con-

Exhibit 8-1. Sales formation analysis for R&R

						Weeks following introduction						
	1	2	3	4	5	6	7	8	9	10	11	12	13
Availability (a_v) (million)	3.2	3.2	3.2	8.0	8.0	8.0	8.0	8.0	12.8	12.8	12.8	12.8	12.8
Awareness (a_w)	0.07	0.13	0.20	0.20	0.20	0.20	0.20	0.20	0.20	0.20	0.20	0.20	0.20
Price ($)	25	25	25	25	25	25	25	25	20	20	20	17	17
Purchase intention (b_c)	0.02	0.02	0.02	0.02	0.02	0.02	0.02	0.02	0.03	0.03	0.03	0.04	0.04
Weekly Sales (M)	4.2	8.3	12.5	31.2	31.2	31.2	31.2	31.2	74.9	74.9	74.9	87.4	87.4
Cumulative Sales (M)	4.2	12.5	25.0	56.2	87.4	118.6	149.8	181.0	255.8	330.7	405.6	493.0	580.3

Notes:
Availability: R&R introduced the product first in high-end retailers, then in department stores, and finally in discounters.
Awareness: We focus on the *TV Guide* ads, because we do not have details on the cooperative ads placed by retailers. There were five ads in total.
Purchase intention: Purchase intention is a function of price (this is characterized by the demand curve). The price of the *TV Guide* game dropped over time, primarily because of the pricing policies of the stores in which it was sold. Dropping the price increases the number of people willing to purchase it. Thus there are two effects increasing demand when moving from Bloomingdales to Walmart—one is greater availability (more people shop in Walmart stores than in Bloomingdales stores). The other effect is the price effect. More people will buy the game at $16.97 than will buy it at $25.00 (regardless of whether it is in Bloomingdales or Walmart).

210

joint analysis. We do not have demand variance in this case, but will demonstrate its application in the Epigraphs example.

Historical Analogy

The use of historical analogy for demand forecasting arises from the observation that new product adoptions (first purchase) by individuals follow a predictable pattern. In general, cumulative adoptions follow a logistic (S shape) growth curve. The rate (per period) of adoptions correspondingly follows a normal curve. The basic formula for a logistic curve is:

$$Yt = L / (1 + ae\text{-}bt)$$

Where:

Yt	is cumulative adoption through period t
L	is the growth limit (this corresponds to the point estimate of potential demand from conjoint)
e	is the base of the natural logarithm
t	is time
a	is the intercept
b	is the slope of the growth curve

The inflection point in the curve occurs at $t = (\ln a)/b$, where cumulative sales have reached 50% of total demand ($Y=L/2$).[5] Exhibit 8-2 shows adoption rates (as % of total firms or households) versus time since introduction for five product innovations: color TV, ultrasound, mammography, air conditioners, and clothes dryers. On average, product adoptions peak in the 8th year following introduction, at a rate of 7.5% households per year, but there is substantial variance across products.[6]

The variance is captured by two parameters: the rate of adoption, b (some products diffuse more rapidly than others), and the extent of adoption, L. Products with high *rates* of adoption (color TV) peak before year 8. Those with

Exhibit 8-2. Sample adoption rates for new products

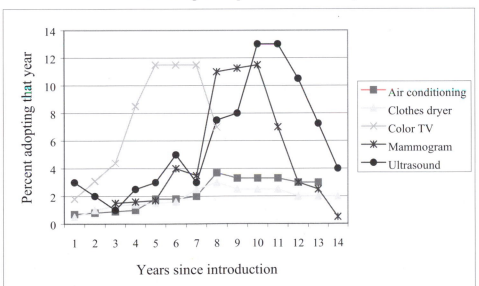

Reprinted by Permission, Lenk P. and A. Rao, "New Models from Old: Forecasting Product Adoption by Hierarchical Boyes Procedures, Marketing Science, Vol 9, No 1, pp. 42-53. Copyright © 1990, The Institute of Management Sciences (Informs), 901 Elkridge Landing Road, Suite 400, Linthicom, Maryland, 21090-2909 USA.

high *levels* of adoption (ultrasound), peak above 7.5% of households/population. Note that there is no requirement that rate and level be correlated.

If we have L and b, we can forecast both cumulative sales adoption and per-period sales. The challenge in forecasting, of course, is estimating L and b. The art of historical analogy is choosing prior products whose L and b are likely to be similar to the new product.

Appropriate choice of analogous products requires some understanding of the factors affecting diffusion. We turn again to the diffusion literature. In Chapter 7 we used the diffusion literature to learn about the relative effectiveness of mass media versus interpersonal channels in various stages of the product life cycle. This informs "what to do when" to facilitate adoption. Here we are interested in the contributions of the diffusion literature for understanding "inherent adoption propensities" of new products.

Five inherent attributes of products affect 49% – 87% of the variance in the rate of their adoption, b:[7]

Relative advantage of the new product over the product it supercedes

Compatibility of the new product with the values, experience, and needs of users

Complexity or the perceived difficulty to understand and use the product

Trialability or the extent to which the product can be used on trial basis

Observability or the ability of potential adopters to observe the product's benefits

Oddly enough, little research has been done to characterize the relative impact of each of these attributes.

We can compute b for each of the consumer products in Exhibit 8-2, and add three more recent innovations to get a rank ordering of products according to their rate of adoption (Exhibit 8-3). The products diffusing most rapidly are color television and Nintendo. Color televisions had obvious *advantage* over black and

Exhibit 8-3. Diffusion coefficients for some major innovations

	Y (% households adopting)	t (years observed)	b (rate of adoption)
Color TV	53.6	8	0.498
Air conditioning	31.1	14	0.246
Clothes dryer	26.2	14	0.233
Cellular phones	15.0	10	0.271
Nintendo	50.0	7	0.559
Personal computers	33.0	25	0.140

white TVs, but benefited greatly from the fact that consumers had experience with black and white. This ensured *compatibility* of color TV with existing experience. Similarly, since color television operation was identical to black and white, uncertainty/*complexity* were removed. *Triability* and *observability* were facilitated by store displays.

Nintendo is a little harder to explain—while Atari superseded it, Atari's introduction led Nintendo by only a year or so. Thus, the diffusion of Nintendo is taken to be diffusion of consumer video games as a product class. Comparing video games to television makes some sense, since the games utilized the displays of home televisions. *Trialability* and *observability* were comparable to TV, in that games could be tried in all outlets in which they were sold. In addition, home games were comparable to arcade games (facilitating *compatibility* and reducing *complexity*). The real *relative advantage* of Nintendo is probably with respect to arcade games. Home games are far more convenient and accessible, and have lower lifetime cost (since games at arcades cost 50 cents or more per play).

The product with the slowest diffusion is the personal computer (PC). Here, the slowness is explained through *complexity* and *relative advantage*. Early PCs were only accessible to techies, who could build their own systems from parts. Even after user-friendly turn-key systems, such as the Apple, and packaged software were available, few households could perceive a utility for PCs that would justify their price.

These are subjective assessments. One means to obtain quantitative estimates of the relative importance of these factors is through regression.

One study has done this in the context of industrial products,[8] examining the diffusion of 12 innovations throughout 4 industries (Exhibit 8-4). The study modeled the diffusion rate (b in the equation above) of a given innovation, in a given industry, as a function of the profitability impact of that innovation to the target industry, P_{ij}, the cost of adopting the innovation in that industry, S_{ij}, and a set of dummies for each industry. This simple model explained 90-98% of the variance in the diffusion rate, b_{ij}.

$$b_{ij} = \underset{(0.015)}{.530\, P_{ij}} - \underset{(0.014)}{.027\, S_{ij}} + \text{industry dummies}$$

> Where: P is the average payout period to justify investments divided by the average payout period for investment in the innovation.
> S is the average investment in the innovation divided by firm assets.

Exhibit 8-4. Characterizing the diffusion of twelve industrial products (from Mansfield 1968)

Innovation	Data			Parameter Estimates		
	# adopting	profitability	cost to adopt	aij	bij	R-squared
Diesel locomotive	25	1.59	0.015	-6.64	0.20	0.89
Centralized traffic control	24	1.48	0.024	-7.13	0.10	0.94
Car retarders	25	1.25	0.785	-3.95	0.11	0.90
Continuous wide-strip mill	12	1.87	4.908	-10.47	0.34	0.95
By-product coke oven	12	1.47	2.083	-1.47	0.17	0.98
Continuous annealing	9	1.25	0.554	-8.51	0.17	0.93
Shuttle car	15	1.74	0.013	-13.48	0.32	0.95
Trackless mobile loader	15	1.65	0.019	-13.03	0.32	0.97
Continuous mining machine	17	2.00	0.301	-14.96	0.49	0.98
Tin container	22	5.07	0.267	-84.35	2.40	0.96
High-speed bottle filler	16	1.20	0.575	-20.58	0.36	0.97
Pallet-loading machine	19	1.67	0.115	-29.07	0.55	0.97

Mansfield's quantitative factors explaining diffusion correspond roughly to the qualitative factors that Rogers defined above. Profitability captures *relative advantage*, the cost of adopting the innovation is comparable to the *complexity of the innovation* (or psychic cost), and industry dummies are characteristics of the market segments (such as wealth) that help explain differences in diffusion. Of these variables, most of the action is in profitability or relative advantage. This makes sense—rational firms considering innovations examine first the extent to which the innovation will affect their unit margins. They then compare the improvement in margins to the fixed cost of implementing the innovation to assess the break-even point.

This range of estimates for b & L, and their subjective assessments provide guidelines for estimating the rate of diffusion of new-to-the world products. Often historical analogy is much simpler. In industries marked by regular innovation, there likely is secondary data on the distribution of sales volume over product lives, as well as the profile of sales over the life. For example, in wall coverings, the average product line sales are 7 million rolls (minimum and maximum are 2 million and 200 million, respectively). Modal product life is 3 years (with a maximum of 10 years). In general, 60% of product sales occur within the first 12 months of introduction.

This diffusion pattern is different from the logistic curve. It is skewed left (heavy sales early) (Exhibit 7-6). If we are interested in forecasting sales of a new wallcovering, then we can take advantage of these "stylized facts" of the sales pattern to form a monthly sales profile that we apply to the point estimate for demand from conjoint.

Industry data can help identify other temporal patterns in demand. One important pattern is seasonality. Many business services experience slower sales in the summer; many retail sales peak in December. These patterns are largely outside the control of the new venture. Others that may be within your control have to do with response to events. Catalog sales follow a predictable pattern of sales following each mailing.[9] Similarly, advertising, promotions, and trade shows will cause sales spikes. Secondary data will help you understand sales patterns arising from both controllable and uncontrollable events in your industry.

EPIGRAPHS DEMAND FORECAST

We will use the wallcovering-specific diffusion curve in Exhibit 7-6 as the historical analogy on which to build the top-down Epigraphs forecast. The primary role of the top-down forecast is to test the plausibility of the bottoms-up forecast—does the bottoms-up forecast fall within the observed range for past wallcoverings? To develop the bottoms-up forecast for Epigraphs, we combine data gathered over several chapters:

- A point estimate of potential demand, given awareness and availability in the target market (from conjoint analysis, Chapters 4 and 5)
- An estimate of target market size (from industry studies of the annual market for wallcovering, Chapter 2)
- A distribution channel with known reach (from the channel decision in Chapter 6)
- An advertising policy driving awareness (from the advertising decisions in Chapter 7)
- An historical analogy for demand distribution over the life cycle of a given wallcovering (Chapter 2)

Historical Analogy

We have already discussed information from historical analogy in the previous section. The analogy of past wallcovering sales patterns provides the skewed shape of the distribution curve (Exhibit 7-6), as well as the distribution of lifetime sales over the population of wallpaper patterns. This distribution indicates that the average wallpaper sells 7 million rolls, but there is substantial variance across wallcoverings. Minimum lifetime sales is around 2 million rolls; the maximum is approximately 200 million rolls.

In addition, from industry analysis we estimate that the target market for all wallcovering is 10 million households per year. We obtain this estimate by comparing annual wallcovering sales at retail of $2 billion, with average dollar value per transaction of $200. Thus the number of transactions is 10,000,000 (or 2,500,000 per quarter). This market size is given in row 3 of the Epigraphs demand forecast (Exhibit 8-5).

Point Estimate of Total Demand

The initial point estimate for total demand from conjoint was the intercept value of 4.03 rolls per customer. This estimate can only be achieved if 1) everyone in the target market is aware of the product, 2) they all have access to it, 3) all colors and genres are available, and 4) we price the product at $35.00. The goal of the last several chapters was to determine how much of this potential demand is actually profitable. We found that we were better off by raising price, restricting the range of colors and genres, and limiting distribution and advertising.

While we made a tentative decision to distribute through chains, we continue to examine both Internet and chain distribution. The optimal price differs between the two channels. There are two opposing factors that affect demand through chains relative to demand through the Internet. The first factor is distributor markups—unit revenues to the manufacturer from chain sales are less than retail price; for Internet sales, unit revenues equal retail price. The second factor is observability—customers are able to see the actual installed product in chain displays—this provides greater assurance of the installation outcome than an image over the Internet.

For distribution over the Internet, the optimal price to the nearest $5.00, is $40.00. This corresponds to demand of 2.45 rolls per person (both optimal price and corresponding demand come from Exhibit 5-4). For distribution through chains, the optimal price to the nearest $5.00 is $50.00. This corresponds to demand of 2.72 rolls per person.

In addition to truncating demand by choice of distribution channel and price, we also truncated demand by choice of two colors and two genres. Our analysis in Chapter 5 indicates that those restrictions cause us to forego another 35.4% (100%- 64.6%) of potential demand. Thus, the point estimate for Internet distribution becomes 1.58 rolls per person (2.45*.646) and the point estimate for chain distribution becomes 1.76 rolls per person.

Finally, we know that respondents tend to be optimistic in reporting their purchase intentions, and we need to adjust for that. Exhibit 4-7 indicated that respondents overstate purchase intentions for durable goods by roughly a factor of 2.5. Thus we adjust our point estimates by dividing by 2.5. Our revised point estimates for demand are 0.63 rolls per person over the Internet, and 0.70 rolls per person through chains. We insert the per person point estimates in rows 1 and 2 of Epigraphs demand forecast spreadsheet (Exhibit 8-5).

If we apply these estimates to the target population (10 million households purchasing wallcovering each year), we arrive at point estimates of 6.3 million rolls per year over the Internet, and 7.0 million rolls through chains (row 3 of Exhibit 8-5).

These point estimates assume uniform sales over the three-year period. To generate dynamic sales forecasts, we need to incorporate the industry lifetime sales profile, with awareness and availability estimates arising from our advertising and distribution channel decisions. The sales profile is a temporal pattern outside our control. The advertising and distribution decisions generate a temporal pattern of awareness and availability that is within our control.

Lifetime Sales Profile

If we assume that these point estimates accurately capture first-year sales, then we can apply the rule of thumb that 60% of lifetime sales are in the first-year to generate the lifetime sales estimate. Using this approach, total lifetime

Exhibit 8-5. Epigraphs Sales Formation Forecast

	Q1	Q2	Q3	Q4	Q5	Q6	Q7	Q8	Q9	Q10	Q11	Q12
Demand estimate												
Rolls/person in target												
Internet	0.63	0.63	0.63	0.63	0.63	0.63	0.63	0.63	0.63	0.63	0.63	0.63
Chain	0.70	0.70	0.70	0.70	0.70	0.70	0.70	0.70	0.70	0.70	0.70	0.70
Target market:												
households purchasing wallcovering (thousand)	2500	2500	2500	2500	2500	2500	2500	2500	2500	2500	2500	2500
Lifetime Sales Profile	0.32	0.60	0.80	0.72	0.52	0.36	0.24	0.16	0.12	0.08	0.04	0.04
Awareness (% of households)	0.11	0.21	0.21	0.21	0.21	0.21	0.21	0.21	0.21	0.21	0.21	0.21
Availability (% of market)												
Internet purch penetration	0.18	0.21	0.24	0.27	0.29	0.32	0.35	0.38	0.40	0.43	0.45	0.48
Chain	1.00	1.00	1.00	1.00	1.00	1.00	1.00	1.00	1.00	1.00	1.00	1.00
Quarterly Sales (1000 rolls)												
Internet	9	41	63	64	50	38	28	20	16	11	6	6
Chain	59	221	294	265	191	132	88	59	44	29	15	15
Quarterly Sales ($1000)												
Internet	378	1637	2510	2553	1986	1522	1113	807	638	453	240	254
Chain	2100	7875	10500	9450	6825	4725	3150	2100	1575	1050	525	525
Cumulative Sales (1000 rolls)												
Internet	9	50	113	177	227	265	292	313	329	340	346	352
Chain	59	279	573	838	1029	1161	1250	1308	1352	1382	1397	1411
Cumulative Sales ($1000)												
Internet	378	2014	4524	7077	9063	10585	11698	12505	13144	13597	13837	14090
Chain	2100	9975	20475	29925	36750	41475	44625	46725	48300	49350	49875	50400

sales are 10.5 million rolls (=6.3/.60) over the Internet, or 11.7 million rolls through chains. (Row 4 of Exhibit 8-5 generates the entire pattern of sales over the three-year product life from Exhibit 2-7.)

Awareness

Our preliminary plans for advertising are the same for Internet and chain distribution. Ultimately, we assume that the Internet will require more advertising in that it has no counterpart to the store displays that provide supplemental "free" advertising. We adopt the advertising plan from Chapter 7, which provides advertising on HGTV and *Home* magazine in the first three months of product introduction. This produces the three exposures generally needed to stimulate sales. After that period, we will terminate advertising, so that the product does not become overexposed.

HGTV has an audience of 1.1 million and *Home* magazine has an audience of 1 million. For simplicity, and because neither HGTV nor *Home* has data on overlap, we assume that the two audiences are distinct. Thus the advertising program should create awareness in 2.1 million households. We assume that this audience is a complete subset of the market for wallcovering—that neither vehicle is "wasting" advertising outside the market. Both these assumptions may be optimistic, but because we are ignoring the free advertising associated with Internet and store displays, we feel the assumptions are warranted.

Our estimates of awareness are captured in row 5 of Exhibit 8-5. In all periods after the first quarter, we assume awareness of 21% of the target households (2.1 million audience/10 million households purchasing wallcovering annually). In the first period, we assume awareness is half the ultimate value, as the ad exposures accumulate.

Availability

Internet – The Internet truncates reach, in that only 17.8% of households purchased over the Internet as of 1999 (Forrester, March 2000). The penetration rate of Internet purchasing is growing rapidly, but at a decreasing rate. Given past growth trends, we assume that the penetration growth rate in each future year will be 65% of its growth rate in the prior year. Thus, by the end of year 3, we anticipate 48% of households will be making Internet purchases. The corresponding quarterly penetration rates are given in row 6 of Exhibit 8-5.

Chains – We assume that the product will be distributed through Sherwin-Williams. The chain has approximately 2200 stores, with 1500 transactions per quarter. This number exceeds the number of wallcovering transactions per month, and the markets are assumed to be identical, thus we conclude that distribution through Sherwin-Williams provides 100% availability to the target market (row 7 of Exhibit 8-5).

Sales Projections

We obtain quarterly sales projections by merely multiplying per person demand, bi_j, awareness, awi_j, availability, avi_j, market size, and lifetime sales profile within each of the distribution channels. This leads to the quarterly unit sales in rows 8 and 9 of Exhibit 8-5, and the cumulative sales in rows 12 and 13. Total sales over the Internet peak at 64,000 rolls in Quarter 4; total sales through chains peak at 294,000 rolls in Quarter 3. Cumulative Internet sales over the three-year life are 352,000 rolls; cumulative sales for chains are 1,411,000 rolls.

We can assess the plausibility of this estimate by comparing it with the historical wallcovering sales. Our estimates in either channel are well below the mode of 7 million rolls over a pattern life. Furthermore, our first year sales represent only 1% of annual wallcovering sales. Both comparisons tend to suggest our estimates may be conservative.

Note that we would ordinarily form optimistic and pessimistic versions of these forecasts using the variance in the conjoint demand estimates as the basis for variance in the summary forecasts. Our regression results exhibited very little variance. The standard error on the demand estimate was 0.29 versus a mean of 4.01 (variance = 7.5% of the mean). Optimistic and pessimistic forecasts that provide a 67% chance of capturing the true estimate of total chain demand are 1.30 million rolls and 1.51 million rolls, respectively.

Exhibit 8-5 also provides revenue forecasts. These are formed by multiplying the optimal price in each channel by the sales in that channel. (Rows 10 and 11 provide quarterly revenues; rows 14 and 15 provide cumulative revenues.) These will form the basis of our financial forecasts in Chapter 11.

Summary

We continue to validate the conclusion to distribute Epigraphs through chains—creating total revenues four times than that through the Internet. Moreover, we find that our sales estimates appear to be conservative relative to industry standards.

CONCLUSION

In this chapter, we combined secondary data from Chapter 2 with primary data and strategic decisions from Chapters 4, 5, 6, and 7 to define the dynamic demand forecast for the venture. While Chapter 4 defines a point estimate for potential demand that is outside our control, the decision in Chapters 5 through 7 determine how much of that potential to capture, and when. The price and product configuration decisions in Chapter 5 define how much of the potential demand to exclude by virtue of low willingness to pay and/or obscure tastes. When we apply these decisions to potential demand, we still have point estimates.

Chapters 6 and 7 introduce dynamics. The distribution decision determines how many buyers in each period will have access to the product. The advertising decision determines how many buyers in each period will be aware of our product. Since these decisions are within the control of the venture, there is some opportunity to smooth demand.

In addition to dynamic factors within the venture's control, some temporal patterns are inherent characteristics of the industry and thus outside the venture's control. We discuss some of these patterns and their impact on demand.

This primary approach to the dynamic forecast is a bottom-up approach. However, as a test of reasonableness, you should also look for historical analogies. The analogies define levels and rates of product diffusion based on the new product's attractiveness relative to the product it replaces.

The dynamic forecast defines the scale of the venture. This scale is a critical input to all subsequent decisions. In the next chapter, we consider the final strategic decision—organizational scope.

Chapter 8 Worksheet

Dynamic Demand Forecast Worksheet

You will create demand forecasts two ways: *Bottoms-up* from the conjoint data and the product configuration, advertising and distribution channel decisions and *top-down* from historical analogy.

Bottoms-up

1. How many individuals, households or firms are in the target market? _____

   Show in all cells of row 2 of the worksheet (From Chapter 2)

2. Show the demand curve from conjoint analysis, what is the optimal

   price?_____

   (from Chapter 5)

3. What is the point estimate for demand from conjoint analysis, given your choice

   of price and product configuration? (Should be expressed as units per person in

   the target)_____

   Remember to adjust for respondent optimism

   Show in all cells of row 1 of the worksheet (from Chapter 5)

4. What is the reach of your distribution channel over time? _____% of target

   Show in row 3 of the worksheet (from Chapter 6)

5. What is the reach of your advertising policy over time? _____% of target

   Show in row 4 of the worksheet (from Chapter 7)

6. Find calendarized unit demand by multiplying rows 1,2,3 and 4. Show in row 5

7. Find calendarized revenues by multiplying row 5 by unit price. Show in row 6.

8. Find cumulative unit demand by summing current and all prior demand in row 5.

   Show in row 7

9. Find cumulative revenues by summing current and all prior revenues in row 6.

   Show in row 8.

	Q1	Q2	Q3	Q4	Q5	Q6	Q7	Q8	Q9	Q10	Q11	Q12
Demand estimate Units/person in target												
Target market: people or firms in target												
Awareness percentage of target												
Availability percentage of target												
Quarterly Sales (units)												
Quarterly Sales ($1000)												
Cumulative Sales (units)												
Cumulative Sales ($1000)												

Historical Analogy

10. What products/services are similar to that in your venture?

11. For each analogous product, define the total sales and the rate of sales growth.

12. Is your demand forecast from the bottoms-up approach within the range of the analogous products?

Analogous product	Total diffusion, L	Rate of diffusion, b

[1] One caveat here--some products, such as Furbys and Pokemons are driven by a social process (as discussed in Chapter 7). For these products, purchase intentions will be understated because the survey is conducted in isolation from the social effects.

[2] If the product is a durable good, like a refrigerator, which is purchased by consumers only once, then S is interpreted as cumulative sales up through that period. If, however, the product or service is a repeat good, like shampoo, which is purchased on a regular basis, then S is interpreted as sales during the period.

[3] Mossi, J. and H. Stevenson, 1985. "R&R," Harvard Business School Case 9-386-019.

[4] Krugman, Herbert, 1972. "Why Three Exposures May Be Enough," Journal of Advertising Research, 12, pp. 11-14.

[5] Forecasting is facilitated by transforming to log linear form: $Y = -\ln(a) + bt$ (a plot of Y on semi-log paper is linear).

[6] Lenk, P. and A. Rao, 1990. "New Models from Old: Forecasting Product Adoption by Hierarchical Bayes Procedures," Marketing Science, 9 (1), pp. 42-53.

[7] Rogers, Everett M., 1995. "Diffusion of Innovations," New York: The Free Press.

[8] Mansfield, Edwin, 1968. "The Economics of Technological Change," New York: W.W. Norton and Company.

[9] See Werssowetz, R., R. Kent and H. Stevenson, 1985. "Ruth M. Owades." HBS Case 9-383-051 for a typical catalogue response pattern.

chapter 9

scope of operations

INTRODUCTION AND GOALS

One of the most important strategic decisions that a firm makes is that of its operational scope—which activities should the firm execute internally versus outsource to other firms. This is the last of the strategic decisions we make in the venture design. What makes the scope decision strategically important are the facts that it is largely irreversible, and that it affects the long-term viability of the firm.

On one extreme of operational scope are highly vertically integrated firms like General Motors. General Motors designs and manufactures not only the automobile, but most of its components, and then distributes the finished goods through its own dealers. At the other end of the spectrum are "virtual firms" like Compaq Computer. Compaq outsources its design and manufacturing, and distributes its products through independent retailers. Since both firms are highly successful, it is not true that one form dominates the other. In general, most firms are hybrids of the two forms—outsourcing some activities and internalizing others.

Our goal in this chapter is to develop a framework for determining which activities to outsource and which to execute internally to ensure the long-term viability of the firm. The objective in making the decision is to provide reliable provision of high quality goods and services at the lowest cost, while building/preserving the capabilities that lead to sustained competitive advantage.

The chapter first reviews the principles underlying the decision—transaction cost economics and the resource-based view of strategy. Next, we present an analytical process for making the scope decision, and then we apply that process to Epigraphs.

PRINCIPLES

The principles underlying this chapter on the scope of the firm are closely related to those in Chapter 6 pertaining to the distribution decision. Both chapters deal with the level of vertical integration of the firm. Chapter 6 deals with

225

forward integration into market activities, while this chapter deals with backward integration into various stages of supply. Accordingly, we might expect the theoretical foundations to be identical.

While both issues draw from the literature on vertical contracting, there is a subtle difference that justifies separate treatment. In particular, the central concern in the forward-contracting literature is the principal agent problem of designing contracts (or choosing channels) where the incentives of the agents in the channel are aligned with those of the firm. In contrast, the central concern in the backward-contracting literature is the hold-up problem—that suppliers will control critical resources, and accordingly will extract the rents from those resources at the expense of the firm.

This literature has a decidedly defensive posture, focusing on mechanisms that prevent or minimize supplier hold-up. We argue that even if there is no problem of supplier hold-up, there may be reasons to internalize a given activity. Thus we augment the transaction cost perspective in the vertical-contracting literature with other perspectives from the management literature.

Transaction Cost Economics

Transaction cost economics tries to explain when economic activity will be organized in hierarchies (firms) rather than markets. The basic assumption in the literature is that markets provide powerful incentives for price to be driven toward marginal cost, and even for marginal cost to fall over time through learning and scale economies. Thus the "anomaly" that the literature tries to explain is the existence of firms—non-market activity.

The answer to the firm anomaly is that some transactions are more costly to conduct across markets. This occurs a) when there are firm specific assets (to be defined momentarily), b) when it is difficult to observe or measure the quality of an output, c) when there are coordination problems, and d) when there are externalities. We will discuss each of these, and their implication for firm scope.

Firm specific assets are costly assets (both physical and human) that are significantly more valuable in the provision of a particular good or service, than they are in their next best use. Assets can become specific in any of three ways. *Site specificity* pertains to physical assets that are co-located with a particular customer. This is the case if a supplier of engines to Toyota, chooses to locate its plant next door to Toyota to minimize transportation costs. If it later chooses to supply engines to Nissan, the net cost to Nissan for each engine is much higher than the net cost to Toyota for the same engine. If there are other comparable firms located more centrally, then Nissan will prefer the centrally located firms.

Physical asset specificity pertains to physical assets that are tailored to a given producer. This is the case, for example, if a supplier creates molds for the production of a new toy. Once the molds are created, they are of no use to any other producer. Finally, *human asset specificity* pertains to employee training or on-the-job learning of skills that are valuable only to a given firm. This might be the case with workers on an assembly line, who have no technical training, but who through years of experience have become adept at their particular task (unique to the firm and sometimes even to a specific product).

When a supplier's assets are likely to become specific to a particular buyer, there are two (seemingly offsetting) hold-up problems. The first problem is that once the supplier has made the investments, their specificity causes those investments to become sunk. Accordingly, the supplier will become powerless in price negotiations with the buyer, and will ultimately be willing to drop price to marginal cost, never recouping the investment from the specific asset (*buyer hold-up* of supplier). Knowing this, a rational supplier would be unwilling to make such investments. This market failure forces "buyer" firms to integrate into the supply of the input requiring the specific investments.

A symmetric problem to buyer hold-up is the *supplier hold-up* that occurs when a firm is the sole source of supply for a given input. This allows the supplier to charge a price equal to the input's marginal product, leaving little opportunity for producer profit. Oddly, once a supplier has made investments in specific assets, *it* becomes the sole source of supply for the good/service from that asset. Thus, we might expect that the buyer and seller have comparable hold-up power, and could reach an equitable solution. However, both asset specificity (buyer hold-up) and lack of competition in the supply chain (seller hold-up) tend to produce backward vertical integration by the producer.

The other circumstances under which transaction costs may be high and we therefore expect activity to be organized in firms rather than markets include:

- When it is difficult or costly to assess the quality of an input. This is the case for example with Dairy Queen. Dairy Queen, the franchisor, requires individual outlets to purchase ice cream mix directly from headquarters to prevent outlet owners from purchasing poor quality mix at lower cost. Neither Dairy Queen nor outlet owners have the capability to continuously monitor the quality of other suppliers' mixes. Since the quality of the final product critically depends on the mix, the best solution is to control the mix quality by producing it internally.
- When there is high interdependence among activities requiring coordination. This is the case in the early stages of new devices. Go Corporation, the first developer of a tablet computer (with script input), had to develop both hardware and software simultaneously because the capabilities of each were evolving over time.
- When two or more goods are complements—one good is only valuable if the owner has (or has access to) a complementary good. This is the

case, for example, with Switch Manufacturing.[1] The firm developed a new quick-release binding for snowboards, but the binding required the redesign of boots (typically manufactured by different firms). Thus, Switch faced the choice of developing its own line of boots, or forming alliances with existing boot manufacturers. Initially it developed its own boots, but ultimately the firm was acquired by Vans, a leading boot manufacturer.

The transaction-cost perspective is an efficiency perspective—where is it most efficient for a given economic activity to be organized? Thus we might expect that all firms in an industry would behave identically. Since all firms face comparable input requirements, they should reach similar conclusions about which activities to execute internally versus which to outsource. This is not the case. Several industries—auto manufacturers and personal computers, for example—all have firms that appear to outsource all activity (virtual firms), while others appear to be fully integrated. We demonstrated this earlier for autos (GM is highly integrated, while Chrysler is largely a virtual firm) and PCs (IBM is highly integrated, while Compaq is virtual). Thus, transaction-cost economics is not sufficient in explaining firm scope. It appears instead that firm scope decisions are intrinsically linked to firm strategies for competitive advantage.

Interestingly, a number of economic trends have eased many of the factors that previously pushed firms in the direction of vertical integration. In particular, the integration of the global economy has led to more competitive markets, minimizing the likelihood of sole suppliers. In addition, flexible production technology has enabled "mass customization"—the ability to produce products to order with a speed comparable to mass production. McDonald's, for example, is now rolling out "made-to-order" technology that actually reduces the average order time and cost relative to its "made-to-stock" process. Flexible production technology reduces the prevalence of specific physical assets. Finally, information technology, such as Electronic Data Interchange (EDI), has facilitated highly coordinated activities between buyers and sellers.[2]

Strategic Perspective

While the transaction-cost perspective is geared toward efficiency (cost minimization) of firm scope decisions, the strategic (competitive advantage) perspective is geared toward demand maximization of firm scope decisions. The goal of the strategic perspective is to develop and protect capabilities deemed important to maintaining the firm's basis for differentiation.

If the venture is founded on a proprietary concept that is not patentable (or patented, but easy to invent around), then the guiding principle in scope decisions is to internalize activities that would otherwise cause the proprietary information to be divulged. This is particularly true if the supplier is capable of integrating forward into your activity. A salient example here was Go Corporation's decision to team with Microsoft to develop companion software for its tablet computer. Even though both firms had signed non-disclosure, non-compete agreements, once Microsoft fully understood Go's operating system, it severed the alliance and began developing a competing operating system.[3] While this was not the only source of Go's $100 million failure, it was certainly a significant factor.

In addition to a defensive posture of internalizing activities to prevent disclosure, is an offensive posture of internalizing activities to further develop capabilities that are linked to the firm's core benefit proposition. The underlying principle here is that while rivals are attempting to imitate your initial offering, you will be developing capability to improve your offering. This applies both to cost advantage strategies as well as differentiation strategies.

E-steel, for example, is an Internet broker of steel products. Its core benefit proposition is that it bypasses brokers—it creates a more efficient market by pooling more buyers and sellers, such that buyers pay lower prices, while sellers receive higher prices. This is inherently a cost advantage strategy—buyers and sellers prefer E-Steel to brokers because it is a lower cost means to exchange steel products.

The concern with the basic venture concept is that it is easily imitated. In fact, Vertical Net is a firm that creates business-to-business intermediaries in a whole range of markets. Thus, Vertical Net is a likely entrant into the steel products market. While E-steel would like its reputation to form a barrier to entry, the fact that E-Steel was able to create a reputation sufficient to generate several million dollars in revenues, is evidence that reputation is either easy to achieve or unimportant in this setting. Moreover, Vertical Net can transfer its reputation from other markets to the steel market. Since Vertical Net can transfer both reputation and technology, it could be a formidable player in a matter of days should it choose to enter. While loyalty may be important in consumer markets because tastes often dominate budget considerations, business customers are focused on the bottom line and thus are prone to disloyalty.

The issue then is that E-Steel's core benefit proposition requires it to continually reduce its cost so as to maintain advantage over likely rivals. Whereas Go's scope decisions should have internalized activities that required divulging proprietary knowledge, E-Steel's scope decisions should internalize activities that allow it to reduce its operating cost over time.

Similar logic applies when a venture's core benefit proposition is differentiation rather than lower cost. C-Pen, a product introduced by a new firm, C-Technologies, is a pen-sized scanner that allows users to digitally record "highlighted" text. While the product may be patent-protected, the long-term survival of the firm will require product innovation. In fact, several firms have already introduced competing products. Thus C-Technologies will want to internalize activities that enhance its ability to do product innovation. These activities may include customer service—so that the firm learns about the reliability of existing components, and learns about additional capabilities that customers would like to have.

Complementarity considerations

A final consideration for the scope decisions is activity complementarities. Complementary activities is a concept that is similar to that of complementary products introduced in Chapter 2. When two activities are complements, the payoff to performing one activity increases when the firm also performs the second activity. In these circumstances, both activities should be performed by the same firm, regardless of whether they are performed internally or externally. These complementary activities can be thought of as modules. Two factors influence the modularity of activities. The first factor pertains to the intrinsic properties of the activities; the second factor pertains to the maturity of the product/process design.

Two activities, A and B, are intrinsically coupled if the output of A is required for B, but the quality of the output of A is not observable, except as it is manifest in the output of B.[4]

Activities A and B are also intrinsically linked if they share a common knowledge base such that learning from activity A enhances learning from activity B, and vice versa. This is the case for production and product development. Intimate knowledge of the production process enhances the likelihood that product development will lead to designs that can be efficiently produced. This was one of the contributions of "lean production" in the Japanese auto industry. When development and production were coupled, both production cost and product development time were reduced.

Even if activities aren't intrinsically coupled, they may be functionally coupled if a) a firm produces custom rather than standard products/services, or b) if technology is in the ferment stage such that interfaces between component technologies have not been standardized. In these instances, new ventures will need to internalize more activities than they would like.

Empirical Evidence

A number of empirical studies have examined when firms outsource a given activity versus execute it internally.[5] The general observations from these studies are summarized in Exhibit 9-1. The exhibit demonstrates that both efficiency factors and strategic factors affect the scope decision.

Exhibit 9-1.   Summary of findings on firm scope

Factor	Activity Internal When…	Industry Setting	Study Leading To That Result
Relative cost to make versus buy	The cost to produce internally is lower than outsourcing	Auto components	Walker & Weber
Number of suppliers	Few suppliers	Auto components Semi-conductors	Walker & Weber Leiblein, Reuer & Dalsace
Threat of forward integration by suppliers	High threat of forward integration		
Complementary products	Product depends on availability of another product	Polaroid (cameras and film) Go Corp (hardware and software)	Historical record
Asset specificity	Provision of inputs requires investments in assets specific to the end product	Alaska Pipeline Fisher Auto-body Semi-conductors	Historical record Klein, Crawford & Alchian Leiblein, Reuer & Dalsace
Demand uncertainty	Demand is uncertain, and there are few suppliers	Auto components Semi-conductors	Walker & Weber Leiblein, Reuer & Dalsace
Technological uncertainty	Activity is outsourced when technology is uncertain, and there are large number of suppliers	Auto components	Walker & Weber
Proprietary technology	Technology is not patented		
Customization	When input is non-standard	Aircraft subsystems	Masten
Product complexity	When input is complex	Aircraft subsystems	Masten
Input autonomy	When input is interdependent with other inputs	Bicycles	Ulrich & Ellison

Adapted from Walker, Gordon, "Changing the Boundaries of the Firm"

231

A particularly nice study is summarized in Exhibit 9-2. In this study, Ulrich and Ellison examined the scope decisions of firms in the Mountain Bike industry. They took into account efficiency considerations and strategic considerations, as well as complementarities. They attempted to predict firm scope (design =circle, production=square) as a function of the design strategy (whether the firm used a unique suspension), the materials strategy, the materials processing capability, and the scale of the firm (less than 50,000 bikes is below minimum efficient scale). These factors accurately predicted the scope decision in 20 of 23 firms.

Outsource Bias

Before getting into the nuts and bolts of the scope decision process, it is useful to establish a default decision—which direction the decision will go in the absence of a compelling reason to do otherwise. While it is not essential to do so, it does ease the decision process.

The issue then is whether the default should be internalizing or outsourcing. In the case of a startup venture with severe resource constraints, both financial and managerial, we advocate outsourcing as the default decision for the provision of each activity in the value chain. This bias offers four advantages: first, it minimizes *operational risk* of the venture by reducing the managerial task, not only technically, but also administratively. By the technical managerial task, we mean the diversity of activities over which management must maintain expertise and oversight. By the administrative managerial task, we mean the human, resources tasks of recruiting, training, counseling, and replacing employees who execute the activities.

The second advantage of the outsourcing bias is that it minimizes the *financial risk* of the venture. Because the firm makes minimal investments in physical and human assets, it requires less funding (and has lower overhead and financial carrying costs). The lower fixed costs translate into a lower breakeven volume. The combined effect of low operational risk and low financial risk is superadditive in increasing the odds of venture success. As an illustration of the value of minimizing operational and thereby financial risk, two-thirds of the 1999 Inc 500 firms were started with less than $50,000 in capital. Only 21% required more than $100,000.[6]

The third advantage of the outsourcing bias is that outsourcing is a rapid response decision. Once the decision to internalize has been reached, the firm still needs to wait for delivery, installation, and integration of physical assets, and recruiting and training of human assets. Since there is attendant uncertainty of the outcomes of both processes, the firm needs to allow additional time for the system (both human and physical capital) to perform reliability. In contrast, suppliers should be fully operational with demonstrated performance on compa-

Exhibit 9-2. Organization scope versus activity characteristics for bicycle manufacturers [10]

Firm	Unique Susp.	Lack Scale	Unique Mat'ls Proc.	New Mat'ls	Internalization/ Integration Factors	Observed Organizational Structure	Consistent with Theory?
Teton	0	0	0	0			√
Vesuvius	0	0	0	0			√
Everest 3	0	0	0	1			
Washington	0	1	0	0			√
Whiteface 1	0	1	0	0			√
Whiteface 2	0	1	0	0			√
Whitney	0	1	0	0			√
Olympus 2	0	1	0	1			√
Denali	1	0	0	0			√
Matterhorn	1	0	0	0			√
Everest 2	1	0	0	0			
Mitchell	1	0	0	0			√
Everest 1	1	0	0	1			√
Kilimanjaro	1	0	0	1			
Baker	1	0	0	1			√
Cannon	1	0	1	1			√
Crestone	1	0	1	1			√
Mont Blanc	1	1	0	0			√
Olympus 1	1	1	0	0			√
Ranier	1	1	0	0			√
Ras Dashan	1	1	0	1			√
Snowmass	1	1	0	1			√
Shasta	1	1	1	1			√

Source: Ulrich, K. and D. Ellison, "Beyond Make-Buy: Internalization and Integration of Design and Production.

rable activities. They should only need time to accommodate the aspects of the process that are idiosyncratic to your venture.

Finally, and perhaps most importantly, the outsourcing decision is more easily reversed than an internalization decision. Once a firm has made investments in both human and physical assets for a particular activity, it becomes difficult to displace them. In contrast, the outsourcing decision is largely reversible (an exception is long term contracts, which start to approach vertical integration). Experience with your suppliers, the quality of their outputs, and the impact of that quality on your final product/service, will refine your understanding of which activities are critical or strategic. Once you have this information, you can make more informed choices about which activities to internalize.

Dynamics of Firm Scope

The discussion of outsourcing bias suggests that there are venture-specific dynamics of firm scope. There are also industry-specific dynamics of firm scope that are driven by industry maturity. In emerging industries, there is limited opportunity to outsource activities, since support industries have not yet developed. Generally, support industries will not emerge until the primary industry has demonstrated viability and adequate scale to justify creation of the support industries. Thus for example, the e-tailing pioneers like CDNow had to create search software, purchase transaction software, customer tracking software, and the fulfillment interface. New e-tailing ventures not only can purchase each of these components, they can purchase whole suites that integrate all the components, or more convenient still, they can merely customize a storefront provided by an Internet service provider. The Internet service provider will register the domain name, host the site, and process the credit cards.

Thus, the outsourcing options available to a firm are a function of industry maturity. In the early stages of an industry, firms must internalize most transactions. In the growth stage, as support industries emerge, many firms will outsource a large fraction of their activities to quickly meet the needs of the growing market, and focus on those activities at which they excel. Ultimately, as the industry matures, and competition begins to weed out inferior competitors, firms may internalize more activities to enhance the bases for competitive advantage.

This evolution of outsource activity as a function of industry development is depicted in Exhibit 9-3. It is interesting to note that this evolution is not ensured. Route 128 in Boston and Silicon Valley in California were largely engaged in similar industries. While Route 128 is primarily associated with mini-computers, and Silicon Valley is associated with personal computers, both regions were highly involved in most stages of electronics innovation since World War II. An interesting distinction between the two regions, often cited as the reason Silicon Valley has ultimately been more successful, is the fact that Route 128 comprises

Exhibit 9-3. The Evolution of Firm Scope in Emerging Industries

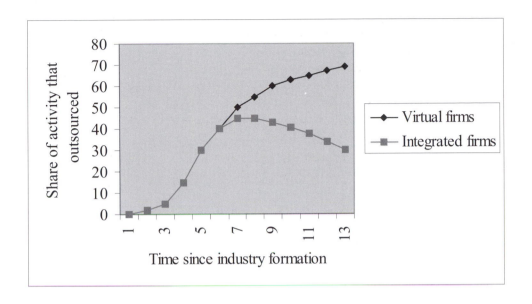

large, vertically integrated electronics firms, while Silicon Valley is primarily single function and virtual firms.[7]

A Note on Strategic Alliances

One very popular trend for both established firms and new ventures is alliance formation. Strategic alliances can take on many forms: technology alliances are formed to jointly develop new technologies, marketing alliances allow a new venture to tap into the distribution channels of established firms, while allowing the established firm to fill out its product line, and sourcing alliances allow representatives from the buyer organization to reside within the supplier organization for more effective development and incorporation of the supplied parts.

The concern with strategic alliances is that rather than combining the benefits of markets and hierarchies, they actually tend to combine the detriments. Alliance partners forego the high power incentives and efficiency of outsourcing through the market, and also lose the protection of proprietary knowledge afforded by internalization. In addition, alliances require as much, if not more, oversight and communication as internalization. Those resources strain an established firm, much more so a new venture.

For some really nice stories of alliances forced upon a new venture by its investors, read the accounts of Go Corporation.[8] In one case, with Microsoft, the

235

problem was loss of proprietary knowledge. In another case, with a large insurer, it was inordinate effort dealing with a reluctant buyer, who ultimately never committed.

This is not to say that strategic alliances are to be avoided completely. It is to say strategic alliances should not be entered casually.

New ventures can form valuable alliances when those ventures have well-defined objectives and a comprehensive strategy for exploiting the alliance. One very successful example of a new venture that exploited strategic alliances with powerful established firms is Millenium pharmaceuticals.[9] Millenium had proprietary bio-technology that was attractive to the large Pharmaceuticals firms. In a series of alliances, Millenium was able to successively enter more stages of the value chain, such that within its seven-year life, it was in sight of being a fully integrated pharmaceutical firm.

The recommendation, then, is that you consider strategic alliances only if there are problems with your outsourcing (no reliable firm is willing to supply you) and internalization options (your venture lacks capability), and only if you have the resources and foresight to manage the alliance strategically.

ANALYTICAL PROCESS

Having identified the venture's core benefit proposition in Chapter 3, and having established the default decision above as outsourcing all activities, we proceed with the process for determining when activities should be internalized. The process begins by characterizing the venture's value chain. From there, we develop a profile of the relative efficiency and relative advantage from internalizing each activity. This allows us to rank activities by their long-term value-added. The firm then internalizes activities with the greatest value-added up to the point at which the firm scope becomes too large for the current management. Other activities that add value, can be internalized at some point in the future (remembering that it is easier to integrate activities in the future than it is to sever them).

Value chain

The first step in the scope decision is to characterize the venture's value chain. The value chain is the sequence of activities that convert a firm's inputs into outputs. Exhibit 9-4 is a generic, top-level value chain for a manufacturing firm. The primary activities (those performed for each unit of output) are inbound logistics (purchasing, inventory holding, and materials handling), production, outbound logistics (warehousing and distribution), sales and marketing, and customer service.

In addition to the primary activities is a set of support activities. These include finance, accounting, information systems, legal services, research,

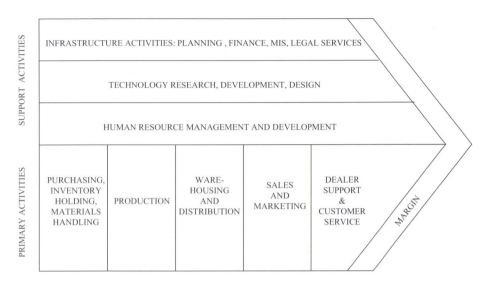

Exhibit 9-4. Generic Value Chain for a manufacturing firm

design and development, and human resources. Support activities occur on a continual or as-needed basis, related to the scale, but not the pace of primary activities. A simple means of distinguishing between the classes of activities is to partition them into tasks that enter into costs of goods sold (primary activities) versus everything else (support activities).

Exhibit 9-4 characterizes activity at too high a level to aid in decision-making, but it is helpful in triggering a complete, more detailed, value chain for specific ventures. We have translated the high-level depiction into a detailed value chain for Epigraphs in Exhibit 9-5. Here we have distinguished a third type of activity—development. While primary and support activities are recurring, development activities occur only once (or once per product development). The goal in characterizing the value chain (fleshing out Exhibit 9-5 for your venture) is to be as thorough as possible. This framework not only supports the scope decision, but also provides the template for specifying resource requirements in the next chapter.

Scope Worksheet

Once the value chain has been fully characterized, we gather details on each activity. We assess the structure of the supply industry, the cost to execute the

Exhibit 9-5. Epigraphs Value Chain

Select Materials		Design patterns			Develop displays	Develop Advertising
Materials purchase	Inventory Materials	Create Die	Package rolls	Inventory Packaged rolls	Take orders	Fulfillment
		Produce rolls				
			Design Packaging			
		Produce Prototype		Develop Dealer Site	Develop Consumer site	
		Design Instructions		Computer support	Dealer support	Customer service
				Advertising Promotion	Accounting	Legal
					Human Resources	

Primary Activities
Support Activities
Development Activities

activity both internally and through outsourcing, the current level of firm competence in executing the activity, the degree of strategic value, as well as the extent of complementarities between activities. This "Scope Worksheet" has been completed for Epigraphs in Exhibit 9-6. Information on the structure of the supply industry comes from the analysis in chapter 2; information on costs is from bids from potential suppliers.

The worksheet can be used in a number of ways to draw conclusions about which activities to internalize. One approach is to compute the break-even volume and cross-over volume for each activity (or each module), just as we did for distribution channel analysis in Chapter 6. At this point, given our outsource bias, that analysis may be overkill. Instead, one of the columns that captures the spirit of breakeven analysis, but not the details, is minimum efficient scale. Minimum efficient scale (MES), as the name implies, is the scale of operations below which it makes little sense to internalize an activity. Think of MES as a flag for us to revisit the scope decision when we reach that scale in the future.

We advocate following simple decision rules, like those in Ulrich and Ellison for mapping the activity characteristics into a scope decision. These decision rules are summarized in Exhibit 9-7. If the activity is strategic, then internalize it *unless* the supply industry is competitive, or your venture has limited competence. If the activity is non-strategic, then outsource it unless a) the supply industry is non-competitive, b) there is substantial threat of forward integration by the supplier, or c) outsourcing would require you to divulge proprietary information to the supplier.

EPIGRAPHS

Epigraphs is somewhat unique, in that it is a transient venture—one product with a three-year lifespan, with no plans to develop new products beyond that. Thus the venture has an even more pronounced outsourcing bias than other new ventures. Having said that, the scope decisions suggest it is not a virtual firm.

We have already developed and discussed Epigraphs' value chain (Exhibit 9-5) and the activity worksheet (Exhibit 9-6) in the previous section on analytical process. We now apply the decision rules in Exhibit 9-7 to the Epigraphs activity worksheet in Exhibit 9-6 to make internalization/outsourcing decisions for each module. We examined modules rather than activities to keep interconnected activities together regardless of whether the activities were to be outsourced or internalized. This mapping process led us to the following scope decisions:

Design module (Design of the product and packaging): **Internalize**
> Two things argue in favor of internalization. First, this module is of strategic importance—it is the most fundamental element of the venture.

Exhibit 9-6. Epigraphs Scope Worksheet

Activity	Number suppliers	Fwd integration Potential*	Tech uncer-tainty	Avg unit cost outsource	Avg unit cost internal	Min effic Scale	Current comp-etence	Strategic Value	Interdep activities	Comments
Primary										
Materials	One	Low	Mod	-	$3.00/roll	-	-	High	Manufg module	Done by mfr if outsourced
Inventory materials	-	-	-	-	.03/roll**	-	-	Low	Manufg module	Done by mfr if outsourced
Manufact Rolls	Compet-itive	Low	Low		$7.70/roll	500 roll/mo	None	High	Manufg module	Done by mfr if outsourced
Package rolls	Compet-itive	Moderate	Low		$1.00/roll		None	Low	Mfg or fulfill	Done by mfr/ fulfill if outs
Inventory goods	Compet-itive	Low	Low	-	$.10/roll		None	Mod	Fulfill module	Done by fulfill if outsourced
Take orders	Compet-itive	Low	Low	Check Call ctr	2.50/order***	100/mo	None	High	Customer Int mod	With EDI could be $0
Fulfillment	Compet-tive	Low	Low	Check fulfill	2.50/order	100/mo	None	Low	Fulfill module	
Support										
Accounting	Compet-itive	Low	Low	$125/hr		160 hrs/mo	Mod	Low		
Legal	Compet-itive	Low	Low	$300/hr		160 hrs/mo	None	Low		
Computer support	Compet-itive	Low	Low	$50/hr		160 hrs/mo	Mod	Mod	Customer Int mod	
Human resources	Compet-itive	Low	Low	_%_ payroll		50 em-ployees	Mod	Mod		
Advertising /Promotion	Compet-itive	Low	Low	Included In ad fees	-	$1 mill adv	Low	High	Adv module	

Dealer support	-	-	-	-	_ hrs/dealer/month	-	Mod	High	Customer Int mod	
Customer service	-	-	-	-	_ hrs/month rolls	-	Mod	High	Customer Int mod	
Develop										
Design patterns	-	-	-	-	Founder hours	-	High	High	-	
Create template/die	-	-	Mod	Check Mfr	-	-	-	High	Mfr module	Done by mfr
Select materials	-	-	-	-	Founder Hours	-	High	High	Mfr module	
Produce prototype(s)	-	-	Mod	Check Mfr	-	-	-	High	Mfr module	Done by mfr
Develop advertising	Competitive	Low	Low	Inc in Ad fees	-	-	Low	High	Adv module	
Develop displays	Competitive	Low	Low	?	-	-	Low	High	Adv module	
Develop dealer site	Competitive	Low	Low	$25,000	-	-	Mod	High	Customer Int mod	
Consumer site	Competitive	Low	Low	Inc with Dealer site	-	-	Mod	High	Customer Int mod	
Produce instructions	-	Low	Low	$5000 production	-	-	Low	Mod	-	

Exhibit 9-7. Simple Rules for scope decision, given activity or module characteristics

Strategic Value	Need to divulge Propri tech	Number of suppliers	Supplier threat of integration	Current competence	**Scope Decision**
High	-	Low	-	Mod+	**Internalize**
High	No	High	Low	Low	**Outsource**
Low	No	Low	Low	High	**Outsource**
Low	Yes	High	Low	-	**Outsource**
Low	Yes	High	High	Mod+	**Internalize**

Second, much of this task has already been done in generating the prototype for the focus group, and analyzing the refinements from conjoint data. The only work remaining is to determine the sources of materials and select the quotes. (If we were to outsource the relevant supply industry is product designers, which is competitive.)

Customer interface module (Order taking, dealer support, customer service): **Internalize**

This module is also of strategic importance because we plan to use a single distribution channel. Thus, maintaining a good relationship with the channel is critical. In addition, tight links with the channel and the order data base provide rapid feedback on any issues end-users have with the product.

Manufacturing module: (Material purchase and inventory, manufacture rolls): **Outsource**

While product quality is of strategic importance, two factors argue in favor of outsourcing. First, the two potential supply industries, sign makers and die-cutters, are both competitive. Second, the venture has no expertise or facility with which to begin manufacturing, and investments in expertise and facilities make little sense for a venture with a three-year life. The major caveat is that if Epigraphs uses die-cutting technology, the dies will be specific assets, thus the die-cutters have hold-up potential. (Note: We will revisit this decision in the next chapter on resource requirements.)

Fulfillment module: (Package and inventory rolls, fulfill orders):

Outsource

> Fulfillment is the tail-end of the relationship with the channel, thus it is potentially important. However, this module, like the manufacturing module, requires investments in facilities and equipment that seem unwarranted given the venture's short life. Moreover, fulfillment is a competitive industry.

Misc. support activities: (Advertising, human resources, legal, accounting):

Outsource

> These services are all in competitive supply, and the venture has inadequate scale to justify bringing any of them in house. By definition, none of them is of strategic importance.

Thus, the Epigraphs venture becomes similar in scope to R&R (*TV Guide* Game). While Epigraphs tends toward a virtual configuration, the firm maintains competence and control over design activities as well as dealer/customer interface. The strategic value of the dealer/customer interface is that it provides data on product demand and quality to facilitate rapid reconfiguration of manufacturing and the product mix. (It may also provide insights for future venture ideas.)

CONCLUSION

In this chapter we examined the last of the strategic decisions—that of firm scope. The two extremes of firm scope are complete vertical integration on one end, and a virtual firm (complete outsourcing) on the other. We discussed issues that would drive the venture toward one direction versus the other.

We outlined a process for decomposing firm activities and assessing the decision separately, and within modules, for each activity.

This is the final step in venture design. We've designed both the product and the firm. In the remaining chapters we outline the resources that are required to execute that venture design. The first step is to identify the necessary human and physical resources. We do that in the next chapter.

Appendix 9-1
Operational Scope Worksheet

Our goal in this chapter is to determine which activities to outsource and which to execute internally, to ensure the long-term viability of the venture.   To make that decision, you need two to characterize the venture's value chain, and you need to analyze each activity.

1. Characterize the venture's value chain. Distinguish between primary activities, support activities, and development activities. Show interdependencies between activities, where they exist. (Use Exhibit 9-5 as an example)

2. Complete the scope worksheet (use Exhibit 9-6 as an example)

| Activity | Supply industry structure | | | | | Internal capability | | | | | | |
	Number suppliers	Fwd integration Potential*	Tech uncer-tainty	Avg unit cost outsource	Avg unit cost internal	Min effic Scale	Current comp-etence	Strategic Value	Interdep activities	Internalize Or Outsource
Primary										
Support										
Develop										

3. Make the scope decision for each activity based on the information in the worksheet and the principles in the chapter (enter decision in last column of table above).

1 Caggiano, Christopher, 1996. "Kings of the Hill," Inc Magazine, August 1996, pp. 46-53.

2 These observations were drawn by James A. Brickley, Clifford W. Smith, and Jerold L. Zimmerman, 2000. "Managerial Economics and Organization Architecture," New York: McGraw-Hill.

3 Kaplan, Jerry, 2000. "Startup: A Silicon Valley Adventure," New York: Penguin Books.

4 King, Andrew, 1999. "Retrieving and transferring embodied data: Implications for the management of interdependence within organizations." Management Science, 45(7): 918-935.

5 The Inc 500 represent the most successful (fastest growing) privately held new ventures. To qualify for the 1999 Inc 500, a company had to have sales of at least $200,000 in base year, 1994. The fastest growing firm had 20332% (377%AGR) growth from 1994 to 1998, while firm 500 had growth of 595% (156% AGR) over the same period.

6 Source: Walker G., 2000. "Changing the Boundaries of the Firm," Chapter 5 in "Strategic Thinking," forthcoming, Irwin-McGraw, pp. 17.

7 For a detailed comparison of the two regions, see Saxenian, Annalee, 1996. "Regional Advantage: Culture and Competition in Silicon Valley and Route 128," Cambridge, MA: Harvard University Press.

8 Kaplan (op cit)

9 Thomke, Stefan and Ashok Nimgade, 2000. "Millenium Pharmaceuticals, Inc. (A)" HBS Case 9-600-038.

10 Source: Ulrich, K. and D. Ellison, "Beyond Make-Buy: Internalization and Integration of Design and Production."

11 This is particularly important if there is proprietary knowledge/technology that is NOT protected by patent

12 Assumes 12% cost of capital, and 30 days material inventory.

13 Assumes 15 minutes labor at $10.00 (may be costless with EDI).

14 This is particularly important if there is proprietary knowledge/technology that is NOT protected by patent.

determining requirements

resource requirements and capacity planning

INTRODUCTION AND GOALS

Up until this point, we have been making major strategic decisions for the venture: whom to target, with what product, at what price, through what distribution channel and advertising program, and with what internal operations. Now we move from strategic decisions to operational implementation—given the decisions we have made, what resources are required to execute those decisions. In this chapter we consider physical and human resource requirements. In the next chapter, we translate the physical and human resource requirements into financial requirements.

The goal in this chapter and the next is to provide adequate resources to satisfy the forecasted demand. In Chapter 8, we emphasized that an accurate demand forecast is the linchpin of the business plan. We said that an optimistic forecast will lead to over-investment in human and physical capital resources, and that the carrying costs of those investments could strangle an otherwise healthy venture. Similarly, a pessimistic forecast can lead to under-investment in resources. Such under-investment will render the firm unable to satisfy demand, and may lead to permanent losses in potential market share as customers go elsewhere. In this chapter, we specify the internal resources that are commensurate with demand, so that we avoid both under-investment and over-investment.

The chapter presents three new tools: the operating cycle, the bill of capacity, and the master production schedule. We combine these tools with the demand forecast developed in Chapter 8 and the scope decision in Chapter 9 to develop the human and physical resource requirements for the venture. We apply this approach to the Epigraphs example.

PRINCIPLES

Whereas in the previous chapters our principles have been more or less theoretical, in this chapter the principles are decidedly operational. The chapter first translates the demand forecast into the resource requirements (labor hours, machine hours, and floor space). These resource requirements are then used to make venture capacity decisions: how many people to employ and how much equipment to secure (either lease or buy).

The important distinction between requirements and capacity is that while requirements can be expressed in divisible units, actual investments in capacity are lumpy. A firm can't, for example, add 0.5 machines. While it can in principle add human resources in partial units (through the use of part-time labor), a practice of doing so to solve the lumpiness problem will lead to a larger (and less committed) workforce than the corresponding full-time force.

These problems of adding capacity are particularly acute for new ventures. A 10% increase in demand for a large manufacturer with 20 workstations translates into the fairly straightforward addition of two workstations. A 10% increase in demand for a new venture operating at capacity with one workstation, implies a dilemma between overtime on the existing workstation (and therefore overtime labor, and higher equipment maintenance costs) and committing to the second workstation (despite the fact that it will likely operate below breakeven volume).

The goal of capacity planning is to recognize at what point it is optimal to add units of capacity. This is a long-term planning approach to adjusting capacity. It is also possible to adjust capacity in the short term. However, short-term adjustments are costly, because they generally involve the use of overtime labor (with wage premiums). They are also disruptive. Not only are new employees not immediately functional, but worse, their training requires valuable labor hours from more experienced employees who are already working beyond capacity. It is for these reasons that short-run marginal cost curves are upward sloping, even though most industries exhibit scale economies. Thus, a secondary goal in defining resource requirements is to minimize the need for short-term adjustments in capacity.

ANALYTICAL PROCESS

This chapter is closely related to the last chapter on firm scope. Both chapters require knowledge of the value chain and of the technology associated with each stage of the value chain. Whereas in the last chapter this knowledge was at the rather high level of activities, here we work at the more detailed level of task execution. We actually specify over time the types of equipment and labor required to produce forecasted demand.

To establish the resource requirements for the venture's internal operations, we need to define or characterize four things:

- The relevant unit of output

- The operating cycle
- The "bill of capacity"
- The master production schedule

Output units

While defining the unit of output is trivial in many industries, in some it is less obvious. We therefore take a moment to review standard industry definitions. The goal in defining the unit of output is to capture the limiting resource. In the case of auto production, the obvious output measure is the number of vehicles. In the case of airlines, the limiting resources are the number of seats in each aircraft and the number of trips that each aircraft can make. Thus, the standard output measure in the industry is seat-miles. Both these measures (vehicles and seat-miles) obscure the fact that there is a good deal of variation in the types of vehicles (Toyota produces the Corolla as well as the Lexus), and the types of flights (short-hops versus long-hauls). This variation becomes important in detailed operations planning, but we leave those details to more operations texts.

Operating cycle

The operating cycle is the schedule of activities that convert the venture's inputs into delivery of its outputs. In the case of a multi-product or multi-service firm, there will be a set of operating cycles. In McDonald's for example, there are separate cycles for hamburgers, french fries, and shakes. Even in the case of a single product firm, there may be two operating cycles: the external cycle of processing orders, and the internal cycle of producing the goods to fulfill the orders. Relatedly, direct mail catalogs (and their e-tailing equivalents) have separate cycles for "catalog" production (website updating), and order processing.

The objective in characterizing the operating cycle is to "calendarize" the utilization of assets. This is necessary because peak demand in November, may not correspond to peak labor in November if, for example, the operating cycle is two months.

The value chain developed in Chapter 9 is a good starting point for characterizing the operating cycle. To convert the value chain to an operating cycle, we focus on the primary activities. For each activity we specify its duration. Since the value chain implies the ordered sequence of activities, we can also characterize each activity in terms of its start time and completion time, relative to the start of the entire cycle. This is done for Epigraphs in Exhibit 10-1. (Note that in Chapter 9 we determined that Epigraphs would outsource production. Thus this exercise is primarily for illustration, and to confirm the scope decision.) The Exhibit makes an assumption that there are no queues in any of the processes. Under this assumption, the elapsed time from receipt of order to delivery at the shipping dock is 2:05 (2 hours and 5 minutes). Whether the item ships on the

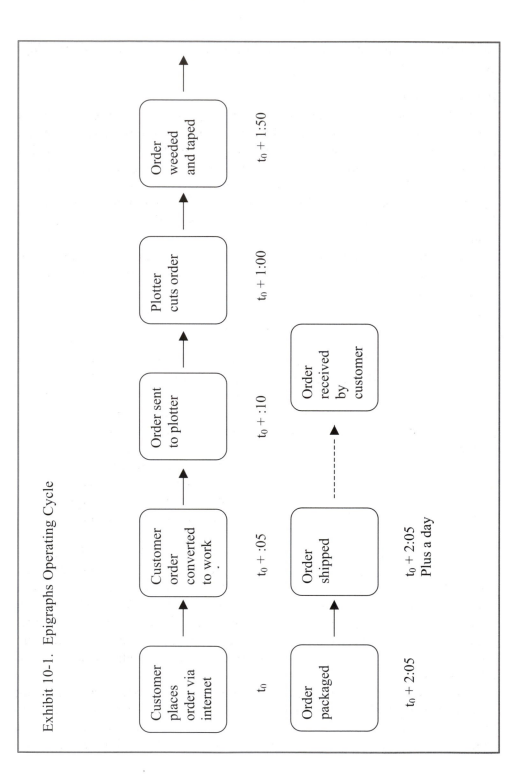

Exhibit 10-1. Epigraphs Operating Cycle

day of order receipt is a function of the time of day it is received relative to shipper pick-up times.

Bill of Capacity

While the operating cycle characterizes the sequence of activities that convert inputs to a given unit of output, the "bill of capacity" specifies the total standard time of each piece of equipment, and each type of labor required to produce that unit of output.[1] Standard time is the number of equipment or labor minutes (or hours) required to execute a task. These standards can be developed from micro-detail of the motions involved in executing each task using universal standards. In general however, standards are historical firm-specific averages of the time required to perform tasks.

A particularly charming example of an effort to simultaneously design a plant layout and develop time standards for firm activities comes from the early history of McDonald's:

> The McDonald brothers showed similar inventiveness when they designed the kitchen for the new building. It was more than twice the size of the one in San Bernardino, and the brothers wanted to be certain that its design accommodated their well-defined production system. They had a brainstorm. They drew the outline of the new kitchen on their home tennis court, and after closing one night at Fourteenth and E, they invited the night crew over to go through all the hamburger assembly motions. As the crew members moved around the court making imaginary hamburgers, shakes and fries, the brothers followed them, marking in red chalk exactly where all the kitchen equipment should be placed. By 3:00 A.M., the tennis court markup was completed; and for a fraction of the cost of conventional design work, the brothers had a detailed kitchen layout.[2]

As the McDonald's story illustrates, developing the bill of capacity requires fairly detailed knowledge of the operational processes. Since we are designing new ventures, this problem is particularly difficult. We won't yet have our own historical standards. Possibly the best source of operational knowledge for new ventures is equipment suppliers. Because suppliers sell the equipment to firms who use it in their operations, they must understand those operations in sufficient detail to argue that their equipment offers efficiency advantages over that of other vendors.

In cases where there is no equipment, and thus no equipment suppliers, you may be able to get the information from firms within your own industry. Though this seems counterintuitive, there are cases when you don't compete directly with other firms in the industry. This is the case, for example, in fragmented industries such as restaurants and auto repair, where each firm serves a local market. Such industries are most easily recognized by the presence of franchises. If you plan to operate in a single region, you may be able to get someone in a distant region to share information with you (possibly for a fee). This was the approach followed by Tables to Teapots. The founders of the venture discovered a store very similar to the one they hoped to start, and convinced the owners to mentor them in exchange for $1500 and an agreement not to compete within 50 miles.[3] Relatedly, if you are in a diversified industry, such as trade-journal publishing, where firms serve highly targeted market segments, you may be able to get information from firms who serve a segment unrelated to the one you plan to serve.

Exhibit 10-2 provides the bill of capacity (and materials) for Epigraphs production process. A separate bill of capacity is necessary for order processing.

Exhibit 10-2. Bill of capacity for Epigraphs production
(Requirements to produce one 50 foot roll)

	Units	Required Units	Cost/unit	Cost/roll
Graphics computer				
Machine	Hours	0.08	0.50	0.04
Labor	Hours	0.08	10.00	0.80
Cutter/plotter				
Vinyl	Roll	0.11	35.00	3.85
Machine	Hours	0.833	0.50	0.42
Labor	Hours	-	-	-
Slitter				
Machine	Hours	0.14	0.17	0.02
Labor	Hours	-	-	-
Weeding/Taping				
Transfer tape	Case	0.014	100.00	1.40
Table	Hours	0.833	0.02	0.01
Table	Sq feet	150		
Labor	Hours	0.833	7.00	5.83
Total unit cost				12.37

The estimates for the production process came from a potential subcontractor. The bill indicates that each roll of wallcovering requires 0.08 hours of graphics computer time, 0.83 hours of cutter time, and 0.14 hours of slitter time. The corresponding labor requirements are 0.08 hours of computer operation and 0.83 hours of weeding/taping. We have incorporated costs for each of the equipment, labor, and material requirements, to form the fully burdened unit cost for a produced roll of $12.37. Note that this bill of capacity is specific to a particular configuration of technology.

Demand Forecast/Master Production Schedule (MPS)

A master production schedule (MPS) is the anticipated build schedule for manufacturing end products. It is a statement of production, rather than a demand forecast. The MPS and the demand forecast are the same however, if the venture plans to produce to demand. Alternatively, the venture could produce to inventory (to smooth work, for example). In those cases, the MPS and the demand forecast will be different. As a first step, you will want to look at unsmoothed demand.

For Epigraphs, the demand forecast pertains to sales at the distribution channel. Assuming setbacks for shipping and stocking at the chains of 1 month, the MPS for Epigraphs is merely the demand forecast shifted by one month. This is shown in Exhibit 10-3. The Exhibit indicates that production peaks in Quarter 3 at 294,000 rolls. This peaking reflects the industry sales profile over a pattern life.

Exhibit 10-3. Epigraphs Master Production Schedule

	Q1	Q2	Q3	Q4	Q5	Q6	Q7	Q8	Q9	Q10	Q11	Q12
Quarterly Sales (1000 rolls)	59	221	294	265	191	132	88	59	16	11	6	6

The low-early sales help the venture ramp-up production. The low sales after Quarter 6 suggest a strategy of level production in Quarters 2 through 6, followed by shutdown thereafter. You wouldn't want to smooth production over all twelve quarters. Doing so would leave customers with unmet demand, thus alienating them and inviting entry. For now, we will ignore the smoothing issue, and continue with the assumption of producing to demand to help illuminate the next two stages of analysis.

Calendarized Resource Requirements

The bill of capacity is combined with the MPS to specify the requirements for each type of equipment, and each type of labor. The resource requirements are merely the hours required for each unit of production times the planned units in the MPS in each quarter. These are shown for Epigraphs in Exhibit 10-4.

The Exhibit indicates that the equipment resources required to produce the level demand of 294,000 rolls are: 23,520 hours of graphics computer time, 244,902 hours of cutter time, 41,160 hours of slitter time, and 244,902 hours of table time per quarter. The corresponding human resources are 23,520 hours of computer operators, and 244,902 hours of a weeder/taper. Finally, peak quarterly production consumes 32,340 rolls of vinyl and 4116 rolls of transfer tape. Next we translate these hourly requirements into capacity requirements—numbers of equipment to purchase or lease and number of employees to hire.

Associated Capacity Requirements

The calendarized resource requirements in Exhibit 10-4 are expressed in hours. To convert these resource requirements into capacity plans, we translate the hours into full-time equivalent. We make an assumption that all resources are utilized for a single shift only. Thus over three months, each employee or piece of equipment is productive for 504 hours (40 hours per week times 13 weeks—less 2 days holiday per quarter).

The peak in Quarter 3 establishes the necessary capacity of all resources. These are elucidated in Exhibit 10-5. The most significant requirements—those driving the venture scale are for plotters (equipment), and weeders (labor). Single shift operations dictate a requirement for 486 plotters, 486 tables, and 486 weeders (as well as other equipment and labor).

While we could ease the equipment requirement by operating double shift, this would not ease the labor requirement. One advantage of single shift operation is that servicing can take place in the second shift, where it does not disrupt production. In a double shift operation, we would need to add machine service downtime to the hourly equipment requirements. Thus, if a machine requires 10 hour servicing for every 200 hours of operation, we would need to rescale the hours above by 1.05 (210/200)—thus 244,902 hours of cutter time becomes 257,147 hours. Another advantage of single shift operation is that only one management team is required. A thorough examination of the shift decision would require that these advantages of the single shift be weighed against the cost savings from cutting the equipment resources in half, and cutting the physical plant size accordingly.

Exhibit 10-4. Calendarized Resource Requirements for Epigraphs

	Required Hours	Q1	Q2	Q3	Q4	Q5	Q6	Q7	Q8	Q9	Q10	Q11	Q12
Quarterly Sales (1000 rolls)		59	221	294	265	191	132	88	59	16	11	6	6
Graphics computer													
machine	80	4,720	17,680	23,520	21,200	15,280	10,560	7,040	4,720	1,280	880	480	480
Labor	80	4,720	17,680	23,520	21,200	15,280	10,560	7,040	4,720	1,280	880	480	480
Cutter/plotter													
vinyl	110	6,490	24,310	32,340	29,150	21,010	14,520	9,680	6,490	1,760	1,210	660	660
machine	833	49,147	184,093	244,902	220,745	159,103	109,956	73,304	49,147	13,328	9,163	4,998	4,998
Labor	0												
Slitter													
machine	140	8,260	30,940	41,160	37,100	26,740	18,480	12,320	8,260	2,240	1,540	840	840
labor	0												
Weeding/Taping													
Transfer tape	14	826	3,094	4,116	3,710	2,674	1,848	1,232	826	224	154	84	84
Table	833	49,147	184,093	244,902	220,745	159,103	109,956	73,304	49,147	13,328	9,163	4,998	4,998
Labor	833	49,147	184,093	244,902	220,745	159,103	109,956	73,304	49,147	13,328	9,163	4,998	4,998

Exhibit 10-5. Capacity Requirements for Epigraphs

Resource	Maximum Hours*	Required Capacity**
Graphics computer		
Machine	23,520	47
Labor	23,520	47
Cutter/plotter		
Machine	244,902	486
Labor		
Slitter		
Machine	41,160	82
Labor		
Weeding/Taping		
Table	244,902	486
Labor	244,902	486

*From Exhibit 10-4, Quarter 3

**Assumes 504 hours per quarter (13 weeks*40 hours-2 holidays)

EPIGRAPHS

Details for Epigraphs resource requirements analysis have been outlined above in the process section, thus we won't duplicate them here. We do however, want to comment on a venture design implication that arises from this analysis. In particular, the capacity requirements in Exhibit 10-5 define a very large scale operation—in fact, twenty times the size of an average sign shop. Such scale is infeasible for a new operation without prior production expertise. Even if the managerial challenges could be solved, the financial investment is significant—the 486 plotters are approximately $3.1 million. Moreover, the physical space necessary to accommodate the plotters and the weeding tables is approximately 200,000 square feet. Even in an industrial location, this implies monthly rent of $200,000 (with a likely requirement for a long-term lease). Given the short expected life of the venture, these investments seem unwarranted. Thus, the resource requirements analysis supports the decision reached in Chapter 9 on scope—that Epigraphs should outsource production.

CONCLUSION

In this chapter we translated all the prior venture decisions into a set of physical and human resource requirements to implement the venture. To do this we had to define a unit of output, generate an operating cycle, create a master production schedule (MPS), and specify the bill of materials to produce the unit output. We then applied the bill of materials to the MPS to quantify the equipment and employment necessary to satisfy demand.

In the next chapter, we apply wage rates and equipment purchase/lease costs to these physical and human resources to define the necessary financial resources.

Appendix 10-1
Resource Requirements Worksheet

Our goal in this chapter is to specify the resource and capacity requirements of the venture. To make that decision, you need to characterize the venture's operating cycle, the bill of capacity for internal activities, the master schedule (may be the same as the top level demand forecast), the calendarized resource requirements, and the capacity requirements.

1. Characterize the operating cycle for the venture. This is the like the value chain for the primary activities in the last chapter, but it adds information about the time it takes to execute the activities (See Exhibit 10-1 for an example).

2. Create the bill of capacity (set of equipment and labor hours required to execute one cycle of the primary activities) (See Exhibit 10-2)

	Units	Required Units	Cost/unit	Cost/roll
Activity 1				
Material				
Machine	Hours			
Labor	Hours			
Activity 2				
Material				
Machine	Hours			
Labor	Hours			
Total unit cost				

3. Characterize the master "production" schedule (See Exhibit 10-3). This may be the same as the demand forecast if there are no lags in the operating cycle.

	Q1	Q2	Q3	Q4	Q5	Q6	Q7	Q8	Q9	Q10	Q11	Q12
Sales (units)												

4. Combine the information from the "bill of capacity" on the requirements for each unit, with the output levels in the master production schedule, to create a calendar of resource requirements (See Exhibit 10-4).

		Q1	Q2	Q3	Q4	Q5	Q6	Q7	Q8	Q9	Q10	Q11	Q12
Sales (units)	Required Hours												
Activity 1													
Material													
Machine													
Labor													
Activity 2													
Material													
Machine													
Labor													
Activity 3													
Material													
Machine													
Labor													
Activity 4													
Material													
Machine													
Labor													

5. Determine the capacity requirements for the venture by examining the maximum hours of each piece of equipment and type labor in each period. Divide the required hours by the usable hours. For example, in a single shift, there are approximately 168 hours per month for each piece of equipment and each employee. (See Exhibit 10-5)

Resource	Required Capacity
Activity 1	
Material	
Machine	
Labor	
Activity 2	
Material	
Machine	
Labor	
Activity 3	
Material	
Machine	
Labor	
Activity 3	
Material	
Machine	
Labor	

[1] This term is similar to the "bill of materials" which is an ordered list of all materials necessary for the production of a single unit. We ignore materials requirements in this text.

[2] Love, John F., 1986. "McDonald's: Behind the Arches," New York: Bantam Books, pp. 21.

[3] McLaughlin, Shane, 1998. "Hands On: Mentor for Hire," Inc Magazine, Dec 1, 1998.

chapter 11

valuation and financial requirements

INTRODUCTION AND GOALS

Having designed the venture and defined its human and physical resource requirements, we can now do the final analysis for the venture—financial analysis. The goals of financial analysis are three-fold. First, we want to characterize the profit potential of the firm through its valuation. Second, we want to determine the funding required to implement the venture design, and third, we want to determine if there is anything we can change in the operational design to improve profits or minimize financial risk.

These three elements are linked. The financial requirements define how much outside investment is required; the valuation determines how much equity is available in exchange for investment; and the risk analysis helps establish the required rate of return for investments. Together these three elements define how much equity in the venture must be given up to gain the necessary funds to ensure the venture's success.

The chapter begins by reviewing the principles of financial analysis and valuation. Next we present the steps in the analytical process: developing financial statements, performing diagnostics on the operational design using those statements, defining the financial requirement, and performing the valuation. We apply all these tools to the Epigraphs example.

PRINCIPLES

The two basic principles that we deal with in this chapter are operating economics and valuation. Operating economics are the translation of your operational practices into their financial impact, both the demands for outside financing, and the financial risk of that financing. Valuation is the process of assigning a price tag to your business—what is the value of your venture as an ongoing concern. The two constructs are linked in that the operating economics define how much outside financing the venture requires, while valuation defines the equity price of those outside funds.

The basic building blocks for the operating economics and the valuation are

265

the same. The primary inputs are the demand forecast from Chapter 9, and the operating cycle and resource requirements from Chapter 10. From these, we develop intermediate inputs: the pro forma financial statements (income statement, balance sheet and cash flow statement) and the cash conversion cycle.

The perspective we take in this chapter is that the venture has not yet raised any funds, either from outsiders or from the founders themselves. Thus we define the total funding requirement. Accordingly, we ignore financial structure issues (amount of debt versus amount of equity) as well as their impact on subsequent valuation. The financial structure of the firm contributes an additional component of risk to the venture. Operating economics define the business risk of variability of *operating income*. Financial structure adds to overall risk through its impact on *net income*.

Operating Economics

The operating economics characterize the economic efficiency of the venture—to what extent is the operational design of the venture driving the requirement for outside financing. We utilize two tools to assess operating economics: ratio analysis and the cash conversion cycle. Ratio analysis is a comparative tool to assess your venture's operating economics relative to those of other ventures. In some sense, the use of ratio analysis at the "paper stage" of the venture seems premature, since the real value of the analysis is as a diagnostic tool. However, it is useful at this stage in testing the reasonableness of the operations design, and in setting operating targets. The cash conversion cycle is an absolute tool for assessing the impact of the operations design on its cash requirements.

Cash conversion cycle. The cash conversion cycle is a financial interpretation of the operating cycle developed in Chapter 10. The cash conversion cycle measures the length of time that the venture needs to fund the costs to produce a unit of output. Functionally, it is the length of time between incurring the expenses associated with production, and actually receiving the payment for the goods or services produced. This is depicted graphically in Exhibit 11-1. The cycle is triggered by the receipt of raw materials, but the cycle actually begins when the firm makes payment for the materials. The length of time between receipt and payment of materials is defined by the accounts payable (AP) policy. Once materials are received they are inventoried as raw materials, as work-in-process, or as finished goods. The length of time in each stage is a function of the venture's inventory and delivery policies. At some point goods are sold, and at some later point payment is received for those goods. The length of time between sale and actual payment is a function of the venture's accounts receivable (AR) policy. The total time that the venture funds the unit of output is computed as the number of days between payment for final goods and payment for the corresponding raw materials.

Exhibit 11-1. The Cash Conversion Cycle

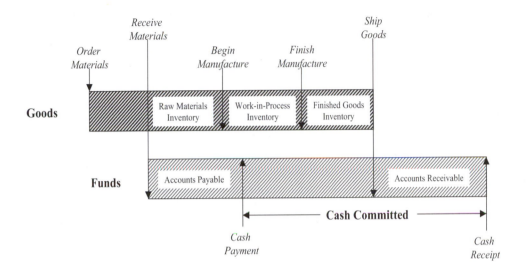

Let's look at the cash conversion cycles of two very different ventures, a manufacturer and an e-tailer. Let's assume that the manufacturer purchases raw materials monthly. If so, the average length of time in raw materials inventory is 15 days. If it makes four different products, and they each are produced one week of the month, then on average, goods are inventoried as work-in-process for another 15 days. Assuming further that the venture produces to stock, and that on average goods are stored as finished product for another 15 days, the total inventory cycle is 45 days.

We make two additional assumptions. The first very credible assumption is that as a new venture, suppliers require payment on receipt, thus the AP period is 0 days. The second assumption is that the venture is an industrial supplier, and thus buyers expect an industry norm of 45 day payment period (invoices are collected throughout the month, billed at the end of the month, and due 30 days later).

Thus the cash conversion cycle is the average days in inventory (45), plus the

AR days (45), minus the AP days (0). In this example then, the venture funds materials for 90 days (3 months). The corresponding working capital requirement is the cost of materials times the demand forecast times the cash conversion cycle. If I forecast demand of 10,000 units per month, and the cost of materials for those units is $100, with the cash conversion cycle of three months, then I require working capital of $3,000,000 ($100*100,000units/month*3months). The associated carrying cost for that working capital might be $60,000 per month.

Let's look at a contrasting example of an Internet retailer who takes title to the goods it sells, but not possession. This would be the case if distributors shipped from their inventory to the end customer, but billed the retailer. Let's assume that the retailer has favorable payment terms with the distributors (30 days), and that payment from customers is by credit card, so that the venture receives payment within 2 days of the order. There is no inventory, so the cash conversion cycle is merely the AR days (2) minus the AP days (30). Thus the cash conversion cycle is actually a *negative* 28 days. Here rather than having to fund production, the venture actually makes money on float. In particular, if we assume parity with the above example—10,000 transactions per month at $100 —the venture has a cash balance of $1,000,000, on which it might earn approximately $5,000 per month.

Thus, despite comparable revenues and cost of goods sold, firm two will have $780,000 higher net income ($65,000 monthly). If both firms look to the equity markets to fund their development costs, firm one will have a lower valuation due to lower net income, and thus will have to give up more equity to obtain the same funds. However, it is even worse off because it needs greater funds. The implication is that operations policies (inventory) and payment policies (AR and AP) have a significant impact not only on the funding requirements for the venture, but also on its financial risk, and its valuation.

Ratio Analysis. Ratio analysis is a diagnostic tool to examine the performance of the venture relative to comparable firms, and to track changes in its own performance over time. Ratios are used internally to make operational decisions; they are used externally to gauge the quality of the venture as an investment. In general, ratio analysis is used to examine realized performance relative to a goal. Here however, we merely have a venture design and the corresponding pro forma statements, so the analysis will test the quality and reasonableness of the design. There are basically four categories of ratios used to evaluate a firm: *liquidity ratios, leverage ratios, efficiency ratios,* and *profit ratios. Liquidity ratios* assess the ability of the venture to meet short-term financial obligations. *Leverage ratios* characterize the financial stability of the venture. *Efficiency ratios* assess the ability of the venture to make effective use of its assets. *Profitability ratios* measure the overall performance of the venture. Since liquidity ratios and leverage ratios pertain to the financial structure of the venture, and we will not be discussing financial structure, we will treat them only superficially. We deal primarily with the performance (efficiency and profitability) ratios.

Exhibit 11-2 summarizes the standard ratios, their calculation, and typical values. For the most part, efficiency ratios are measures of the constructs we discussed for the cash conversion cycle. The ratio, *average collection period*, is the measure of Accounts Receivable (AR) days in the cash cycle. It is computed using AR turnover. A collection period of 45 days corresponds to an AR turnover of 8 (365 days/45 days). Similarly, the ratio, *average purchase credit period*, is the measure of Accounts Payable (AP) days in the cash cycle. It is computed

Exhibit 11-2. Typical Firm Ratios

	FORMULA	OBJECTIVE	RULE OF THUMB
LIQUIDITY RATIOS			
Current ratio	Total current assets / Total current liability	Tests ability to meet short term obligations	>2
Acid test (quick ratio)	Cash +Securities +AR / Current liabilities	Tests ability to meet immediate obligations	>1
LEVERAGE RATIOS			
Debt ratio (leverage ratio)	Total liabilities / Total assets	Measure of debt level	
Debt-to-Equity ratio	Total liabilities / Total equity		
Interest coverage ratio (times interest earned)	EBIT[i] / Interest expense	Tests ease of meeting interest expense	
EFFICIENCY RATIOS			
Accounts receivable turnover	Annual revenues / Average AR balance	Assesses effectiveness of credit policy	>8
Average collection period	365 / AR turnover	Period over which firm is financing customers	< credit period +10
Inventory turnover	Annual COGS[ii] / Average inventory	Assess effectiveness of inventory mgmt	
Average inventory holding period	365 / Inventory turnover	Time to convert materials to sales	
Accounts payable turnover	Annual COGS / Average AP balance	Assesses ability to obtain supplier credit	>8
Average purchase credit period	365 / AP turnover	Period over which firm is financed by supplier	> credit period +10
Asset turnover	Annual revenue / Total assets[iii]	Assesses ability of firm to make use of assets	
PROFITABILITY RATIOS			
Return on sales	Net income / Sales		
Return on equity	Net income / Shareholder equity	Measures return on investment	Compare to stock market
Return on assets	Net income / Total assets	Alternative measure of return on investment	

[i] Earnings before interest and tax
[ii] Cost of Goods Sold
[iii] Important to designate whether the assets are characterized by book value or market value (market value preferred)

using AP turnover. Finally, the ratio, *average inventory holding period*, is the measure of days in inventory in the cash cycle. It is computed using inventory turnover. The main distinction between the AP and inventory turnover ratios versus the AR turnover ratio is that the numerator for AR turnover is revenues, while for AP and inventory the numerator is cost of goods sold (COGS). As we implied in the cash cycle discussion, the goals are to minimize the inventory holding and collections periods, while increasing the purchase credit period. These collectively reduce the need for working capital.

The one efficiency measure not captured by the cash cycle is asset turnover. Whereas the cash cycle measures focus attention on working capital, asset turnover takes into account the effective use of all assets, including physical capital. Asset turnover is improved when firms reduce the cycle time on machines (the time to produce one unit of output), when their maintenance policy minimizes down-times, or when they operate multiple shifts. Three really nice examples of firms that are driven to continually improve operational efficiency are Lincoln Electric,[1] Walmart,[2] and McDonald's.[3]

The profitability ratios are measures of the venture's investment quality. Return on Sales (ROS) varies substantially with industry, and thus is best examined relative to other firms in a given industry. A more useful measure, in large part because it transcends industry, is Return on Equity (ROE). This allows investments in a firm to be compared to investments in other financial instruments (these comparisons however, must take into account the higher risk and lower liquidity of privately held firms).

Valuation

The market value of your venture will ultimately be determined by equity investors, as their investment divided by their equity share. While current market valuations seem to have no relation to a venture's financial forecasts: (A solid team and a business plan is going for $5 million valuation in series A", and "Series C valuation is a balancing act between the funds you require, and desired ownership targets for VCs, founders and owners") you will want to have developed your own valuation to help you decide whether investment offers are attractive to you.

The foundation for venture valuation is securities valuation, but there are special adjustments for privately held firms. There are three basic approaches to valuation: cash flow valuations, asset valuations, and market valuations. We discuss each of these in turn.

Asset-based valuations. Asset-based valuations define the firm's value as the value of its assets minus its debt. There are three basic approaches to asset-based valuations: book value, replacement value, and liquidation value. Generally these approaches are used for purposes other than seeking equity financing, since they disregard the firm's potential to generate income. *Book values* are based on the historical costs of assets, less accumulated depreciation. They are primarily of interest for loans against assets. *Replacement values* take into account the fact that current market prices for the firm's assets may differ from book value. Replacement valuations are important for securing adequate insurance, and for entrepreneurs/firms contemplating entry into new industries or markets. To the extent Greenfield startups (purchase of new assets) in your industry or market are more expensive than the book value of assets, then there is opportunity for existing owners to sell their ventures to the new entrants profitably. Liquidation values pertain to the net proceeds from selling all the firm's assets in a quick sale. Liquidation value can be used as a test of a venture's merit as on ongoing concern. General Dynamics for example, was worth more in pieces than it was as a diversified corporation[4].

Cash flow valuations. Cash flow valuation is the fundamental technique for valuing financial assets generally and public companies, in particular. The present value of a firm is the sum of its future cash flows (CF) discounted by the cost of capital, r:

$$\text{Value} \quad = \quad \frac{\Sigma \; CF_t}{(1+r)^t} \; + \; \frac{\text{terminal value}_n}{(1+r)^n}$$

Since the venture generates a pro forma cash flow statement, cash flow valuations are fairly straightforward. The real challenge is in choosing the appropriate discount rate. A good starting point for the discount rate of the terminal value is the inverse of price-to-earnings ratio (P/E) of public firms in the industry. Stock prices of public firms should reflect their terminal value, where terminal value assumes stable growth, g, of the annual cash flows:

$$\text{Terminal value} \quad = \quad \frac{CF}{r-g}$$

The P/E ratio is merely the inverse of r-g. The corresponding discount rate, r, is therefore:

$$r \; = \; 1 \, / \, (P/E) \; + \; g$$

Adjustments to discount rate for private firms. We mentioned previously that private firms are valued differently than public firms. In particular, there are four adjustments to the discount rate that potentially come into play. The first is an *illiquidity premium*. Because equity in private firms is not traded in competitive markets, investors' shares are less marketable. Accordingly they expect a premium for the illiquidity of their investments. Historically, this premium is an additional 40% over the discount rate of publicly held firms in the industry[5].

The second adjustment is the *key person discount.* The key person discount typically arises in small businesses where the founder controls relationships with customers and suppliers, and has historically made all the major decisions. Think of Bill Gates in the early days of Microsoft. In these instances, there is a significant risk that business will decline even if a replacement manager is found. In fact, a study by Lerch found that even in public firms the value of securities fell 30% after the unexpected death of the owner.[6]

The third adjustment is the *minority discount/control premium.* The minority discount applies when there is an individual or group of individuals controlling more than 50% of the voting rights of the venture. In those instances, the minority shareholders' equity stakes are discounted by approximately 25% relative to ventures in which there are no majority blocks.[7] The control premium is not quite as straightforward, since it varies with the extent of the majority. The control premium is found by taking the market value of the venture, subtracting the market value of the minority shares (adjusted for the minority discount), and dividing the remaining market value by the majority equity stake and the unadjusted discount rate.

Finally, there are *size premia*, reflecting the higher failure rates for small ventures. The size premium for firms valued at less than $150,000 is roughly 4.0%; for firms valued at less than $600,000, the premium is roughly 2.1%; and for firms valued at less than $2,500,000, the premium is roughly 1.3%. Note, these size premia are **added** to the discount rate, whereas the other adjustments were multiplied by the discount rate.

If all four adjustments apply: a minority shareholder in a private firm valued at less than $150,000, with a key person, in an industry with an average discount rate of 15%, then the effective discount rate that the minority shareholder must achieve is:

(15%)* (1.4 illiquidity)*(1.3 key person)*(1.25 minority) + 4% = 38%

Discount rates for earlier periods. The discussion above pertains to discount rates for the venture's terminal value. The underlying assumption is that the firm is being acquired or going public at that point. For earlier stage ventures with greater risk, investors will seek much higher returns. Exhibit 11-3 summarizes the sources and implicit rates of financing typically associated with each stage of the venture.

Note that none of the adjustments just discussed is as precisely defined as I have depicted it. The main point of the foregoing discussion is to make you aware of the set of adjustments, the rationale behind them, and the likely values they may take.

Exhibit 11-3. Sources and rates of financing versus venture stage

Stage	Seed	Seed/startup	Start-up	Development	Growth	Income	Income	Income
Source	Family & friends	Angels	Venture Capital	Venture Capital	Public Equity	Cash-flow financing	Asset financing	Internal financing
Typical Amounts		<$100,000	$1-2 million	$2-5 million	>$10 million		90% AR 50% f.g. inventory 50-80% equipment 85% real estate	Slow AP Speed AR Speed operating cycle
Typical rates	10-18%	25%	90-100%	40-60%	15-20%	12%	Prime + 2	0%
Share of all outside financing	-------	25%	1%		1%	20%	50%	

Multiples valuations. The final approach to valuation, and probably the one most commonly used by business brokers, is multiples valuations. While multiples of earnings is the equivalent of P/E ratios, and therefore fundamentally a discounted cash flow (DCF) approach, it is common in many industries to use multiples of revenues. While we do not advocate this approach to arrive at a valuation for your venture, you will want to be familiar with the revenue multiples in your industry. This is particularly true if you are an acquisition candidate, or if you are creating your venture through acquisition of existing firms. One particularly notable example of venture creation through acquisition is the serial entrepreneur, Wayne Huizenga, who has created several successful public firms through roll-up of existing private firms in a given industry.[8]

The primary multiple approach used by business brokers is the "Multiple of Discretionary Earnings." Discretionary earnings is defined by the International Business Brokers Association as earnings prior to income taxes, non-operating income and expense, non-recurring income and expense, depreciation and amortization, interest income or expense, and owner's compensation. The important distinction between discretionary earnings and EBITDA is the exclusion of owner's compensation expense. The reason that discretionary earnings excludes owner's compensation is that owners have substantial discretion over whether to take income as wages or profits. Because they pay social security tax on the wage component, but not on the profit component, they may actually prefer to understate the market wage for their services. Thus, discretionary earnings is a more reliable measure of a venture's earnings potential than is EBITDA. Having said that, discretionary earnings overstate "earnings" since they don't account for managerial wages. Accordingly, we would expect the multiples of these private firms to be below the P/E ratios for comparable public firms even after we make the adjustments discussed above.

Exhibit 11-4 is a table of typical multiples in several industries from Bizcomps.[9] These multiples are from sales where the transaction price excluded inventory. Note that these multiples are far below standard P/E ratios, because owners should not have to pay the Net Present Value of the wage component of their earnings. Perhaps more interesting than the multiples themselves is the manner in which they are derived by business appraisers. Exhibit 11-5 is an appraiser's analysis table taken from the Handbook of Business Valuation. In essence, the multiple assigned to a business in its valuation is the weighted sum of its rating points on each of ten attributes of the business. The implicit constraint on the multiple is that it can never exceed 3.

A less common, but occasionally used, approach to multiples valuation is "Gross Revenue Multiples". The underlying logic of this approach is that the revenue stream is the valuable asset, and that it, rather than current earnings, defines the true profit potential of the firm. Revenue multiples are most likely to be used

Exhibit 11-4. Multiples of selling price to discretionary earnings developed from Bizcomps

Type of Business	Eastern US	Central US	Western US
Automotive Repair	1.6	2.0	1.9
Beauty salons	1.8	1.4	1.8
Cocktail lounges	1.6	1.5	2.6
Coin laundries	2.0	2.0	2.8
Convenience stores	1.8	1.2	2.6
Delicatessens	1.8	1.2	1.9
Day care centers	2.4	2.0	1.9
Dry cleaners	2.5	2.7	3.2
Florists	1.6	1.6	n/a
Food markets	1.6	1.9	2.6
Liquor stores	1.9	1.6	3.8
Printing	2.2	2.2	2.2
Restaurant/family	2.2	2.0	2.4
Service stations	1.4	2.0	2.1
Service stations w/mini-marts	1.9	1.5	n/a
Video stores	1.8	1.8	2.3

Source: West, Thomas L. "Handbook of Business Valuation, Copyright © 1991 by John Wiley & Sons. Reprinted by permission of John Wiley & Sons.

in either of two extremes: when income data is unreliable or erratic, or in homogeneous industries where the cost structure is standard, and thus where income is highly predictable from revenues (stable ROS). Examples of such homogeneous industries are travel agencies, insurance agencies, and real estate agencies.

Financial requirement

The financial requirement for the venture is simply the most negative cash balance the venture expects in its future. This occurs near the break-even point. Prior to that point, losses add to the negative balance, whereas after the break-even point, profits help to erode it. The basic requirement is determined from the cash flow statement for the nominal (most likely) demand forecast.

You also want to be aware of the impact of best-case and worst-case outcomes on your funding requirement. It is not necessarily true that the "worst case" demand presents the worst case for funding requirements. Often best-case demand creates more pressure on financing. This is particularly true if the cash conversion cycle is long, driving the need for greater working capital. Thus you will examine the most negative cash balance for both scenarios, determine which is greater, and compare that to the nominal requirement to specify a "contingency requirement." You will ask for the nominal amount, but make provisions up front for the contingency amount.

Exhibit 11-5. Certified Business Brokers Appraisers Analysis Table*

Rating Scale	Description	Weight
Historical Profits		10
0.1-1.0	Negative to break-even	
1.1-2.0	Positive, but below industry norm	
2.1-3.0	Industry norm or above	
Income Risk		9
0.1-1.0	Continuity of income at risk	
1.1-2.0	Steady income likely/3-5 years old	
2.1-3.0	Profitability assured/5+ years old	
Terms of Sale		8
0.1-1.0	Seller requires all cash	
1.1-2.0	Reasonable terms available	
2.1-3.0	Exceptional terms available	
Business Type		7
0.1-1.0	Service business with few assets	
1.1-2.0	Equipment and/or inventory significant	
2.1-3.0	High cost of entry (equipment and/or inventory)	
Business Growth		6
0.1-1.0	Declining and further decline likely	
1.1-2.0	Flat or at inflationary levels	
2.1-3.0	Rapid growth with more expected	
Location/Facilities		5
0.1-1.0	Less that desirable to tolerable	
1.1-2.0	Acceptable to average	
2.1-3.0	Above average to superior	
Marketability		4
0.1-1.0	Limited market--special skills required	
1.1-2.0	Normal market--needed skills available	
2.1-3.0	Large market--many qualified buyers	
Desirability		3
0.1-1.0	No status, rough or dirty work	
1.1-2.0	Respectable and satisfactory	
2.1-3.0	Challenging and attractive environment	
Competition		2
0.1-1.0	Highly competitive or unstable market	
1.1-2.0	Normal competitive conditions	
2.1-3.0	Little competition/high startup costs	
Industry		1
0.1-1.0	Declining and further decline likely	
1.1-2.0	Flat or at inflationary levels	
2.1-3.0	Rapid growth with more expected	

*Multiples of discretionary earnings

Source: West, Thomas L., "The 1997 Business Reference Guide," Copyright © 1997 by Business Brokerage Press. Reprinted by permission of the publisher.

ANALYTICAL PROCESS

Financial statements

The analytical process begins with proforma financial statements. The main statement of interest is the *cash flow statement*, but it generally is easiest to create the *income statement* first and use it to derive the cash flow statement. While the *balance sheet* won't be particularly interesting until you know the structure of financing, it is valuable in characterizing the potential for debt financing. Inventories, accounts receivable, property, plant, and equipment are all assets you can borrow against.

The second issue with regard to financial statements is timing. How far into the future do you need to forecast the financials (time horizon), and how frequently within that period do you need to characterize the financials (reporting interval)? The answer to both questions depends on what the statements will be used for. With respect to the time horizon question, venture capitalists typically envision exit after five years, so you will want to forecast cash flows at least that far into the future to be able to form a valuation. Thus, you will want a five-year summary of cash flows. In principle, since valuation analysis is driving the requirement, you should only need the cash flow statement. In practice, you typically see a five-year summary of all three statements.

With respect to the second question of reporting interval, again the answer depends on what the statements will be used for. Here, the driving requirement is accurately specifying the funding requirement. Typically, the most negative cash balance is going to occur within the first two years, so you will want monthly cash flow summaries over that period. Otherwise the true requirement will be "smoothed" over the year in which it occurs, and the requirement will be understated. For example, if the most negative cash balance, -$1,500,000, occurs in July of year 2, but cash flow statements are year-end summaries, then the cash balances in December of years 1 and 2 are by definition less negative than $1,500,000.

For planning purposes, you may want monthly summaries of the income statement over the same period. Note that if your negative cash balance continues to increase beyond two years you will want to continue with monthly summaries until the breakeven point. Similarly, if you reach breakeven in year one, then you only need the first year of monthly summaries.

The third issue with respect to the financial statements pertains to the scenarios: nominal case, pessimistic case, and optimistic case. Again, since these scenarios are created to assess the financial requirement, you will want cash flow statements for each scenario for the monthly summaries.

The nominal case for your financial statements is defined by the conjoint analysis demand coefficients for the chosen product configuration and price.

This is the *potential demand* that you derived in Chapter 5. The *realized demand* that we developed in Chapter 8 combined that potential demand with your decisions about advertising and distribution channel. To generate the worst-case demand, find the standard error on the intercept coefficient, subtract it from potential demand, then assess the impact on realized demand. This should be a simple matter of changing the potential demand row in the Chapter 8 spreadsheet. Similarly, to find best-case demand, add the standard error to potential demand, and work through the Chapter 8 spreadsheet.

In total then, you will want the following financial statements:

Cash flow statement

Monthly summaries for first 24 months (or until breakeven) – nominal case

Monthly summaries for first 24 months (or until breakeven) – worst case

Monthly summaries for first 24 months (or until breakeven) – best case

Annual summary for first five years

Income statement

Monthly summaries for first 24 months (or until breakeven) – nominal case

Monthly summaries for first 24 months (or until breakeven) – worst case

Monthly summaries for first 24 months (or until breakeven) – best case

Annual summary for first five years

Balance sheet

Annual summary for first five years

Exhibits 11-7 through 11-15 are the pro forma financial statements for Epigraphs. Exhibit 11-7 is the income statement for the nominal case, Exhibit 11-8 is the cash flow statement for the nominal case, and Exhibit 11-9 is the balance sheet for the nominal case. Exhibits 11-10 through 11-12 are the corresponding statements for the optimistic case. Exhibits 11-13 through 11-15 are the corresponding statements for the pessimistic case.

The optimistic scenario was created by adding the normalized standard error to the nominal forecast. The normalized standard error is merely the standard error of a coefficient divided by the value of the coefficient itself. Remember from Chapter 8 that the normalized standard error for Epigraphs was 0.072. To create the optimistic forecast we merely multiply the nominal demand forecast by 1.072.

The pessimistic scenario is simply the mirror image of the optimistic scenario—we subtract the normalized standard error from the demand forecast. Thus we multiply the nominal demand forecast by 0.928 (= 1 - 0.072).

Exhibit 11-7. Epigraphs Income Statement (nominal case)

Income Statement-Nominal Case

	Mo 1	Mo 2	Mo 3	Q1	Q2	Q3	Q4	Q5	Q6	Q7	Q8	Q9	Q10	Q11	Q12
Sales															
Units (1000 rolls)	9.8	19.7	29.5	59.0	221.0	294.0	265.0	191.0	132.0	88.0	59.0	44.0	29.0	15.0	15.0
Sales ($1000)	351.2	702.4	1053.6	2107.1	7892.9	10500.0	9464.3	6821.4	4714.3	3142.9	2107.1	1571.4	1035.7	535.7	535.7
Cost of Goods Sold*	121.6	243.3	364.9	729.8	2733.8	3636.8	3278.1	2362.7	1632.8	1088.6	729.8	544.3	358.7	185.6	185.6
Fulfillment @3%	10.5	21.1	31.6	63.2	236.8	315.0	283.9	204.6	141.4	94.3	63.2	47.1	31.1	16.1	16.1
Gross Margin ($1000)	219.0	438.0	657.0	1314.1	4922.3	6548.2	5902.3	4254.1	2940.0	1960.0	1314.1	980.0	645.9	334.1	334.1
Operating Expenses															
General and Administrative															
Office lease	2000	2000	2000	6000	6000	6000	6000	6000	6000	6000	6000	6000	6000	6000	6000
Computer lease & support**	360	360	360	1080	1080	1080	1080	1080	1080	1080	1080	1080	1080	1080	1080
Telecommunications	200	200	200	600	600	600	600	600	600	600	600	600	600	600	600
Managerial salary & benefits	8333.3	8333.3	8333.3	25000	25000	25000	25000	25000	25000	25000	25000	25000	25000	25000	25000
Depreciation & Amortization	2250	2250	2250	0	6750	6750	6750	6750	6750	6750	6750	6750	6750	6750	6750
Selling Expense															
Customer service staff	3333.3	3333.3	3333.3	10000	10000	10000	10000	10000	10000	10000	10000	10000	10000	10000	10000
Advertising (chapter 7)	40500	45000	36000	121500											
Income before tax ($1000)	162.0	376.6	604.6	1149.9	4872.9	6498.8	5852.9	4204.7	2890.6	1910.6	1264.7	930.6	596.5	284.7	284.7
Income taxes	55.1	128.0	205.6	391.0	1656.8	2209.6	1990.0	1429.6	982.8	649.6	430.0	316.4	202.8	96.8	96.8
Net income	106.9	248.5	399.0	758.9	3216.1	4289.2	3862.9	2775.1	1907.8	1261.0	834.7	614.2	393.7	187.9	187.9

* Assumes unit cost of $12.37 (from Exhibit 10-2)
** Assumes two workstations

Exhibit 11-8. Epigraphs Cash Flow Statement (nominal case)

Consolidated Statement of cash flows

	Mo 1	Mo 2	Mo 3	Q1	Q2	Q3	Q4	Q5	Q6	Q7	Q8	Q9	Q10	Q11	Q12
Net income ($1000)	106.9	248.5	399.0	758.9	3216.1	4289.2	3862.9	2775.1	1907.8	1261.0	834.7	614.2	393.7	187.9	187.9
Adjustments to net income															
Depreciation and amortization	2.3	2.3	2.3		6.8	6.8	6.8	6.8	6.8	6.8	6.8	6.8	6.8	6.8	6.8
Increase in market securities															
Increase/(Decrease) in accounts receivable*	-351.2	-526.8	-526.8		-2541.7	-1303.6	517.9	1321.4	1053.6	785.7	517.9	267.9	267.9	250.0	0.0
Decrease in inventory**					-172.3	-298.0	118.4	302.1	240.8	179.6	118.4	61.2	61.2	57.1	0.0
Increase in inventory	-243.3	-121.6	-364.9												
Increase in pre-paids															
Increase in deferred taxes															
Increase in accounts payable***	121.6	121.6	121.6		455.2	270.9	-107.6	-274.6	-218.9	-163.3	-107.6	-55.7	-55.7	-52.0	0.0
Increase in accounts payable-future inventory	243.3														
Decrease in accrued expenses															
Increase in income taxes payable															
Total adjustments	-227.3	-524.5	-767.8		-2252.0	-1323.9	535.4	1355.6	1082.2	808.8	535.4	280.2	280.2	261.9	6.8
Net cash from operating activity	-120.4	-276.0	-368.8		964.1	2965.3	4398.3	4130.7	2990.0	2069.8	1370.1	894.4	673.9	449.8	194.6
Cash flows from investing activity															
Purchase of fixed assets****	-100														
Website & EDI software	-35														
Net cash from investment activity	-135														
Cash Flows from Financing Activity															
Decrease in notes payable															
Decrease in long-term debt															
Proceeds from stock issue															
Payment of dividends															
Net Cash from financing activity															
Increase in Cash	-255.4	-276.0	-368.8	-900.2	964.1	2965.3	4398.3	4130.7	2990.0	2069.8	1370.1	894.4	673.9	449.8	194.6
Cash Balance	-255.4	-531.4	-900.2	-900.2	63.9	3029.2	7427.5	11558.2	14548.2	16618.0	17988.0	18882.4	19556.2	20006.1	20200.7

*Assumes AR days = 45
**Assumes inventory days=60
***Assumes AP days =30
****Purchase of dies

Exhibit 11-9. Epigraphs Income Statement (nominal case)

Consolidated Balance Sheet

	Mo 1	Mo 2	Mo 3	Q1	Q2	Q3	Q4	Q5	Q6	Q7	Q8	Q9	Q10	Q11	Q12
ASSETS															
Current assets															
Cash	-26.6	-318.4	-657.5	-186.3	254.4	3439.0	8159.8	12593.7	15804.8	18029.5	19504.0	20468.5	21196.7	21684.8	21899.2
Marketable securities at cost															
Accounts receivable--less allowance for bad debt	376.5	941.2	1505.9	1404.8	4230.6	5628.0	5072.9	3656.0	2526.9	1684.6	1129.4	842.3	555.1	287.1	287.1
Inventories	260.8	391.2	729.8	729.8	967.1	1285.5	1159.6	835.8	577.6	385.1	258.2	192.5	126.9	65.6	65.6
Prepaid expenses & other current															
Total current assets	610.7	1014.0	1578.2	1948.2	5452.1	10353.5	14392.3	17085.8	18909.3	20099.1	20891.6	21503.4	21878.8	22037.6	22252.0
Property, plant and equipment															
Land															
Buildings															
Equipment	100.0	100.0	100.0	100.0	100.0	100.0	100.0	100.0	100.0	100.0	100.0	100.0	100.0	100.0	100.0
Software	35.0	35.0	35.0	35.0	35.0	35.0	35.0	35.0	35.0	35.0	35.0	35.0	35.0	35.0	35.0
Leasehold improvements															
Furniture,fixtures, etc															
Total property,plant and equi	135.0	135.0	135.0	135.0	135.0	135.0	135.0	135.0	135.0	135.0	135.0	135.0	135.0	135.0	135.0
Less accumulated depreciation*	2.3	4.5	6.8	6.8	13.5	20.3	27.0	33.8	40.5	47.3	54.0	60.8	67.5	74.3	81.0
Net property, plant and equipm	132.8	130.5	128.3	128.3	121.5	114.8	108.0	101.3	94.5	87.8	81.0	74.3	67.5	60.8	54.0
Intangibles															
TOTAL ASSETS	743.5	1144.5	1706.5	2076.5	5573.6	10468.3	14500.3	17187.1	19003.8	20186.9	20972.6	21577.6	21946.3	22098.3	22306.0
LIABILITIES															
Current Liabilities															
Accounts payable	130.4	260.8	391.2	364.9	879.2	1169.6	1054.2	759.8	525.1	350.1	234.7	175.0	115.4	59.7	59.7
Notes payable															
Accrued expenses															
Income taxes payable															
Other liabilities															
Total current liabilities	130.4	260.8	391.2	364.9	879.2	1169.6	1054.2	759.8	525.1	350.1	234.7	175.0	115.4	59.7	59.7
Long-term liabilities															
Deferred income taxes															
Debentures															
Other long-term debt															
Total Liabilities	130.4	260.8	391.2	364.9	879.2	1169.6	1054.2	759.8	525.1	350.1	234.7	175.0	115.4	59.7	59.7
SHAREHOLDER'S EQUITY															
Preferred stock___ par value															
authorized shares															
outstanding shares															
Common stock___ par value															
authorized shares															
outstanding shares															
Additional paid-in capital															
Retained earnings	118.7	270.7	431.6	825.4	4279.3	8883.6	13031.0	16012.2	18063.6	19421.7	20322.8	20987.5	21415.9	21623.6	21831.3
Less: Treasury stock at cost															
Total shareholder's equity	118.7	270.7	431.6	825.4	4279.3	8883.6	13031.0	16012.2	18063.6	19421.7	20322.8	20987.5	21415.9	21623.6	21831.3
Total Liabilities and share equi	249.1	531.5	822.7	1190.3	5158.5	10053.2	14085.2	16772.0	18588.8	19771.8	20557.5	21162.6	21531.2	21683.2	21891.0

* 5 year straight line

Exhibit 11-10. Epigraphs Income Statement (optimistic case)

Income Statement-Optimistic Case

	Mo 1	Mo 2	Mo 3	Q1	Q2	Q3	Q4	Q5	Q6	Q7	Q8	Q9	Q10	Q11	Q12
Sales															
Units (1000 rolls)	10.5	21.1	31.6	63.2	236.9	315.2	284.1	204.8	141.5	94.3	63.2	47.2	31.1	16.1	16.1
Sales ($1000)	376.5	753.0	1129.4	2258.9	8461.1	11256.0	10145.7	7312.6	5053.7	3369.1	2258.9	1684.6	1110.3	574.3	574.3
Cost of Goods Sold*	130.4	260.8	391.2	782.4	2930.6	3898.6	3514.1	2532.8	1750.4	1166.9	782.4	583.5	384.6	198.9	198.9
Fulfillment @3%	11.3	22.6	33.9	67.8	253.8	337.7	304.4	219.4	151.6	101.1	67.8	50.5	33.3	17.2	17.2
Gross Margin ($1000)	234.8	469.6	704.4	1408.7	5276.7	7019.7	6327.3	4560.4	3151.7	2101.1	1408.7	1050.6	692.4	358.1	358.1
Operating Expenses															
General and Administrative															
Office lease	2000	2000	2000	6000	6000	6000	6000	6000	6000	6000	6000	6000	6000	6000	6000
Computer lease & support**	360	360	360	1080	1080	1080	1080	1080	1080	1080	1080	1080	1080	1080	1080
Telecommunications	200	200	200	600	600	600	600	600	600	600	600	600	600	600	600
Managerial salary & benefits	8333	8333	8333	25000	25000	25000	25000	25000	25000	25000	25000	25000	25000	25000	25000
Depreciation & Amortization	2250	2250	2250	0	6750	6750	6750	6750	6750	6750	6750	6750	6750	6750	6750
Selling Expense															
Customer service staff	3333	3333	3333	10000	10000	10000	10000	10000	10000	10000	10000	10000	10000	10000	10000
Advertising (chapter 7)	40500	45000	36000	121500											
Income before tax ($1000)	179.8	410.1	653.9	1250.5	5233.3	6976.3	6283.8	4517.0	3108.3	2057.7	1365.3	1007.1	649.0	314.7	314.7
Income taxes	61.1	139.4	222.3	425.2	1779.3	2371.9	2136.5	1535.8	1056.8	699.6	464.2	342.4	220.7	107.0	107.0
Net income	118.7	270.7	431.6	825.4	3454.0	4604.3	4147.3	2981.2	2051.5	1358.1	901.1	664.7	428.3	207.7	207.7

* Assumes unit cost of $12.37 (from Exhibit 10-2)
** Assumes two workstations

Exhibit 11-11. Epigraphs Cash Flow Statement (optimistic case)

Consolidated Statement of cash flows

	Mo 1	Mo 2	Mo 3	Q1	Q2	Q3	Q4	Q5	Q6	Q7	Q8	Q9	Q10	Q11	Q12
Net income ($1000)	118.7	270.7	431.6	825.4	3454.0	4604.3	4147.3	2981.2	2051.5	1358.1	901.1	664.7	428.3	207.7	207.7
Adjustments to net income															
Depreciation and amortization	2.3	2.3	2.3		6.8	6.8	6.8	6.8	6.8	6.8	6.8	6.8	6.8	6.8	6.8
Increase in market securities															
Decrease in accounts receivable*	-376.5	-564.7	-564.7		-2825.8	-1397.4	555.1	1416.6	1129.4	842.3	555.1	287.1	287.1	268.0	0.0
Decrease in inventory**	-260.8	-130.4	-338.6		-237.3	-319.4	126.9	323.8	258.2	192.5	126.9	65.6	65.6	61.3	0.0
Increase in pre-paids															
Increase in deferred taxes															
Increase in accounts payable***	130.4	130.4	130.4		514.3	290.4	-115.4	-294.4	-234.7	-175.0	-115.4	-59.7	-59.7	-55.7	0.0
Increase in accounts payable-fu	260.8														
Decrease in accrued expenses															
Increase in income taxes payable															
Total adjustments	-243.8	-562.5	-770.7		-2542.1	-1419.7	573.4	1452.8	1159.6	866.5	573.4	299.9	299.9	280.3	6.8
Net cash from operating activity	-125.2	-291.8	-339.1		911.9	3184.6	4720.8	4434.0	3211.1	2224.6	1474.5	964.6	728.2	488.0	214.5
Cash flows from investing activity															
Purchase of fixed assets****	-100														
Website & EDI software	-35														
Net cash from investment activity	-135														
Cash Flows from Financing Activity															
Decrease in notes payable															
Decrease in long-term debt															
Proceeds from stock issue															
Payment of dividends															
Net Cash from financing activity															
Increase in Cash	-260.2	-291.8	-339.1		911.9	3184.6	4720.8	4434.0	3211.1	2224.6	1474.5	964.6	728.2	488.0	214.5
Cash Balance	-26.6	-318.4	-657.5	-657.5	254.4	3439.0	8159.8	12593.7	15804.8	18029.5	19504.0	20468.5	21196.7	21684.8	21899.2

*Assumes AR days = 45
**Assumes inventory days=60
***Assumes AP days=30
****Purchase of dies

Exhibit 11-12. Epigraphs Income Statement (optimistic case)

Consolidated Balance Sheet

	Mo 1	Mo 2	Mo 3	Q1	Q2	Q3	Q4	Q5	Q6	Q7	Q8	Q9	Q10	Q11	Q12
ASSETS															
Current assets															
Cash	-255.4	-531.4	-900.2	-186.3	63.9	3029.2	7427.5	11558.2	14548.2	16618.0	17988.0	18882.4	19556.2	20006.1	20200.7
Marketable securities at cost															
Accounts receivable--less	351.2	878.0	1404.8	1404.8	3946.4	5250.0	4732.1	3410.7	2357.1	1571.4	1053.6	785.7	517.9	267.9	267.9
allowance for bad debt															
Inventories	243.3	364.9	729.8	729.8	902.1	1200.1	1081.8	779.7	538.8	359.2	240.8	179.6	118.4	61.2	61.2
Prepaid expenses & other current															
Total current assets	339.1	711.5	1234.4	1948.2	4912.5	9479.3	13241.4	15748.6	17444.2	18548.6	19282.5	19847.7	20192.5	20335.2	20529.8
Property, plant and equipment															
Land															
Buildings															
Equipment	100.0	100.0	100.0	100.0	100.0	100.0	100.0	100.0	100.0	100.0	100.0	100.0	100.0	100.0	100.0
Software	35.0	35.0	35.0	35.0	35.0	35.0	35.0	35.0	35.0	35.0	35.0	35.0	35.0	35.0	35.0
Leasehold improvements															
Furniture,fixtures, etc															
Total property,plant and equipment	135.0	135.0	135.0	135.0	135.0	135.0	135.0	135.0	135.0	135.0	135.0	135.0	135.0	135.0	135.0
Less accumulated depreciation*	2.3	4.5	6.8	6.8	13.5	20.3	27.0	33.8	40.5	47.3	54.0	60.8	67.5	74.3	81.0
Net property, plant and equipment	132.8	130.5	128.3	128.3	121.5	114.8	108.0	101.3	94.5	87.8	81.0	74.3	67.5	60.8	54.0
Intangibles															
TOTAL ASSETS	471.9	842.0	1362.7	2076.5	5034.0	9594.1	13349.4	15849.9	17538.7	18636.4	19363.5	19922.0	20260.0	20395.9	20583.8
LIABILITIES															
Current Liabilities															
Accounts payable	121.6	243.3	364.9	364.9	820.1	1091.0	983.4	708.8	489.9	326.6	218.9	163.3	107.6	55.7	55.7
Accounts payable-inventory	**243.3**	**243.3**	**243.3**												
Notes payable															
Accrued expenses															
Income taxes payable															
Other liabilities															
Total current liabilities	364.9	486.6	608.2	364.9	820.1	1091.0	983.4	708.8	489.9	326.6	218.9	163.3	107.6	55.7	55.7
Long-term liabilitites															
Deferred income taxes															
Debentures															
Other long-term debt															
Total Liabilities	364.9	486.6	608.2	364.9	820.1	1091.0	983.4	708.8	489.9	326.6	218.9	163.3	107.6	55.7	55.7
SHAREHOLDER'S EQUITY															
Preferred stock , __par value															
authorized shares															
outstanding shares															
Common stock , __par value															
authorized shares															
outstanding shares															
Additional paid-in capital															
Retained earnings	106.9	**355.5**	**754.5**	758.9	3975.0	8264.2	12127.1	14902.2	16810.0	18071.0	18905.7	19519.9	19913.5	20101.4	20289.3
Less: Treasury stock at cost															
Total shareholder's equity	106.9	355.5	754.5	758.9	3975.0	8264.2	12127.1	14902.2	16810.0	18071.0	18905.7	19519.9	19913.5	20101.4	20289.3
Total Liabilities and share equity	471.9	842.0	1362.7	1123.9	4795.2	9355.3	13110.6	15611.0	17299.9	18397.6	19124.6	19683.2	20021.2	20157.1	20345.0

* 5 year straight line

Exhibit 11-13. Epigraphs Income Statement (pessimistic case)

Income Statement-Pessimistic Case	Mo 1	Mo 2	Mo 3	Q1	Q2	Q3	Q4	Q5	Q6	Q7	Q8	Q9	Q10	Q11	Q12
Sales															
Units (1000 rolls)	9.1	18.3	27.4	54.8	205.1	272.8	245.9	177.2	122.5	81.7	54.8	40.8	26.9	13.9	13.9
Sales ($1000)	325.9	651.8	977.7	1955.4	7324.6	9744.0	8782.9	6330.3	4374.9	2916.6	1955.4	1458.3	961.1	497.1	497.1
Cost of Goods Sold*	112.9	225.8	338.6	677.3	2536.9	3374.9	3042.0	2192.6	1515.3	1010.2	677.3	505.1	332.9	172.2	172.2
Fulfillment @3%	9.8	19.6	29.3	58.7	219.7	292.3	263.5	189.9	131.2	87.5	58.7	43.7	28.8	14.9	14.9
Gross Margin ($1000)	203.2	406.5	609.7	1219.5	4567.9	6076.7	5477.3	3947.8	2728.3	1818.9	1219.5	909.4	599.4	310.0	310.0
Operating Expenses															
General and Administrative															
Office lease	2000	2000	2000	6000	6000	6000	6000	6000	6000	6000	6000	6000	6000	6000	6000
Computer lease & support**	360	360	360	1080	1080	1080	1080	1080	1080	1080	1080	1080	1080	1080	1080
Telecommunications	200	200	200	600	600	600	600	600	600	600	600	600	600	600	600
Managerial salary & benefits	8333	8333	8333	25000	25000	25000	25000	25000	25000	25000	25000	25000	25000	25000	25000
Depreciation & Amortization	0	0	0	0	0	0	0	0	0	0	0	0	0	0	0
Selling Expense															
Customer service staff	3333	3333	3333	10000	10000	10000	10000	10000	10000	10000	10000	10000	10000	10000	10000
Advertising (chapter 7)	40500	45000	36000	121500											
Income before tax ($1000)	189.0	392.3	595.5	1176.8	4525.2	6034.1	5434.7	3905.1	2685.7	1776.2	1176.8	866.8	556.7	267.4	267.4
Income taxes	64.3	133.4	202.5	400.1	1538.6	2051.6	1847.8	1327.7	913.1	603.9	400.1	294.7	189.3	90.9	90.9
Net income	124.8	258.9	393.0	776.7	2986.6	3982.5	3586.9	2577.4	1772.5	1172.3	776.7	572.1	367.4	176.5	176.5

* Assumes unit cost of $12.37 (from Exhibit 10-2)
** Assumes two workstations

Exhibit 11-14. Epigraphs Cash Flow Statement (pessimistic case)

Consolidated Statement of cash flows

	Mo 1	Mo 2	Mo 3	Q1	Q2	Q3	Q4	Q5	Q6	Q7	Q8	Q9	Q10	Q11	Q12
Net income ($1000)	124.8	258.9	393.0	776.7	2986.6	3982.5	3586.9	2577.4	1772.5	1172.3	776.7	572.1	367.4	176.5	176.5
Adjustments to net income															
Depreciation and amortization	2.3	2.3	2.3	6.8	6.8	6.8	6.8	6.8	6.8	6.8	6.8	6.8	6.8	6.8	6.8
Increase in market securities															
Decrease in accounts receivable*	-325.9	-488.9	-488.9		-2257.5	-1209.7	480.6	1226.3	977.7	729.1	480.6	248.6	248.6	232.0	0.0
Decrease in inventory**					-107.4	-276.5	109.9	280.3	223.5	166.7	109.9	56.8	56.8	53.0	0.0
Increase in pre-paids															
Increase in deferred taxes															
Increase in accounts payable***	112.9	112.9	112.9		396.2	251.4	-99.9	-254.8	-203.2	-151.5	-99.9	-51.7	-51.7	-48.2	0.0
Increase in accounts payable-fu	225.8														
Decrease in accrued expenses															
Increase in income taxes payable															
Total adjustments	15.0	-373.7	-373.7		-1962.0	-1228.1	497.3	1258.5	1004.8	751.0	497.3	260.5	260.5	243.6	6.8
Net cash from operating activity	139.7	-114.8	19.3		1024.7	2754.4	4084.2	3835.9	2777.3	1923.3	1274.0	832.6	627.9	420.0	183.2
Cash flows from investing activity															
Purchase of fixed assets****	-100														
Website & EDI software	-35														
Net cash from investment activity	-135														
Cash Flows from Financing Activity															
Decrease in notes payable															
Decrease in long-term debt															
Proceeds from stock issue															
Payment of dividends															
Net Cash from financing activity															
Increase in Cash	4.7	-114.8	19.3	-122.1	1024.7	2754.4	4084.2	3835.9	2777.3	1923.3	1274.0	832.6	627.9	420.0	183.2
Cash Balance	-26.6	-141.4	-122.1	-122.1	902.6	3657.0	7741.2	11577.1	14354.4	16277.7	17551.7	18384.3	19012.2	19432.2	19615.4

*Assumes AR days = 45
**Assumes inventory days=60
***Assumes AP days =30
****Purchase of dies

Exhibit 11-15. Epigraphs Balance Sheet (pessimistic case)

Consolidated Balance Sheet

	Mo 1	Mo 2	Mo 3	Q1	Q2	Q3	Q4	Q5	Q6	Q7	Q8	Q9	Q10	Q11	Q12
ASSETS															
Current assets															
Cash	-26.6	-141.4	-122.1	-186.3	902.6	3657.0	7741.2	11577.1	14354.4	16277.7	17551.7	18384.3	19012.2	19432.2	19615.4
Marketable securities at cost	325.9	814.8	1303.6	1404.8	3662.3	4872.0	4391.4	3165.1	2187.4	1458.3	977.7	729.1	480.6	248.6	248.6
Accounts receivable–less allowance for bad debt	225.8	338.6	729.8	729.8	837.2	1113.7	1003.9	723.5	500.0	333.4	223.5	166.7	109.9	56.8	56.8
Inventories															
Prepaid expenses & other current															
Total current assets	525.1	1012.0	1911.4	1948.2	5402.1	9642.7	13136.5	15465.8	17041.9	18069.4	18752.9	19280.1	19602.6	19737.6	19920.8
Property, plant and equipment															
Land															
Buildings	100.0	100.0	100.0	100.0	100.0	100.0	100.0	100.0	100.0	100.0	100.0	100.0	100.0	100.0	100.0
Equipment	35.0	35.0	35.0	35.0	35.0	35.0	35.0	35.0	35.0	35.0	35.0	35.0	35.0	35.0	35.0
Software															
Leasehold improvements															
Furniture, fixtures, etc															
Total property,plant and equi	135.0	135.0	135.0	135.0	135.0	135.0	135.0	135.0	135.0	135.0	135.0	135.0	135.0	135.0	135.0
Less accumulated depreciation*	2.3	4.5	6.8	6.8	13.5	20.3	27.0	33.8	40.5	47.3	54.0	60.8	67.5	74.3	81.0
Net property, plant and equipm	132.8	130.5	128.3	128.3	121.5	114.8	108.0	101.3	94.5	87.8	81.0	74.3	67.5	60.8	54.0
Intangibles															
TOTAL ASSETS	657.8	1142.5	2039.6	2076.5	5523.6	9757.4	13244.5	15567.0	17136.4	18157.1	18833.9	19354.4	19670.1	19798.4	19974.8
LIABILITIES															
Current Liabilities															
Accounts payable	112.9	225.8	338.6	364.9	761.1	1012.5	912.6	657.8	454.6	303.1	203.2	151.5	99.9	51.7	51.7
Notes payable															
Accrued expenses															
Income taxes payable															
Other liabilities															
Total current liabilities	112.9	225.8	338.6	364.9	761.1	1012.5	912.6	657.8	454.6	303.1	203.2	151.5	99.9	51.7	51.7
Long-term liabilities															
Deferred income taxes															
Debentures															
Other long-term debt	112.9	225.8	338.6	364.9	761.1	1012.5	912.6	657.8	454.6	303.1	203.2	151.5	99.9	51.7	51.7
Total Liabilities	112.9	225.8	338.6	364.9	761.1	1012.5	912.6	657.8	454.6	303.1	203.2	151.5	99.9	51.7	51.7
SHAREHOLDER'S EQUITY															
Preferred stock, __par value authorized shares outstanding shares															
Common stock, __par value authorized shares outstanding shares															
Additional paid-in capital															
Retained earnings	124.8	258.9	393.0	776.7	3763.3	7745.8	11332.7	13910.1	15682.6	16854.9	17631.6	18203.7	18571.1	18747.6	18924.0
Less: Treasury stock at cost															
Total shareholder's equity	124.8	258.9	393.0	776.7	3763.3	7745.8	11332.7	13910.1	15682.6	16854.9	17631.6	18203.7	18571.1	18747.6	18924.0
Total Liabilities and share equi	237.6	484.7	731.7	1141.6	4524.4	8758.3	12245.3	14567.9	16137.2	17158.0	17834.8	18355.2	18671.0	18799.2	18975.7

* 5 year straight line

Diagnostics

Cash conversion cycle. The cash conversion cycle is derived from the operating cycle in Chapter 10. Under the final plan of outsourcing production and distributing through a chain, we make the following assumptions: The purchase credit period for AP and finished goods inventory is 30 days, while the average collection period for AR is 45 days. Thus the cash conversion cycle is: 30 days (inventory) + 45 days (AR) – 30 days (AP) = 45 days. This is a rather long conversion cycle and thus will drive a significant requirement for initial working capital.

Financial ratios. We apply the formulas in Exhibit 11-1 to Epigraphs' income statement and balance sheet to characterize Epigraphs performance, and assess the plausibility of its assumptions. Since ratio analysis is really a comparative technique, we compare Epigraphs' ratios to industry averages. To do this we gathered the ratio summary for SIC code 5231 (note—this is the SIC code for paint, glass, and wallpaper retailers. We might want to do another analysis using SIC code 2671 for wallpaper manufacturers). We present ratios from Robert Morris Associates in Exhibit 11-6.[10]

The average collection period for Epigraphs is 45 days. This corresponds to an AR turnover of 8. Comparing this number to the industry ratios, indicates that Epigraphs is comparable to larger retailers. Smaller retailers have better (higher) AR turns due to cash and credit card sales, whereas larger retailers are more likely to have commercial sales involving purchase credit. Since Epigraphs will be selling exclusively to a single commercial customer, the assumption of a 45 day collection period seems plausible.

The average purchase credit period for Epigraphs is 30 days. This corresponds to AP turnover of 12. This is consistent with medium sized firms in the industry and actually conservative relative to smaller or larger firms. Thus the assumption of a 30 day purchase credit period also seems plausible.

Finished goods inventory is estimated at 30 days. (Since production is outsourced, there are no materials and work-in-process inventories.) This corresponds to an inventory turnover of 12. This assumption appears to be somewhat optimistic. Medium and large retailers turn inventory only about 5 times per year. The argument in favor of higher turns for Epigraphs is that it will only have one product and will control its production through real-time tracking of retailer sales. Thus it should be able to avoid producing inventory that becomes obsolete.

Epigraphs' return on sales in year 1 is 40.5%. This is obtained by adding the net income from all four quarters ($12,127), and dividing by the sales for all four quarters ($29,964). This is substantially higher than the retailer norm of 1 to 3.5%. The higher returns stem from monopoly pricing in a new product class.

Exhibit 11-16. Discounted Cash Flow Valuation Spreadsheet

	M0	M1	M2	M3	Q2	Q3	Q4	Q5	Q6	Q7	Q8	Q9	Q10	Q11	Q12
Net cash from operating activity	0	-120	-276	-369	964	2965	4398	4131	2990	2070	1370	894	674	450	194.6
Net cash from investment activity	-135														
Net cash from financial activity															
Net cash	-135	-120	-276	-369	964	2965	4398	4131	2990	2070	1370	894	674	450	195
Discount factor at 39% rate	1.00	1.03	1.06	1.09	1.18	1.28	1.39	1.51	1.64	1.78	1.94	2.10	2.28	2.48	2.69
Discounted value of cash flows ($1000)	-135	-124	-292	-401	1,137	3,799	6,118	6,242	4,907	3,688	2,651	1,879	1,538	1,115	524
NPV of cumulative flows ($1000)	-135	-259	-550	-951	186	3,984	10,102	16,344	21,250	24,939	27,590	29,469	31,006	32,121	32,645

Financial requirement

Basic requirement. The most negative cash balance for Epigraphs occurs at the end of month 3. The cash flow statement indicates that Epigraphs will need $900,200 of external financing. The requirement in month 3 represents some up-front costs for production of dies, development of customer interface software, and advertising. However, the cash requirement is driven primarily by the need for working capital to fund accounts receivable over the 45 day AR cycle.

By the end of the second quarter this deficit disappears and is replaced by a cash surplus of $63,900.

Contingency requirement. To assess the potential requirement for contingency funds, we examine the cash flow statements for the optimistic and pessimistic cases. We look first to see which scenario poses the greatest funding requirement, and then compare that requirement to the nominal case.

There are considerable differences across the three cases. The optimistic case exhibits a most negative cash balance of $657,700 in month 3. In contrast, the pessimistic case exhibits a modest negative cash balance of $141,400 in month 2. As in the nominal case, the cash requirements are driven largely by accounts receivables. The pessimistic case has relatively low cash requirements because sales, and therefore ARs, are low. In the optimistic case, profits from early sales help to fund ARs from later sales.

The contingency requirement for Epigraphs would ordinarily be the difference between the greatest funding requirement and the nominal funding requirement. In this case the $657,700 requirement in the optimistic forecast, and the $141,400 requirement in the pessimistic case, are both below the $900,200 requirement in the nominal case. Thus there is no contingency requirement.

Valuation

The only relevant valuation for Epigraphs is a cash flow valuation since the extent of physical assets is trivial ($135,000), and below the amount of funding sought. Similarly, multiples valuation pertains primarily to firms for which there is a terminal value. We anticipate that the product's life cycle will be exhausted in three years. The only intangible assets of value at that point will be the brand name and the relationships with both the manufacturer and Sherwin-Williams. If these were to be of value to anyone, it would likely be existing wallpaper manufacturers. We assume wallpaper manufacturers already have comparable brandname and relationships, and therefore would not be interested in those of Epigraphs.

Cash flow valuation is merely the present value of the cash stream discounted at the appropriate rate. To determine a discount rate for Epigraphs we begin with the implicit discount rate for Sherwin-Williams. Sherwin-Williams trades at a price-to-earnings ratio of 14, and its earnings have been growing at 9.9%. The corresponding discount rate is therefore:

$$1 / (P/E) + g$$
$$1 / 14 + 9.9 = 17.04\%$$

Thus, the implicit discount rate for a comparable publicly traded firm is 17.04%. We need to adjust this rate to account for the fact that Epigraphs is a private firm, with a key-person, who is also a majority shareholder. Thus we need to apply an illiquidity premium (factor of 1.4), a key person discount (factor of 1.3), and a minority discount (factor of 1.25). We assume the valuation will exceed 2.5 million dollars, thus no size premium is warranted. The resulting discount rate is therefore:

$$* \ 1.4 \ * \ 1.3 \ * \ 1.25 \ = \ 38.77\%$$

Exhibit 11-16 is a spreadsheet that applies this discount rate to Epigraphs' cash flows for the nominal scenario. The resulting valuation over the three-year venture life is $32,645,000.

Equity stake corresponding to financial requirement

If Epigraphs seeks outside equity financing for the entire financial requirement of $900,200, it should only have to give up 2.8% of the venture. This share is obtained by dividing the requirement of $900,200 by the valuation, $32,645,000. In practice, an equity investor will always discount your numbers, so you will likely have to forego more equity. Similarly, equity investors typically want substantial equity stake. A stake of 2.8% is unlikely to appeal to them. Thus you may want to consider debt financing.

CONCLUSION

In this chapter we translated the physical and human asset requirements into the financial requirement for the venture: How much money is required to execute the venture you've designed?

To answer this question we first developed pro forma financial statements using the demand forecast from Chapter 8 and the corresponding resource requirements from Chapter 9. We created three statements: the income statement, the cash flow statement, and the balance sheet. We did this for each of three scenarios: the nominal case, an optimistic case, and a pessimistic case.

From the cash flow statements we found the most negative cash balance in each of the three scenarios to define the funding requirement. We used the cash flow statement again to develop the venture's valuation. By combining the funding requirement and the valuation, we defined the share of equity that you must forego to obtain the necessary financing.

You and investors will undoubtedly differ on the valuation, the funding requirement, and thus the equity stake. The analysis here provides you with a foundation for assessing alternative valuations. Even if you reject the alternative valuations, you may still want to forego a larger equity stake to obtain the backing of a particular investor. This is your prerogative as an entrepreneur—you may feel that the backing of a particular investor may open doors to other resources such as key suppliers and customers. In that case, at least you will know the associated cost of foregone equity for your decision.

At this stage we have completely designed the venture and identified the resources necessary to execute that design. In the final chapter, we assemble all the analysis from the preceding chapters to create a comprehensive depiction of your venture—the business plan.

1 Berg, Norman and Norman Fast, 1983. "Lincoln Electric" HBS case 9-376-028.

2 Bradley, Stephen P., Pankaj Ghemawat, and Shar Foley, 1996. Wal-Mart Stores, Inc., HBS case 9-794-024.

3 See Love, John F., 1986. "McDonald's: Behind the Arches," New York: Bantam Books.

4 Murphy, Kevin J. and J. Dial, 1997. "General Dynamics: Compensation and Strategy (A)," HBS case 9-494-048.

5 Ibbotson and Associates, 1993. "Stocks, bonds, bills and inflation, 1993 year-book: Ibbotson and Associates, Chicago, IL.

6 Lerch, M., 1992. "Discount for key man loss: A quantitative analysis, Business Valuation Review (December): pp. 183-194.

7 Lerch, M., 1991. "Quantitative measures of minority interest discounts. Business Valuation Review (March): pp. 7-13.

8 The first of these was Waste Management, the most famous is Blockbuster, and the most recent is AutoNation. For a really nice account of his strategy, see DeGeorge, Gail, 1996. "The Making of a Blockbuster," New York: John Wiley and Sons, Inc.

9 West, Thomas L., 1997. "The 1997 Business Reference Guide," concord, MA: Business Brokerage Press, p. 323.

10 Alternative sources of industry ratios are: Schonfield and Associates, "IRS ratio studies" and "The Almanac of Business and Industry Financial Ratios."

11 Earnings before interest and tax.

12 Cost of Goods Sold.

13 Important to designate whether the assets are characterized by book value or market value (market value preferred).

putting it all together

chapter 12

the business plan

INTRODUCTION AND GOALS

The Business Plan is the final chapter—it ties together all the analyses and decisions from the prior chapters in a single document. The Business Plan basically serves two purposes for the venture—as a planning tool for the founders and as a sales document for potential investors and resource providers. This leads many people to conclude that there should be two separate documents—one that provides substance (the planning tool) and another that provides flash (the sales document). We argue, however, that given the criteria of venture capitalists, the well-conceived planning tool is also the best sales document.

To make this argument, we first review the decision criteria of venture capitalists in an effort to characterize what would make a good sales tool. We then review the elements of an effective planning tool. Of course, the entire book has been the planning tool—the business plan is merely the documentation of the process. Finally, we discuss how the elements from each of the chapters are incorporated into the business plan to make the document most effective.

VENTURE CAPITAL CRITERA

One of the primary outside audiences for the business plan is potential investors, the most sophisticated of whom are venture capitalists. Thus the best means for understanding how to make plans compelling is to review the criteria venture capitalists use for their investment decisions. We take advantage of two formal studies of venture capitalists and some additional anecdotal comments from entrepreneurs and venture capitalists about the criteria that appear to be important.

The first study[1] gathered responses from 102 (of 150) members of the National Venture Capital Association regarding the importance of 27 criteria for investment decisions. The results from the survey are summarized in Exhibit 12-1. The main conclusion the authors drew was that the most important investment criteria pertained to the entrepreneurial team. In particular, venture capitalists wanted evidence that the entrepreneurial team was capable of sustained effort, was able to evaluate and react to risk, was thoroughly familiar with the market,

Exhibit 12-1. Results from Macmillan Study

	Mean	SD
The entrepreneur's personality		
Capable of sustained intense effort	3.60	0.57
Able to evaluate and react well to risk	3.34	0.73
Articulate in discussing venture	3.11	0.71
Attends to detail	2.82	0.67
Has a personality compatible to mine	2.09	0.81
The entrepreneur's experience		
Thoroughly familiar with the market targeted by venture	3.58	0.57
Demonstrated leadership ability in past	3.41	0.67
Has a track record relevant to venture	3.24	0.69
Referred to me by a trustworthy source	2.03	0.62
Already familiar with the entrepreneur's reputation	1.83	0.71
Characteristics of the product or service		
The product is proprietary or can otherwise be protected	3.11	0.71
The product enjoys demonstrated market acceptance	2.45	0.74
The product has a functioning prototype	2.38	0.90
The product may be described as "high tech"	2.03	0.96
Characteristics of the market		
The target market enjoys a significant growth rate	3.34	0.64
The venture will stimulate an existing market	2.43	0.76
The venture is in an industry with which I am familiar	2.36	0.78
Little threat of competition during the first three years	2.33	0.72
The venture will create a new market	1.82	0.83
Financial considerations		
I require a return at least 10 times my investment in 10 yr	3.42	0.79
I require an investment that can be made liquid	3.17	0.89
I require a return at least 10 times my investment in 5 yr	2.34	0.81
I will not be expected to make subsequent investments	1.34	0.52
I will not participated in later round of investment	1.20	0.45

Reprinted from MacMillian, I., R. Siegel and P.N.S. Narashima, "Criteria Used by Venture Capitalists to Evaluate New Venture Proposals," Journal of Business Venturing, 1, pp. 119-128. Copyright © 1985 by Elsevier Science Publishing Company with permission from Elsevier Science.

and had a demonstrated track record. The interesting puzzle for entrepreneurs is how to convey this information in a business plan. We argue that a business plan developed from the intensive venture design process in this book will automatically convey much of this. It will certainly demonstrate knowledge of the market and ability to assess risk. We think, too, that the substantial work behind the plan will be indicative of sustained effort.

The second study is the one already discussed in Chapter 4.[2] Remember, that study was used to motivate the use of conjoint analysis. The study asked 66 venture capitalists to evaluate 25 actual ventures that had been characterized by the researchers along eight underlying dimensions. The venture capitalists were asked to make investment decisions for each of the ventures, and in addition to specify the criteria that led to the decisions. The researchers conducted conjoint analysis on the investment decisions using the eight dimensions. They then compared the conjoint criteria to the stated decision criteria in predicting investment decisions. The results of that comparison are presented in Exhibit 12-2. The results for the stated criteria are consistent with those from the Macmillan study. The most important stated criterion is the entrepreneurial team. However, the results from conjoint indicate that venture capitalists actually rely more heavily on market structure—the level of competition and the extent of competitive advantage. While the team is important, one means of evaluating the team is by examining its decisions about which market to target (Chapter 3), the understanding of that market (Chapters 2, 3, and 4) and the plan for gaining advantage within that market (Chapter 5).

Exhibit 12-2. Results from Shepherd & Zacharakis Study

	Actual Decision Policy Rank	Stated Decision Policy Rank
Entrepreneurial Team		
Market familiarity	5	4
Leadership	7	1
Start-ups	8	8
Product		
Proprietary	6	5
Market		
Size	3	3
Growth	4	2
Competitors	1	7
Strength	2	6

Reprinted from Katz (Ed.) "Advances in Entreneurship, Firm, Emergence and Growth, Volume 3, pp. 203-248, Copyright © JAI Press with permission from Elsevier Science.

Other indications of venture capitalists decision criteria emerge from comments from individual entrepreneurs and venture capitalists. These comments are delineated in Exhibit 12-3.

Taken together, the two studies as well as the anecdotal comments indicate that the best investment sales tool is a business plan for an early venture in a rapidly growing market written by a team with sufficient technical and managerial expertise in the market, to be able to define and execute an offering likely to achieve market leadership.

The best sales tool is thus a business plan that conveys sophisticated understanding of the market, the technology underlying the products/services in those markets, a marketing plan that optimizes demand, and an operations plan that ensures efficient exploitation of the demand. Thus, the best sales tool is a business plan that documents a well-conceived venture design. In that sense, the best sales tool is the manifestation of a good planning tool.

PLANNING TOOL

The venture design process is the real planning tool. The business plan is merely a snapshot of the venture design at a particular point in time. At this point, you have a reasonably complete venture design.[3] In all likelihood, your original concept of the venture has changed in response to analytical results. In Epigraphs for example, the original distribution plan that emerged from industry analysis was to use the Internet to circumvent entry barriers. However, during the demand forecasting exercise we realized that Internet distribution substantially truncated demand, while increasing the need for advertising. Similarly, we originally envisioned in-house production using Gerber technology. However, when we went through the resource requirements exercise, we learned that we would have to establish 486 workstations—a substantial investment in technology for a venture with a limited three-year life.

Thus we now have a sense that any venture design is a living organism. The advantage you have over virtually all other entrepreneurs is that your experimentation and evolution have taken place on paper. The most obvious advantage of paper experimentation is that it is costless.[4] If Epigraphs' experimentation had taken place in practice, we would have incurred sunk costs for Gerber technology and advertising geared toward web traffic. Additionally, we may have permanently lost market share and access to the chains as established competitors viewed our product, imitated it, and distributed it through their existing channels.

More importantly, we avoided confusing the customer by changing the product and distribution channel after product launch. Perhaps most important, we avoided the inertial tendency to stick with inferior strategies simply because they

Exhibit 12-3. Informal comments from entrepreneurs and venture capitalists regarding investment decision criteria

Primus Venture Partner criteria[7]

    Competent management with deep experience in the industry or market

    Venture potential to become a market leader, indicated by:

        A distinctive, proprietary product

        Unique services with strong appeal

    Opportunity to harvest in three to five years

    One million to five million dollar investment

John Doerr of Kleiner-Perkins[8]

    Technical excellence

    Outstanding management

    Large, rapidly growing market

    Team sense of urgency

    First or second to market

Peter Ligeti of Keystone Capital

    Recognizable customers, strategic partners, board members

Elisa Parsons of Parts River

    Well-defined need

Typical complaints venture capitalists have with entrepreneurs/business plans:

    Well-defined solution to a problem that is either undefined or non-existent

    Don't place sufficient emphasis on in-depth market analysis

    Rely primarily on intuition to estimate market potential

    Are biased (ignore negative information) when interpreting market information

    Underestimate what is required to market products

    Over 90% overestimate market by 40%; Over 60% overestimate market by 60%

have already been implemented. In the case of new ventures, nimbleness is an asset. You are most nimble on paper, but you run the risk of "experimenting in a vacuum"—creating a perfect venture for a customer group that doesn't exist. Here however our experimentation has involved real contact with the customer—in person during interviews and focus groups, and remotely (via mail or the Internet) during the survey.

Simulation

Continuing with the theme of experimentation and nimbleness, possibly the most valuable output of the venture design approach in this book is that you have now created an entire venture simulation. The set of spreadsheets from Chapters 4 through 11 and their linkages comprise the simulation. The design at any given point in time is merely the most recent numbers in the set of spreadsheets. The business plan is the text that interprets those numbers. Thus, if you choose to change any element of the product design or venture design, you can test its impact on the bottom line by changing the corresponding entry in the spreadsheet. This experimentation can now be done in a matter of minutes rather than weeks.

Say, for example, competition enters your market with a product design that you considered in your conjoint survey. You can now go back to see how many people prefer your product to theirs, and as a result, the profit impact of their entry. You can also test whether any revision to your product or venture design will provide higher profits in this new environment.

There generally is very little time to think strategically once you start the venture. Most entrepreneurs complain of having trouble merely behaving tactically. Having the simulation in place allows entrepreneurs to test changes in strategy in less time than it takes to examine changes in tactics. That is, the opportunity to experiment on paper continues even after the venture is initiated.

GENERAL GUIDELINES ON BUSINESS PLAN CONTENT

Since you have a venture design, writing the business plan is largely packaging. For most other entrepreneurs the business plan is the design tool. In fact, you can buy business plan software programs where the text of the business plan exists, and you merely fill in the blanks with the specifics for your venture.[5] The design process is thus determining what goes in the blanks. By definition, such an approach will merely provide you with a pedestrian business plan—since thousands of other plans will share 90% of your text.

Accordingly, while we provide extensive guidance on the venture design process, we will only provide minimal guidance on writing the business plan itself. What we do offer is an outline of business plan content, some discussion of what the major sections of the outline should accomplish, and guidelines on how the various elements of the venture design process are introduced into the plan. Exhibit 12-4 is the suggested outline for the business plan. The most important element of the business plan is the Executive Summary. In fact, in most cases, it is the only part of the plan that is read. Because the Executive Summary is so important, we recommend writing it last.

A note on length. Entrepreneurs often ask how long the plan should be. As in most business writing, the goal is to convey all the critical information as briefly as possible. Often that leaves the question of what is 'critical". Since the outline below defines what constitutes the critical information, the remaining challenge for you is merely to convey that information in a compelling and succinct manner. Typically this results in a plan that is 20 to 30 pages of double-spaced text. Appendices and Exhibits are in addition to the 20 to 30 pages.

A note on editing. Often a business plan is written jointly by several members of the entrepreneurial team—each member writing the section(s) corresponding to his or her area of expertise. While this is a great starting point, it often leads to a plan that is disjointed. Accordingly, you will want to appoint one member of the team as editor. This person should be the strongest writer of the team. Once drafts of the various sections have been written, the editor will compile the sections into a coherent whole and rewrite them to echo a single voice. Each member of the team should then proof-read the revision.

The complete business plan for Epigraphs is included as Appendix I.

Cover page

The cover page includes the formal name of the company, its legal form (e.g., a Pennsylvania S-corporation), full street address, phone and fax numbers, name of principal contact, and date of the plan. Typically the bottom of the cover page includes a notice regarding the plan's confidentiality:

> *This business plan has been submitted on a confidential basis to selected individuals for the sole purpose of soliciting financing for the company. It may not be copied, faxed, reproduced or distributed without permission.*

Executive Summary

The executive summary is the most important part of the business plan. Often it is the only section of the plan that gets read. Think of the summary as the ad for the entire plan. Its main objective is to gain the reader's interest to induce them to read further, or seek a meeting. Peter Ligeti of Keystone Capital has developed a set of guidelines for writing the summary. These are included as Exhibit 12-5. As mentioned earlier, because the summary is so important you should write it last.

Exhibit 12-4. Detailed Plan Outline

1. Cover page
2. Table of Contents
3. Executive Summary (Most important component of plan—see Exhibit 12-2 for guidelines)
4. The Need (Chapter 3)
   - Characterizing the customer
   - Perceptual Map of current offerings (take credit for having spoken to them in focus groups/interviews)
     i. Why those dimensions
     ii. Current deficiency (use good quotes if you have them)
5. Proposed solution (Chapter 3)
   - Top level description of venture product/service
   - Core benefit proposition-How satisfies the need
   - Pictures/drawings if appropriate
   - Optimal Product Configuration (Chapters 4 and 5)
     i. Table of product attributes, and their marginal value
     ii. Corresponding point estimate of demand
     iii. Corresponding target segments (if applicable)
   - Optimal price (as determined by conjoint) (Chapters 4 and 5)
     i. Show demand curve
6. The industry (Chapter 2)
   - Market size, growth rate
   - The competitors and substitutes: How close are they, what are their shares, how profitable are they
   - Entry barriers: How do they work for and against new venture
7. Marketing Plan
   - The buyers: Number, segments, where are they
   - Structure of existing distribution channels (Chapter 2)
   - Distribution channel decision (Chapter 6)
     i. Characterize existing channels (power, reach, effectiveness)
     ii. Characteristics of product that affect channel length
     iii. Breakeven analysis, Subjective factors, conjoint results if applicable
     iv. Channels chosen
     v. Effective reach
   - Advertising decision (Chapter 7)
     i. Media habits of buyers (MediaMark)
     ii. Advertising plan
     iii. Effective awareness
   - Demand forecast (Chapter 8)
     i. Potential demand (point estimate from conjoint)
     ii. Realized demand (calendarized forecast--considers distribution reach and advertising awareness)

iii. Analogy as test of reasonableness
- Expected competitor response, and any efforts to pre-empt (Chapter 5)

8. Operations Plan
   - Value chain (depict graphically and describe) (Chapter 9)
   - Scope of Firm (Chapter 9)
     i. What activities to internalize, and why
     ii. What activities to outsource, and to whom
   - Bill of capacity (Chapter 10)
   - Calendarized resource requirements (Chapter 10)

9. Operating Economics (Chapter 11)
   - Operating cycle and corresponding cash conversion cycle
   - Cost breakdown for Bill of capacity
     i. Variable cost
     ii. Semi-variable cost
   - Breakeven volume
   - Comparison to industry ratios

10. Management Team
    - Organization structure
    - Key management personnel
      i. Backgrounds
      ii. Compensation
    - Board of advisors

11. Overall schedule

12. Critical risks, problems and assumptions

13. Financial Plan (Chapter 11)
    - Pro Forma Income statements
    - Pro Forma Cash Flow Statements
    - Pro Forma Balance Sheets
    - Required financing
    - Uses of funds
    - (Valuation)

14. APPENDICES
    - Conjoint results
    - Industry ratios

Exhibit 12-5. Writing A Summary

- Typical V.C.: 10-20 plans on desk - summary - not read carefully
  - o Entrepreneur must grab attention, stand out
  - o Groundwork before plan sent
    - ▪ get introduction - plan read more carefully
    - ▪ find out about v .c. firm
- Summary - clear & concise, at most 4-5 pages
- Summary - meat & sizzle: partly promotional & marketing
  - o get attention with few key positive points, lead with strength
    - ▪ entrep: experience background
    - ▪ good management - even if just lined up
    - ▪ recognizable customers - like reference sale
    - ▪ recognizable strategic partners
    - ▪ recognizable board members (board composition)
    - ▪ competitive advantages if strong
  - o nevertheless certain key areas must be covered to show thought
    - ▪ product or service up-front
    - ▪ Why needed? Few key features (not technical), benefits
    - ▪ target market, market size - if large, say so
    - ▪ sales & marketing - brief unless crowded field
    - ▪ competition - brief unless crowded (e.g., Doctor practice mgmt. - how different)
    - ▪ stage of company, product
    - ▪ financials:
      - • 3 years P&L, monthly/quarterly/lst year
      - • keep it credible, reveals thought process
      - • revenues doubling, 50% net margin
      - • historical P&L if helps (eg. 3 year R&D mode), credibility
    - ▪ pricing - affects distribution
    - ▪ $ sought now, later - leave cushion: credibility
    - ▪ use of proceeds
    - ▪ when company started - 2 edged sword
- Avoid:
  - o excessive length
  - o technical detail
  - o unrealistic projections
  - o "no competition"
  - o ignoring sales & marketing
- No Mileage:
  - o "conservative projections"
  - o "customer focused"
  - o "pro-active anything (marketing, etc.)"

Source: Peter Ligeti, Partner, Keystone Capital, 5/7 /97

The Need

Venture capitalists often complain that business plans offer solutions in search of problems. This will certainly NOT be true of your ventures. While intuition may have taken you in the direction of a solution rather than a problem, the focus group exercise and the corresponding perceptual map in Chapter 3 will have forced you to identify the customer need.

The need section of the plan should characterize the problem facing the customer. It should identify the dimensions that customers care about in solving that problem. It should demonstrate where current offerings are positioned along those offerings. It should then highlight the current deficiency. This may be best accomplished with the perceptual map. If you have a perceptual map that concisely depicts the customer need, you should include it as a figure in this section. Similarly, the need section is an opportunity to demonstrate that you have first hand knowledge of the customer from the interviews and/or the focus group. If you have pithy quotes that capture the customer need, this is the place to feature them.

Product description (Proposed solution)

This section should define the core benefit proposition for the venture's product or service, linking the proposition to the customer's need from the previous section. The meat of the section describes the venture's product or service in detail. If there are drawings, block diagrams, or pictures of the product or service they would be included here.[6] The discussion should convince readers that the product fulfills the core benefit proposition, and satisfies the customer's need.

This section will include discussion of the product configuration as determined from conjoint analysis. While you won't want to get into details of the analysis, you will want to discuss what attributes were selected and why. This will include discussion of price and the corresponding demand. You might want to include the demand curve.

The industry

The industry description should characterize the market, define its size (both dollars and units), its growth rate, and discuss any important trends. This section should discuss the competitive structure of the industry. It should identify the competitors and closest substitutes, and summarize their market shares. Finally, the section should describe any entry barriers and discuss the extent to which these work in favor of or against the new venture.

Marketing Plan

The marketing plan is a substantial portion of the business plan. It includes a number of subsections: buyer characterization, choice of distribution channel, the advertising plan, and the corresponding demand forecast.

Buyer characterization. This section should characterize the target market in terms of its size, buyer demographics and psychographics. This information comes initially from MediaMark. To the extent your conjoint results indicate there are segments in the market, you want to define the segments and characterize them in the same terms as the overall market.

Distribution channel. This section should characterize the existing channels in terms of power, reach, effectiveness, and economics (costs/markups). It should also discuss characteristics of the product that drive its distribution in the direction of long or short channels. This should set up the discussion of which channel was chosen and why.

Advertising decision. This section should define the communication objective for advertising. It should then describe the media habits of buyers as specified by MediaMark and the media questions in your conjoint survey. This should set up a discussion of the final advertising schedule (number of ads in what vehicles).

Demand forecast. This discussion should follow the methodology from Chapter 8. You should define potential demand from the conjoint analysis. You should then apply the limits to realizing that demand imposed by your distribution decision (availability) and your advertising plan (awareness). If there is a suitable analogy, you would include it to demonstrate the plausibility of your forecast. Finally, you would discuss the optimistic and pessimistic versions of these forecasts.

Expected competitor response. The demand forecast is predicated on customer choice from among your offering and all existing offerings. In this section you will discuss the likely response of competitors to the introduction of your product. You would then discuss possible counter-responses. Ideally, your initial strategy leaves little room for rational response (as in Chapter 5).

Operations Plan

The operations plan is another substantial section of the business plan. You should characterize the value chain both graphically and textually. From this, you would define which activities will be internalized, which will be outsourced, and the factors driving the decision in each case. For activities that are outsourced, you want to identify the leading supplier candidates. For internal activities, you will specify the bill of capacity. Finally, you would match the demand forecast with the bill of capacity to calendarize resource requirements. Note, lest you think that this is too much detail, one venture capitalist said that his litmus test for a credible business plan is one that not only calendarizes human resource requirements, but also takes into account replacement hiring. Thus, his expectation for business plans was that they specify expected employee turnover rates and the cost of those turnovers: recruiting costs, training costs for new employees, lost production before the old employees are replaced, and less efficient production of new employees before they become fully capable.

Operating Economics

This section applies cost information to the operations plan. Here you will define the operating cycle and the corresponding cash conversion cycle, and draw implications about working capital. In addition, you will apply cost information to the bill of capacity to define unit cost (both variable cost and allocation of fixed cost). From this cost information you should be able to specify a break-even volume. You should also demonstrate that your operating economics are comparable to industry averages, and where different, explain why.

Management Team

The goal of this section is to demonstrate that you have the right team (qualified and committed) and the appropriate allocation of responsibility to execute the venture design. Accordingly, you will provide an organization chart and a brief biographical sketch of key management personnel. If you have a board of advisors, you would provide brief biographical sketches of them as well. The function of the board of advisors is to fill holes in your experience base or to provide links to key industry players that you might not otherwise have access to.

Overall schedule

This schedule defines all the critical development activities leading up to launch and the major milestones that occur after launch. Ultimately, this schedule will be used to trigger funding activities and force periodic reassessment of the venture design.

Critical risks, problems and assumptions

The intent of this section is to provide a sense of the underlying risk in the venture design. You will define the major assumptions upon which the design is based, and will specify any other outstanding risks. This is not the comprehensive boilerplate you might find in a legal prospectus. Rather, it is your best assessment of what risks the venture is most susceptible to, and how you expect to handle those risks. Absence of risks is usually an indication that you have your head in the sand. Ironically, too many risks conveys a similar message. If you list an excessive number of risks, it appears you are just working from boilerplate and thus aren't treating any risk seriously.

Financial Plan

This section is primarily an introduction to the Pro Forma statements. In addition you will specify the amount of financing that is required, and define how those funds will be used. Do not specify the financial structure. This will be defined through negotiation with your investors.

Appendices

Most of the figures that illuminate previous discussions should be imbedded in the text of those sections. However, some exhibits are sizable and complex, and should be left to the appendix section. Examples of these are the financial statements, and data summaries and regression results from conjoint analysis.

CONCLUSION

Congratulations! At this point you have completed your venture design. While the most *visible* output of this work is your business plan, the most *valuable* output is the venture simulation you have created to support your decision making. You now have a set of spreadsheets that stretch from the demand curve for your product or service to the valuation. If you want to modify your strategy at any point in the future, you can test that change in the simulation in minutes before you test it in the real world. If a new competitor enters your market with a different product configuration, you can go back to your raw data to see which product each customer will choose. You can do that not only for your current product configuration/price, but can test alternative configurations/ prices. This kind of costless experimentation makes adaptation far more likely and effective.

Finally, because you have actually done much of the venture design work, you should have momentum. I hope you decide that the marginal effort to start the venture is relatively minor.

[1] Macmillan, Ian, Robin Siegel, and P. N. Subba Narashima, 1985. "Criteria Used by Venture Capitalists to Evaluate New Venture Proposals," Journal of Business Venturing 1, pp. 119-128.

[2] Shepherd, Dean A. and Andrew Zacharakis, 1997. "Conjoint Analysis: A Window of Opportunity for Entrepreneurship Research," in Katz, Jerome A. (Ed) "Advances in Entrepreneurship, Firm Emergence, and Growth, London: JAI Press.

[3] Under some circumstances, there are additional design issues beyond those covered in this text. If you have a retail site, for example, a critical issue is site location.

[4] Except for your time and incidental expenses associated with focus groups and surveys.

[5] See for example, Biz Plan Builder.

[6] Note that these figures should never be sufficiently detailed to allow readers to duplicate your offering.

[7] Bhide, Amar V., 2000. "The Origin and Evolution of New Businesses," New York: Oxford University Press.

[8] ibid.

appendix

Epigraphs

A California S-Corporation

Corporate Offices:
1234 ABC Street
Los Angeles, CA 90045
Phone:
Fax:

Principal Contact is: Anne Marie Knott – President

1. Table of Contents

2. Executive Summary

Epigraphs is a new business venture that will manufacture and distribute an innovative wallcovering product. The product is an affordable, creative, and easy-to-install alternative to wallpaper, targeted primarily at the residential do-it-yourself market. The product line consists of a collection of quotes manufactured in strips of letters with an adhesive backing. The quotes can be used as 1) a border around the perimeter of a room, 2) sidewall to cover an entire wall, or 3) an accent to a room. The letters are applied to a painted wall by simply pulling off the adhesive backing of the letters and pressing them onto the wall with a squeegee that is included in Epigraphs'packaging.

Epigraphs fills a gap in the wallcovering market, particularly in the do-it-yourself segment. For the past three years, sales in the wallpaper market have declined at a rate of approximately 7% per year. This decline has been attributed to at least four factors. First, the industry has failed to innovate. Consumers complain that wallpaper designs are stale because companies have not kept pace with current trends in interior design. Second, wallpaper is difficult to install. Consumers and designers complain that problems with paste mess and seam matching detract from their using the product. Third, wallpaper is considered unsuitable for some spaces due to the architecture of these rooms. Because wallpaper comes in large rolls, it is difficult to paste onto angular spaces. Fourth, wallpaper designs are not unique or exclusive, yet consumers desire products that allow them to express themselves in unique ways.

Preliminary reactions to Epigraphs' prototypes from interior designers indicate that the product is attractive in that it is affordable, whimsical, customizable, and functional in enhancing odd spaces. Consumers echoed the designers' sentiments regarding the product's design features, but because they often do their own installation, they were relatively more impressed with the installation advantages.

Primary market research with consumers estimates a market potential of 1.4 million rolls at the optimal price of $50 per roll. This yields cash flows with a net present value of $32.6 million over the product's three-year life. The estimate of 1.4 million rolls is below historical ranges for wallcovering sales over the product life cycle. On average, wallcoverings generate sales of 7 million rolls over their life (with a minimum of 2 million rolls, and a maximum of 200 million rolls).

Because the product life is short, investments in production facilities are unwarranted. Accordingly, the firm plans to outsource production and fulfillment. Retail sales of the product will be exclusively through Sherwin-Williams. Sherwin-Williams provides complete coverage of the market, and provides an opportunity for consumers to view the product first-hand in store displays before purchase. Thus, the chain serves both a distribution function and an advertising function, in exchange for 40% product markup. We augment store display advertising with highly targeted cable and print media to trigger sales in the first three months surrounding introduction.

Epigraphs seeks an equity investment of $900,000. This amount is required to finance tooling of the production dies, development of the supply chain integration website, initial advertising, as well as working capital to fund initial production over the 45 day cash cycle. The firm expects to achieve positive cash flow by Month 4.

3. The Need

Epigraphs is an innovative do-it-yourself (DIY) wallcovering that combines the distinctive look of wallpaper or faux finishing with the durability, flexibility, and reliability of paint. The initial inspiration for Epigraphs grew out of the founder's desire for a unique look in a room that was ill-suited to wallpaper due to numerous windows, entryways, protrusions, and cutouts. Additional aversion to wallpaper came from the founder's recent experience with an installation in another room: throwing away whole lengths of paper when the matching didn't work, having one side of the paper stretch more than the other side, and having the paper fall down and rip when trying to fit it around a window.

Focus groups with interior designers and surveys of consumers revealed similar widespread dissatisfaction with wallpaper. The goal of the focus group was to elicit detailed qualitative understanding from industry experts of the range of wallcovering options, and the factors that affect choice among those options. The ultimate goal of the consumer survey was to obtain quantitative estimates of demand among end-users, though we used the survey to gather qualitative comments as well.

The interior design group was successful in identifying a broad range of wallcovering products and identifying a set of dimensions along which they compared these products. This set came primarily from discussion of their engagement experiences rather than from direct questions about dimensions and product rankings. For example, the group was asked what wallcovering products they used and why? They were also asked to describe wallcovering successes and wallcovering disasters.

The group identified six categories of wallcovering: paint, vinyl, wallpaper, fabric, faux finishing, and borders. The factors the group felt were important in choosing from among these product categories were budget, durability, ease of installation, uniqueness, versatility, product consistency, and the lag time from ordering the wallcovering to having the installation completed. A diagram ranking each of these products along each of the dimensions is given in Exhibit 1.

In general, each product category represents tradeoffs between the various factors. Paint, for example, is inexpensive, durable and easy to install, but not very distinctive. In contrast, faux finishes are expensive and difficult to install, but create a unique effect. Wallpaper is less expensive than faux finishes, but more expensive than paint. While it offers some degree of uniqueness, it suffers from difficult installation, poor consistency in product quality, and often involves long lead times.

Exhibit 1

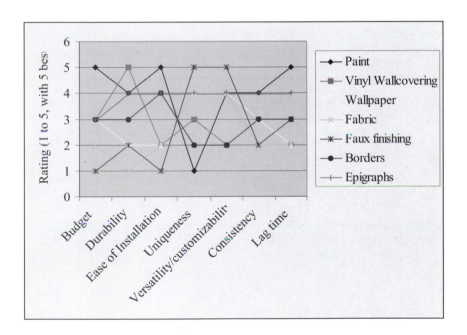

Interior designers were interviewed to represent industry experts. They have extensive experience with a broad range of wallcoverings. Additionally, they are lead users—their current views on design anticipate future mass market views on design. However, because they deal almost exclusively with affluent clients their views will exhibit an affluence bias. Similarly, their experience with wallcovering is second-hand—they neither install the wallcovering nor live with it after the fact. Thus, the designers' focus group was complemented with consumer surveys.

Consumers generally felt that wallpaper installation was tedious, messy, and led to unreliable end results. With regard to the tedium, they complained of the need to strip and prepare walls to create a smooth surface, of having to match the seams, of having to measure and cut around doors and windows, having to work around corners, and of troubles aligning patterns from one sheet to the next. With regard to the mess, they complained about getting glue from the new sheet on the sheets that had just been installed. With regard to the product quality, they complained that wallpaper quality seems to be getting cheaper, that the paper is too thin and tears easily, and that it is too difficult to avoid bubbles, wrinkles, rolled edges, and mismatched seams.

Given the complaints of designers and consumers, it is not surprising that sales of wallpaper have been declining at a rate of 7% a year for the past three years.

4. Proposed Solution

Thus, the interior designers and consumers confirmed the need for a product with the durability, flexibility, and affordability of paint, but with the uniqueness of papers and faux finishes. This forms the core benefit proposition for Epigraphs. This proposition is captured in the preliminary advertising copy (Appendix 1).

We tested interior designer response to Epigraphs using product prototypes, and tested consumer response to Epigraphs using the advertising copy. Both groups indicated sufficient interest in the product to justify going forward with development. While interior designers felt that the product was ill-suited to high-end residential living rooms, they did see a number of other applications:

"I could see doing it where you would do a big floral. I could see doing it in a powder room. It would be kind of fun"

"Media room or game room"

"I could possibly use it in a child's room"

"As a panel at the end of a long corridor"

"Church or library"

"Elevator lobbies"

"I know from personal experience that going into office buildings where there is a waiting room, I will read anything"

"You mentioned elevator lobby, what about the elevator itself?"

In general the designers felt the product was attractive in that it was afford-able, whimsical, customizable, and functional in enhancing odd spaces. Thus, interior designers characteristically focused on Epigraphs' design potential.

Consumers echoed the designers' sentiments: *"novel", "unique", "whimsi-cal", "creative possibilities", "conversation piece", "a new idea in decorat-ing", "adds personal touch, unique, subtle, yet noticeable"*. However, because consumers often do their own installation, they also paid attention to the instal-lation advantages: *"It's a do-it-yourself project", "easily installed", "no messy cleanup", "tool is packaged with product; directions included."*

In addition to assessing general reactions to the product, the survey asked consumers to evaluate various configurations of the product. From thes data we could determine the optimal price, set of features, and distribution channel, and characterize the corresponding demand. To determine the optimal approach we examined the sensitivity of demand to changes in price, distribution channel, and product features. Exhibit 2 presents the demand curve (demand versus price) for distribution through both wallpaper chains and the Internet. (Survey results indi-cated that they saw no difference between the chains and home superstores, so we treat them as synonymous.)

Exhibit 2

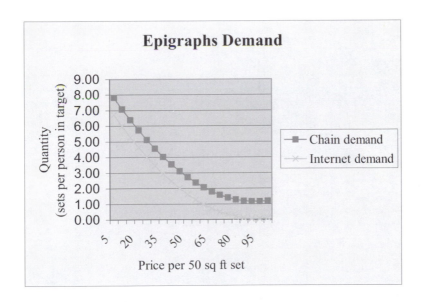

Through a series of sensitivity analyses, including optimal response to likely entrant behavior, we determined that the optimal strategy for Epigraphs is to introduce a product line consisting of 4 color-genre options (Hunter and Black) x (Literary and Inspirational). These products should be sold through wallcovering chains at a price of $50.00 per set.

This strategy appears to be the best strategy not only in monopoly, but also in anticipation of later entry. Epigraphs would cede distribution in superstores to entrants, with the anticipation that the entrant would match Epigraphs' product line. This will reduce the rate of subsequent sales of Epigraphs products by 50%. However, since 60% of product line sales occur in the first year, and the entrant will take time to respond, the net impact on lifecycle sales is minimal.

5. The Industry

Epigraphs would compete most closely with wallcovering. Thus we examined that industry (SIC 267952) to assess the likely environmental conditions we would face. The structure of that industry is summarized in Exhibit 3.

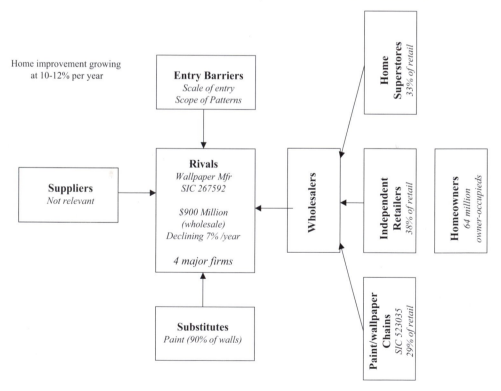

Rivals. The wallpaper industry appears be a mature industry of good size. The wholesale value of industry sales is $870 million (roughly $2 billion at retail). The maturity conclusion is based on the recent steady sales decline (7% in each of the last three years), and the trend toward consolidation—four major US manufacturers control 92% of the market. The market leaders and their respective market shares are given in Exhibit 4. Consistent with consolidation, the behavior of rivals does not appear to be particularly competitive. If the industry were competitive we would expect to see greater advertising expenditures (currently less than 1% of sales), and greater innovation. The fact that "the product was sorely lagging behind other home textiles in terms of trends" is evidence that there isn't sufficient innovation, much less "hyper-innovation" (innovations whose aggregate industry cost exceeds resultant profits). One of the reasons rivalry is likely to be suppressed in the industry is that the product is highly differentiated. There are hundreds of patterns, no two of which are perfect substitutes.

Exhibit 4

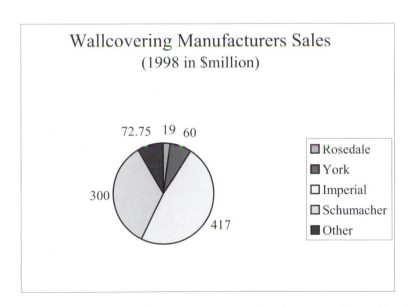

Product life cycle. The life of a typical collection (set of coordinating patterns/colors) is three years. The minimum life cycle is 1 year; the maximum is 10 years. Sixty percent of sales occur in the first year. This information can be combined to form a characteristic sales profile for wallpaper sales. This is shown in Exhibit 5.

Exhibit 5

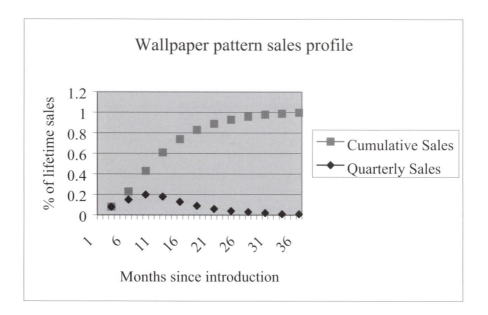

Average lifetime sales over this cycle is 7 million single rolls, while the minimum is roughly 2 million rolls, and the known maximum is 200 million rolls.

Buyers (intermediaries). Wallpaper is sold through three channels: Paint/wallpaper chains (SIC 523035), building supply/department stores, and independent retailers (through wholesalers). Shares of distribution through each channel are summarized in Exhibit 7.

The relative balance between the various channels tends to suggest that no single channel is crucial to the success of a manufacturer. However, there are dominant players in two of the channels: Home Depot in the department stores, and Sherwin-Williams in the paint/wallcovering chains. It is possible that there are also dominant wholesalers in the independent channel as well. The fact that retailers have to buy pattern books is some evidence of limited channel power, however this should be offset by the evidence that the manufacturer holds large inventories.

One recent trend is that independent retailers' share of market is increasing at the expense of chains. Customers are attracted to independent outlets because they believe it is less likely to see the same wallpaper in their neighbor's house.

Exhibit 7

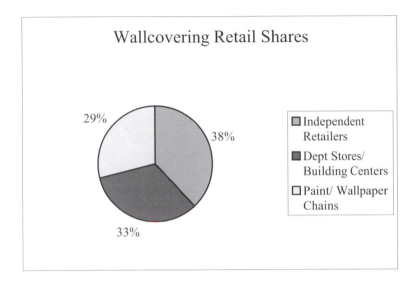

While consumers are moving toward independent retailers, manufacturers are moving in the opposite direction. The recent sales decline has prompted changes in manufacturers' distribution strategy. One of these changes is a manufacturer emphasis on sales through the chains and superstores where the margins are higher (no wholesaler). Additionally, manufacturers are attempting to differentiate themselves in terms of service and availability (in addition to product design). Recognizing that 90% of sales come from stock rather than special orders, manufacturers are offering retailers a 30% discount on any pattern for which retailers stock a 24 roll minimum inventory. Additionally, manufacturers are offering 24 hour delivery for book orders. (90% of sales are from stock, 10% are orders from pattern books.)

Suppliers. We don't dwell on suppliers since the new product uses vastly different materials and technology than conventional wallcoverings. The relatively low cost of materials in the wallcovering industry tends to suggest that suppliers have little impact on industry profitability.

Substitutes. The dominant substitute for wallpaper is paint, "Approximately 90% of American Walls are painted." To assess the power of a substitute, we are interested in assessing cross price elasticity. Since the prices are so widely divergent to begin with, it seems unlikely that demand for wallpaper is affected by a decrease in the price of paint. Paint is roughly $20 for 400 square feet of coverage (excluding labor). In contrast, wallcovering is approximately $200 for the same coverage (excluding labor).

Entry Barriers. The final consideration is entry barriers. These seem to be inconsequential. Fixed costs are minimal (sales/fixed assets = 1000%), production scale economies also seem to be minimal (this makes sense given the fact the product variety is wide—if there were large scale economies we would expect to see fewer wallcovering patterns). Branding does not seem to be terribly important since consumers can rely on the brand of the retailer for quality assurance. Note however that there is a trend toward designer labeling of patterns—a means of "taste assurance" rather than quality assurance. Here, the wallcovering manufacturers form license agreements with prominent designers from other arenas to provide wallcovering designs that bear their name. Thus consumers who are uncertain of their own taste can rely on a designer's.

The most scarce resource seems to be access to the distribution channels, but as mentioned previously, there are multiple channels. Since entry appears to be unimpeded, the profitability of the industry is puzzling. The main entry barrier must be a required scale and scope of entry. New entrants must provide at least a whole pattern of books (probably more), and must produce sufficient number of those books to fill the distribution channel.

Industry summary

The preliminary conclusion is that wallcovering is an attractive industry. There is limited competition among existing rivals, little threat from suppliers and buyers, and no close substitutes. Ratio analysis confirms that this is a profitable industry—Return on Sales (ROS) is 5.5%, return on fixed assets is 48%.

The paradox here is that there appear to be minimal entry barriers. Normally the absence of barriers would tend to suppress industry profitability. The dominant entry barrier appears to be a relatively high minimum scale and scope of entry. Scope (variety of patterns) is required to make your offering attractive to retailers; scale is required to fill the distribution channels.

Thus entry into this attractive industry is feasible for large-scale ventures (a large firm play) OR for small ventures that innovate around the distribution system. Some feasible innovations are forming an exclusive arrangement with a single chain, working through designers rather than retailers, or selling direct to consumers.

6. Target Market

The broadest definition of the target market for Epigraphs is homeowners. The Statistical Abstract of the United States indicates that there are roughly 64 million owner-occupied households, and that the annual expenditures by those households on paint (there is no breakout for wallpaper) were roughly $6.5 billion, growing at 12% per year.

An alternative cut at the target market is to look at data on home textiles. Data from *American Marketplace* indicates that home textile expenditures grow with age, reaching a peak of $150 per household at age 45-54. Thereafter, expenditures decrease fairly rapidly as homeowners enter retirement. Expenditures also rise with income. Households with incomes greater than $70,000 spend an average of $250 per year on home textiles. With regard to household composition, textile expenditures are most likely in two-person households (married without children).

We gathered demographic data in our consumer survey and found general patterns to be similar to those of *American Marketplace*. There were exceptions however. First, we tested more income brackets, and found that sales peaked at $100,000-$150,000 for Epigraphs. This matched the focus group intuition that the product is ill-suited to the high-end market. Second, while textile expenditures are most likely in two-person households (married without children), we found instead that Epigraphs was most popular in households with children. The opposing results may have to do with the fragility of many home textiles vis-a-vis the durability of Epigraphs. Finally, while *American Marketplace* tested households, we also tested individuals. We found that females are twice as likely to purchase the product as males. This may have implications for advertising.

7. Distribution

Industry analysis indicated that there were approximately 15,000 independent retailers served by 100 distributors with an estimated reach of 10 million consumers. Because there are 40% markups both at the distributor and at the independent retailer, the unit revenue through independent retailers is 0.51*retail price (=price/$(1.4)^2$).

While there are fewer chain/superstore outlets, approximately 3000, they have approximately the same reach as independents. This is due to the branding advantages of the chains. Because manufacturers sell directly to the chains and superstores, without distributors, there is only a single mark-up of 40%. The unit revenues through this channel are therefore 0.71*retail price.

We combined these contribution numbers with considerations for inventory and other fixed costs to derive the break-even volume for each channel. Break-even analysis indicates that the channel with the least operational risk is direct sales through the Internet. The three channels have break-even volumes that differ by an order of magnitude: break-even volume for the Internet is 626 units; for sales through chains or superstores, break-even volume is 6556 units; for sales through distributors to independents, break-even volume is 50,038 units.

While this suggests that the Internet is the most attractive channel, there were two other issues: the demand issue—will the Internet attract sales, since the customer can't "feel" the product, and if so, at what volume? The other issue is the advantages of a channel that packages design consulting with the wallcovering sales. The relative ranking of the three channels on this dimension are independents, chains, superstores, and finally, the Internet.

To answer these questions we turn to the results from the survey analysis. Exhibit 4 indicated that the optimal price for distribution through chains was $50. This yields demand of .27 rolls and contribution of $6.79 per person in the target market. The Internet has a lower sales forecast (.24 rolls), at its optimal price of $40, but this is still very healthy demand. Moreover, it yields higher profit per person: $7.17. Thus if consumers have equal access to both channels, then the Internet is most lucrative.

8. Advertising

Audience. We identified the broadest target market for wallcovering as the 67 million owner-occupied households. However, in any given year only about 10 million households purchase wallpaper. Thus we are more interested in focusing advertising on that group. *American Marketplace* indicated that peak household textile use among households was for married couples, age 45-54, with annual incomes in excess of $70,000. Our market survey generally confirmed these basic trends for Epigraphs demand. However, we found that demand was highest for households with children with incomes of $100,000-$150,000.

It is unclear whether the same 10 million households purchase wallpaper annually or whether subsets of the homeowner population cycle in and out of the market. Regardless, we make the plausible assumption that those currently in the market for wallcovering will be actively seeking decorating information. Thus, any movement in and out of the market for wallcovering will be matched by movement in and out of the decorating audience.

Objectives. Before discussing more specific objectives, it is worth commenting on some idiosyncracies of the wallcovering market. First, sales are "skewed left." An average wallpaper pattern sells 7 million single rolls over a 3 year life. Sixty percent of the rolls are sold within the first year. (This was shown in Exhibit 6.) Second, ratio studies of the industry indicate an advertising intensity of less than 1%. Thus a wallpaper firm with first-year sales forecast of $75 million at wholesale ($105 million retail) only spends $750,000 on advertising. The low level of advertising, as well as the fact that sales peak early, tend to suggest that advertising is a relatively unimportant component of the communication process. It appears rather that 20-25% of homeowners decide to purchase wallcovering each year irrespective of advertising, and *then* shop among patterns. In fact, our survey data indicates that store displays are the second most prominent source of ideas.

An additional issue, raised in the focus groups, is that consumers seek uniqueness in their décor. To the extent that customers repeatedly see a wallcovering in advertisements, they may reject it as something that is no longer unique. The skewed three year life cycle corroborates the importance of uniqueness—a wallcovering's greatest sales occur when it is new and unique, and then diminish as it becomes more common.

The implications for advertising in this context are first that ads at most play an attention/interest role. The final stages of the decision process occur at the retailer, where the consumer makes on-site comparisons of wallcovering alternatives. Second, and more importantly, any advertising beyond that point may truncate sales by overexposing the product and eliminating its novelty. Thus wallcovering by nature, rather than strategic choice, is a low advertising intensive industry.

If we examine the wallcovering life cycle once again, we see that demand peaks in quarter three. We recommend advertising to create awareness only until the product reaches this critical mass, and rely on the retailer to stimulate sales thereafter.

Message. While we will leave the structure, format, and source decisions of the message design to an ad agency, we need to supply the content. The content of the message is the core benefit proposition that emerged in the focus group and was confirmed by the consumer survey. The proposition is a whimsical and affordable wallcovering with the versatility and uniqueness of custom finishes (faux, stenciling), with greater durability, and easier installation than wallpaper. This core benefit proposition was captured in the preliminary ad copy used in the consumer survey (Appendix).

Vehicles. Exhibit 7 summarizes circulation, demographic, and rate information for a subset of home and shelter advertising vehicles. In general, the demographics are comparable across the vehicles: the audience is predominately female, 40-45 years old, median household income of $50,00-$60,000, and 80% home ownership.

Exhibit 7

	Living	BH&G	HB	Home	HDTV
Audience size	2,236,000	7,600,000	865,000	1,024,000	1,140,000
Female	87%	78%	84.10%		66%
Age (Median)	40.8	44.1	46.1		45
HHI (Median)	$60,146	$48,688	$53,524		$55,000
Married	65%	66.00%	64.50%		
% with children		45.60%	39.50%		
Own Residence	76%	79.00%	80.80%		
1/3 page color ad	$48,571	$120,600	$24,730	$27,100	$1,500
% medium devoted to home furnishings	25%	25.90%	100%	100%	100%
CPM	$21.72	$15.87	$28.59	$26.46	$1.32

Plan and budget. Our goal is to reach the 10 million homeowners who purchase wallcovering in a given year. Because we don't want to destroy product uniqueness through over-exposure, we only want to achieve awareness/interest through advertising—thus, only one or two attention episodes per target member. Assuming failure to gain attention in some episodes, but no forgetting between episodes, we estimate two exposures per attention episode. Thus total exposures per target is (1 to 2) * 2 = 2 to 4.

HGTV appears to be the most cost-effective means to reach the target. While each show has only 1.1 million viewers, the total subscribers to the channel is 55 million. Thus there is the possibility of reaching the entire target. If so, the total advertising budget would be:

15,000,000/1000 * 1.32 * 3 exposures = $59,400

One caveat is that our primary research indicates that magazines outrank television by a factor of 2:1 as a source of decorating ideas. Thus we plan to augment HGTV advertising with print advertising in three issues of *Home*: 3 * $27,000 = $81,000.

Combining advertising expenditures of $140,000 with forecasted first-year sales of $25.7 million at wholesale yields an advertising intensity of 0.6%. This is comparable to the industry average.

9. Demand Forecast

We examine the demand forecast in two ways. The primary approach is aggregating demand utilizing survey data and decisions specific to Epigraphs, but as a test of reasonableness of that approach we first examine historical analogy.

Aggregated demand forecast. The potential demand for Epigraphs is defined by survey responses for our chosen price and product features. The dynamic unfolding of that potential demand is driven by our decisions regarding distribution and advertising. Exhibit is a spreadsheet that builds the dynamic forecast given our decisions. The spreadsheet applies survey estimates for demand-per-person to the total market size in each quarter, and adjusts that for awareness and availability, and the skewed sales profile for wallcovering sales over the product life. That forecast indicates that sales peak in Quarter 3 at_____ rolls. Total sales over the three-year product life are ____.

10. Operations

Epigraphs is somewhat unique, in that it is a transient venture—one product with a three-year lifespan, with no plans to develop new products beyond that. Accordingly, it makes little sense to make substantial investments in facilities and equipment. However, we want to ensure successful execution of the plan defined so far. Thus, we carefully assess where each of the major activities in the value chain is best performed.

The overall value chain for Epigraphs is given in Appendix I. That diagram distinguishes between development activities (those that occur only once up-front), primary activities (those that are recurring and whose level of effort is a function of the level of output, essentially those things driving variable cost), and support activities (recurring activities unrelated to the level of output, essentially fixed costs). We link interrelated activities into modules, since in general, activities with a high degree of inter-relatedness ought to be performed together. The major modules and corresponding decision on whether to internalize or out-source the activities in the module are as follows:

Design module: (Design of the product and packaging):
Internalize *because these activities determine the extent to which the product satisfies the core benefit proposition*

Customer interface module: (Order taking, dealer support, customer service):
Internalize *since this is the critical link to the sole customer (distributor)— ensures their satisfaction, but also helps to facilitate rapid production response to changes in demand*

Manufacturing module: (Material purchase and inventory, manufacture rolls):
Outsource *since manufacturing requires substantial investment in equipment and facilities that won't be needed after year 3. Also Epigraphs has no expertise, and the necessary manufacturing capability is competitively supplied*

Fulfillment module: (Package and inventory rolls, fulfill orders):
Outsource *since not strategic, no expertise, and fulfillment is competitively supplied*

Misc. support activities: (Advertising, human resources, legal, accounting):
Outsource *since Epigraphs' scale is too small to justify maintaining in-house*

While Epigraphs tends toward a virtual configuration, the firm maintains competence and control over design activities as well as dealer/customer interface. The strategic value of the dealer/customer interface is that it provides data on product demand and quality to facilitate rapid reconfiguration of manufacturing and the product mix. This minimizes the risk of obsolete inventory on one side, and product shortages on the other. It may also provide insights for future venture ideas.

11. Operating Economics

While our plan is to outsource production, we wanted an understanding of the scale of resources required to produce the product in-house. Accordingly, we developed a bill of capacity (machine and labor hours, plus materials required to produce a unit of output). We applied the bill of capacity to the demand in Exhibit 9 (shifted to accommodate shipping and inventory lags) to develop the calendarized resource requirements. The resulting capacity requirements define a very large-scale operation. Such scale is infeasible for a new operation without prior production expertise. Even if the managerial challenges could be solved, the financial investment in equipment is approximately $3,000,000. Moreover, the physical space necessary to accommodate the equipment was approximately 200,000 square feet. Given the short expected life of the venture, these investments seem unwarranted. Thus, the resource requirements analysis supports the decision reached earlier—that Epigraphs should outsource production.

12. Management Team

Epigraphs is largely a virtual corporation, thus we do not plan to build a large organization. The firm consists of two managers/officers.

13. Overall schedule

Week ending	2-Jun	9-Jun	16-Jun	23-Jun	30-Jun	7-Jul	14-Jul	21-Jul	28-Jul	4-Aug	#####	#####	#####	1-Sep	8-Sep	15-Sep	22-Sep	29-Sep
Distribution channel																		
Research Sherwin–Williams (EDI?)																		
Meeting																		
Train outlets																		
Receive initial order																		
Advertising																		
Hire agency																		
Develop ad copy/product lit sheet																		
Produce TV clip/instruction video																		
Develop store displays																		
Trade show displays																		
Interior designer mailer																		
Attend trade shows																		
Manufacturing																		
Research materials (3M, Dan)																		
Identify candidates (Thomas register)																		
RFQ for manufacturers																		
Produce dies																		
Initial production																		
Fulfillment																		
Identify candidates																		
RFQ for fulfillment																		
Procure/ship boxes, labels, instructions																		
Ship initial production																		
Website																		
Customer interface																		
Manufacturing interface																		
Fulfillment interface																		
Administrative																		
Licenses																		

14. Critical risks, problems and assumptions

The main risk in the venture is that we are unable to secure a distribution agreement with Sherwin-Williams on favorable terms. We believe this risk is low. We are offering Sherwin-Williams exclusive retail distribution of the product (we will retain rights to distribute the product through interior designers). Additionally, we will be providing free promotion for Sherwin-Williams in all of Epigraphs' magazine and cable television advertising. If we are unable to secure such an agreement, we will revert to Internet distribution.

The second risk is that we are unable to identify a material for the product that will reliably adhere to walls, but has the capability to be cleanly removed (possibly through the application of heat) when the consumer redecorates. If we are unable to identify such a material, we will give priority to a known material with good adhesion (the one used for the prototype).

The third risk is that the full demand forecast is not realized, and we are left with obsolete product. Since we will be using EDI technology, we will be able to detect when demand slows, and can adjust production accordingly. Additionally, we will not give retailers the option to return unused product.

The final risk is that demand exceeds expectations, that we therefore experience delivery lags, and induce entry by rivals. If this happens, we assume we will cede half of the market from that point forward (as discussed in section 4). Since sales peak in Quarter 3, and 60% of sales will have been achieved by the end of Quarter 4, this risk is considered minimal.

15. Financial forecast

The appendix contains pro forma financial statements for Epigraphs. We present the statements for the nominal forecast. We also developed optimistic and pessimistic forecasts based on the demand variance in the consumer survey. Because the nominal case presented the greatest financial demands on the venture, we do not present the alternative forecasts.

Financial requirement

Basic requirement. The most negative cash balance for Epigraphs occurs at the end of Month 3. The cash flow statement indicates that Epigraphs will need $600,000 of external financing. The requirement in Month 3 is driven by the upfront costs for production of dies, development of customer interface software, and advertising. The real cash requirement however arises from funding early production over the 45 day cash cycle.

By the end of the second quarter this deficit disappears and is replaced by a cash surplus.

index

E

F

N

O

P

T

about the author

Anne Marie Knott is Assistant Professor of Management at the Wharton School, of the University of Pennsylvania, where she has taught Entrepreneurship since 1995. She received a B.S. in Math from University of Utah, an MBA at UCLA in marketing and operations management, and a Ph.D. from UCLA in Management. Her general research interest is the interplay between firm strategies, industry structure and economic growth. Her work is published in the *Journal of Economic Behavior and Organization* and *Management Science*.

Prior to her academic career, Professor Knott spent 1 year managing her father's startup print shop, 15 years at Hughes Aircraft Company doing R&D on guidance systems, and 7 days on Family Feud. A clip from one of the episodes can be seen every 30 minutes on the Family Feud slot machine at the MGM Grand in Las Vegas.